CARTEL

THE COMING INVASION OF MEXICO'S DRUG WARS

SYLVIA LONGMIRE

palgrave
macmillan

This book is dedicated to the men and women of US law enforcement who work every day to defend our borders from the violent criminals who would dare encroach upon them.

CARTEL
Copyright © Sylvia Longmire, 2011.
All rights reserved.

First published in 2011 by PALGRAVE MACMILLAN® in the U.S.—a division of St. Martin's Press LLC, 175 Fifth Avenue, New York, NY 10010.

Where this book is distributed in the UK, Europe and the rest of the world, this is by Palgrave Macmillan, a division of Macmillan Publishers Limited, registered in England, company number 785998, of Houndmills, Basingstoke, Hampshire RG21 6XS.

Palgrave Macmillan is the global academic imprint of the above companies and has companies and representatives throughout the world.

Palgrave® and Macmillan® are registered trademarks in the United States, the United Kingdom, Europe and other countries.

ISBN: 978-0-230-11137-0

Library of Congress Cataloging-in-Publication Data
Longmire, Sylvia.
    Cartel : the coming invasion of Mexico's drug wars / Sylvia Longmire.
        p.   cm.
    Includes bibliographical references and index.
    ISBN 978-0-230-11137-0
    1. Drug traffic—Mexico.   2. Cartels—Mexico.   3. Drug dealers—
Mexico.   4. Organized crime—Mexico.   5. Drug control—Mexico.   I. Title.
HV5840.M4L66   2011
363.450972—dc22

2011005475

A catalogue record of the book is available from the British Library.

Design by Letra Libre

First edition: October 2011

10 9 8 7 6 5 4 3 2 1

Printed in the United States of America.

CONTENTS

AUTHOR'S NOTE

THE EVENTS DEPICTED in this book are true. However, some names and details have been changed to protect the privacy or security of real people. In a few situations, the realities of the drug wars are described but are presented in hypothetical situations using composite characters.

LIST OF ACRONYMS AND ABBREVIATIONS

AFO	Arellano Felix Organization
AMOC	Air and Maritime Operations Center
ATF	US Bureau of Alcohol, Tobacco, Firearms, and Explosives
BLO	Beltran Leyva Organization
CBP	US Customs and Border Protection
DEA	US Drug Enforcement Administration
DHS	US Department of Homeland Security
DoD	US Department of Defense
EPIC	El Paso Intelligence Center
FBI	Federal Bureau of Investigation
FFL	Federal firearms license
GAO	Government Accountability Office
HIDTA	High-Intensity Drug Trafficking Area
ICE	US Immigration and Customs Enforcement
LFM	La Familia Michoacana
NDIC	National Drug Intelligence Center
NICS	National Instant Check System
NRA	National Rifle Association
NVGs	Night vision goggles
ONDCP	Office of National Drug Control Policy
POE	Port of entry
USBP	US Border Patrol
USDOJ	US Department of Justice
VCFO	Vicente Carrillo Fuentes Organization

ACKNOWLEDGMENTS

EVEN THOUGH I'VE BEEN writing about Mexico for several years, the idea of consolidating my work into a book hadn't really crossed my mind until early 2010. In March, I was contacted by writer/director/producer Don Sikorski, who had some questions for me about the Barrio Azteca street gang for a *60 Minutes* piece he was working on. After I told him what I could, he asked me if I had ever thought about packaging my work into a TV pitch or a book. I told him I hadn't, but it sounded like an interesting idea. My thanks go out to Don for starting me on a path I hadn't really intended to explore but am now so grateful I did.

Once I made the commitment to write *Cartel*, I started doing a lot of research on the very daunting book publishing process. Fortunately, that brought me to my agent, Diane Stockwell at Globo Libros. I have so appreciated her enthusiasm for this project, and her feedback on my work has been invaluable. Her hard work also connected me with my editor at Palgrave Macmillan, Luba Ostashevsky, and her assistant, Laura Lancaster. Their expert guidance helped me make the transition from analyst and blogger to a bona fide book author.

Speaking of that transition, it was interesting making the switch from writing analytical products for the Air Force and California state government to writing for a general audience. Barnard Thompson at MexiData.com gave me the opportunity to start doing just that for his website, and his ideas for articles helped me explore aspects of the drug war I might never have come across on my own. I'm also eternally grateful to David Silverberg, editor at *Homeland Security Today* magazine. He took a big risk by putting my first-ever magazine article on his December 2009 cover, and it's led to a great and lasting professional relationship.

I've found over the last few years that the community of people who regularly follow developments in Mexico's drug war—both personally and professionally—is really quite small. Some of these folks who have kindly helped me by bouncing around ideas, providing feedback, writing endorsements, or just giving me inspiration for *Cartel* include Dr. George Grayson of the College of William and Mary, Fred Burton of Stratfor, author and journalist Samuel Logan, Lt. John P. Sullivan, Paul Hagerty, Dane Schiller, Nick Valencia, Leo Miele, Garrett Olson, Molly Molloy, Tony Kail, Gerardo Carrillo, MGen (ret.) Jim Dozier, and Tom Boerman.

There are dozens of analysts who are fighting the good fight for border security and who have my utmost respect. We worked long and hard together across the miles—and teleconferences—to make sense of the threats to our southwest border states. Special thanks go to my "partners in crime" Tom Carroll (editor and mentor extraordinaire), James Parker, Tony Frangipane, Juanita Guy, and Lora Mae Stewart. I'm also thankful to officials like ATF SAIC Bill Newell and former Arizona attorney general Terry Goddard for taking time out of their busy schedules to help me with my fact-checking and for providing some overall context on the southbound weapons trafficking problem.

There are thousands of agents, inspectors, police officers, and deputies who bust their tails every day to make sure drugs don't come into our country and guns and cash don't go out. I've been lucky to have met many of these folks who work along our southwest border and I have a lot of respect and appreciation for what they do and the dangers they often face.

Some were also gracious enough to take the time to tell me some of their "war stories" for inclusion in this book. I thank them for their service, and for helping secure our borders despite the challenges, frustrations, and obstacles that sometimes seem insurmountable.

My expansion into the blogosphere started as a side gig—a way for me to write about other events in the drug war that weren't related to California. Since I started my blog in March 2009, my readership has slowly increased, and I've made some great contacts because of it. I've also developed a decent following on Twitter and my Facebook fan page, and I'm continuously humbled by the fact that people I've never met are regularly following what I write. Special thanks have to go out to my blog readers and followers, whose comments have encouraged civil and engaging debates and helped me expand my analytical horizons.

Writing about Mexico's drug war on a regular basis can be pretty depressing. Fortunately, my daily life has nothing to do with illegal drugs and guns. I have to give credit to the people around me for keeping me sane, and reminding me that there are more important—and uplifting—things than work. Thanks to Warren, Adrianne, Sarah, and Ally for your support, and for always being ready and willing to help when help was needed. If I ever make it on *The Daily Show*, I'll be sure to get you all front-row seats and a handshake from Jon Stewart. My Metro-East MAM friends, you are the greatest bunch of ladies around! Your strength, humor, and giving spirit make me feel so blessed to have you in my life. To Erin and Alana, even though you are many miles away, I know your advice, feedback, friendship, and love are no more than a phone call, text message, or Skype session away.

Last, but not least, the greatest and most enthusiastic thanks go to my family—immediate, extended, and in-laws. It's not easy trying to strike the right balance between being an author, consultant, wife, and mother. Thanks to them, I've had the opportunity to write *Cartel* and get an important message out to America. I've also managed to stay grounded and (relatively) humble during this process. They don't care how much I know about Mexican cartels, or how often I'm on the radio or TV; they just want to know what they're having for lunch and if there are any clean undershirts in the laundry basket. Last, but not least, I have to thank my parents for being my biggest promoters, and for reading every single word I've ever written.

INTRODUCTION

IT WAS ONE OF THOSE Southern California days late in the year when it could be eighty degrees in the high desert during the day and quickly drop into the fifties or even forties after the sun went down—and the sun was going down more quickly with each passing day. US Border Patrol Agent Mike Miller was on the swing shift, and it was a simple task for him to fall into that temperature trap; he wore his rough-duty uniform with only a short-sleeved shirt and maybe a vest, just for an extra layer. A light jacket typically decorated his passenger seat—its exact location when he would miss it later in the evening. His only weapon was the issued handgun he carried, a .40-caliber Beretta disdainfully nicknamed "Tomahawk" by agents, with the insinuation that it was more useful as a projectile than a firearm. At the time, there were shotguns and M-16 rifles in the station armory, but very few agents carried them. The shotgun was like an anchor if an agent got into a foot pursuit or an extended trek, and management was not wild about sending young agents into the field with a fully automatic M-16.

The area where Miller was patrolling was typical high desert along the California-Mexico border. Squat live oaks and ruddy, twisted manzanita bushes stood out from the typical low-lying vegetation and made attractive stopping points for groups of migrants and drug mules who followed the slight canyons, arroyos, and rain-cut gullies leading down to the rural high-way below. The bad guys had the tactical high ground along most of the stretch he was patrolling. The area was just coming back from a massive fire that had swept through the year before, scorching the rocks black against the red caliche clay and sparing only the hardiest of small trees and shrubs. Looking at this stark landscape, Miller couldn't help but think back to images painted in his head as a boy by H. G. Wells stories read in the spooky comfort of a dim lightbulb in his older sister's closet.

The positive benefit from the destruction caused by the fire was the elimination both north and south of the border of much of the vegetation that had been used as cover and concealment by adversaries. Miller was lingering in the area of a tall hill, identified by the numbered border monu-ment perched atop it. Although the monument was clearly positioned fifty yards south of the northern overlook or face of the hill, the smuggling scouts would routinely situate themselves among the boulders at the over-look. There they could observe Border Patrol activity in the area, guide groups north to the highway along routes that they thought avoided the patrollers' sensors, and communicate with vehicles cruising the highway looking to pick up smuggled aliens or narcotics.

There was no road cut to the top of the hill, so one had to be very quiet and stealthy to sneak up on the smugglers undetected, not to mention fairly fit when climbing hundreds of feet through rocks at three thousand feet of elevation. Miller went into the Border Patrol Academy an avid surfer, mountain biker, and racquetball player and came out in even better shape when they were through with him. That didn't stop him from being com-pletely outdistanced by a fifty-year-old Oaxacan lady during a foot chase on the very first group he busted as a trainee.

Back to the hill. The good thing was that it was situated such that if he approached from the west, he could come out of a series of turns and hug the cut bank where the border road had been shaved into the base of the hillside. Parking there, he could keep his vehicle out of sight from anyone on the top, and he could ascend the west side of the hill and take the high ground or surprise anyone up there. On this day, Miller had gotten out to the site quickly, finished looking for evidence of foot or vehicle traffic, and laid down a good fresh tire track before the sun went down. Another benefit of the brush fire was that the large tracts of open ground layered in ash and pulverized burnt clay made for easy sign-cutting, or tracking, right after a fire. Unfortunately, after many people have gone through such an area, it becomes saturated with footprints and patrollers can't get a good idea of what type of prints they're tracking when they start. This is the reason for "dragging" the border road or laying down fresh tire prints.

Miller had accomplished both along his whole patrol route and was planning a nighttime assault on the hill with the intention of using his night-vision goggles (NVGs) to spot groups or drive-through vehicles that might be mustering up to his south. Here, trails cut by smuggling trucks and vans snaked through the brush and arroyos on the Mexico side and didn't stop at the lonely barbed-wire fence that had been cut and retied with baling twine so many times.

Miller killed some time chatting with another agent operating an infrared scope to his east, and after it was good and dark, he slowly rolled back toward the hill, doing his best not to be seen. At the time, driving with the headlights turned off was a common practice, and some of the vehicles had kill switches specially installed in them to shut down all light sources. A couple of bumps and dents here and there were enough to make someone in management decide that it was not a best practice, but agents always figured out a way to get by. Just as he was getting into place, he got a notification from dispatch that a sensor had fired. It was one he recognized as being located about a quarter of the way up the eastern slope of his hill, right at a common crossing point.

His adrenaline immediately kicked in. Miller acknowledged the sensor trip with Border Patrol Dispatch and waited a few minutes to make sure the group got north of the road. They would certainly hear him coming, so there was no point in turning off his lights. If he came in too quickly, though, they would simply run back across the border and they'd be playing cat and mouse the rest of the shift. No, if he let them get a little bit north, the guides would separate from the others when they heard him coming. He would probably catch the group hiding nearby in the brush, and the smugglers and Miller could later exchange pleasantries about their mothers from their respective sides of the border.

He went lights-on and slowly rolled around to the east side of the hill, pretending to be conducting a routine "cut" of the roadway looking for footprints. Miller imagined eyes staring down at him from the top of the hill and furtive movements and warnings whispered into cheap two-way radios. He almost expected to see the tail end of a group running across the road as he rounded the bend or blanket squares abandoned during quick exits from the roadway as he approached, but there were none. A sudden paranoia came over him, and he hit the gas and angled his vehicle to the right and slightly uphill, bathing the fence in light. He revealed, to his relief, that it was still intact and he had not unwittingly allowed a vehicle to drive through with his ill-thought strategy of "delayed response."

Miller repositioned his Ford Bronco, grabbed his flashlight, and jumped out to have a look around. People weren't the only creatures who regularly crossed back and forth; coyotes, bobcats, rabbits, mountain lions, and deer all made their passage without regard for either border security or his valuable time. He was half resolved that he'd be dismissing the sensor alert as "animal" activity and had revealed his location for nothing. That theory rapidly dissolved as he treaded uphill and almost immediately spotted fresh footprints in the soft dirt leading north along the hillside toward the border road.

The adrenaline rush made the hair on his arms stand up, and Miller suddenly felt the chilly night air for the first time. He knew the prints had not been visible crossing the road when he had passed around the hill, so the people must be close, and he decided not to return to his truck for the jacket. Miller began following the tracks, unconcerned with anything but the thrill of the chase and a sudden satisfaction that his gambit had apparently paid off. But something was nagging him, something that he couldn't quite put his finger on for the first few minutes, until it finally registered: the footprints he was following, about four sets of them, were all made by boots like his.

Illegal aliens almost never wear jungle boots, and neither do the drug mules, for that matter. That tank-tread outline with the distinct cloverleaf designs throughout the sole meant something was wrong. Had he stumbled onto a group of his Special Operations people conducting a low-key operation, or maybe some Navy Seals doing training exercises? It didn't seem likely, but it was possible. Then, just short of dropping down to the roadway, about fifty yards north of the border, the tracks turned around and headed south. He followed them back to the fence where they crossed into Mexico, almost exactly at the point where they had clearly come north.

Miller figured that whoever they were, they had seen him coming and been deterred. They were probably hiding back in the brush, he figured, and he wished he'd brought his NVGs with him when he jumped out of the truck. With the adrenaline subsiding, he also began wishing he had his jacket. But he was already at the fence, so he swept his light to the left to clear the area. That's when he saw them.

There were six that Miller saw at first—hunched down, motionless. They were facing away from him, and their black jackets concealed the rest of their clothing and appearance. Black jackets are common, so he thought nothing odd of it and began calling out to them in an attempt to get the group's foot guide to talk to him. He'd had many conversations with foot guides under similar circumstances. They try to convince agents to let them cross and ask what time they're planning to leave. The agents then ask them what time they intend to cross and tell them that they're welcome to cross right then, though they always politely decline. It can actually be very entertaining when agents get a guide with a sense of humor who likes to banter in a respectful way, and the agents have the advantage of already knowing who the guide is if they later catch the group.

Miller called to the group, which wasn't more than twenty feet from him. He identified himself and explained that he had no intention of pursuing them across the barbed-wire fence and that he just wanted to talk to the guide for a moment. After several attempts at making contact, he observed two of the subjects turn their heads to talk to one another. He also realized they were wearing balaclavas that covered their entire heads, except for their eyes. Miller then clearly saw the muzzle of a machine gun that was slung across the chest of the individual on the right and what appeared to be the butt of another rifle protruding against the jacket of the subject on the left. He suddenly felt very alone and outgunned. He began backing up toward a clump of rocks and sweeping the area with his flashlight.

To the left of the first group of men, Miller then saw about a dozen others, all clad in black and hunched down in the brush. Some began moving as his light passed over them, and he saw that they were all heavily armed with automatic weapons. He also noted that, despite what was probably purposeful positioning by the armed men to conceal them, he could see several large black duffel bags on the ground. The bags were packed full and squared off just as he had seen in numerous prior narcotics smuggling events in the past. But this time he was by himself, convinced that he had just stumbled into a very bad situation.

Miller decided to continue to try to speak to a leader in the group in an attempt to make them comfortable, despite his rudimentary Spanish skills, and to convince them that he was not an immediate threat. He felt that getting on his radio at that point might incite some unwanted action, and he wanted to keep the situation calm and increase his chances of survival. Miller asked if the men were Mexican military and requested to speak to their commander on the scene to share information. After what seemed like an eternity, one of the men stood up, stated that the group was Mexican army, and identified himself as the captain. To Miller, this was progress, even if the man was lying and he was actually a cartel member. He explained that he felt a little nervous about all of the heavy weapons and requested that the man take his mask off, disarm, and come to the fence. The man agreed and walked closer to the fence; then Miller didn't have to yell from his semi-concealed position, which he was not about to vacate.

Miller asked the "captain" what the group was doing and told him that he might have some information that could help his patrols. The man, who was in his thirties, clean shaven, with the bearing of a person in charge, explained that they were a special military group assigned to counter narcotics operations. Following this perfunctory identification, he immediately began asking Miller questions in a casual manner about Border Patrol operations in the area—specifically, the distance from their location to the highway below, and how long the trek was, and other inquiries that were obvious attempts to gather intelligence. Miller played dumb for the most part, saying that he was newer to the job than he really was, and explained that he was familiarizing himself with the area when he came across some footprints. The captain apologized and replied that they, too, were new to the area and did not recognize the barbed-wire fence as the international boundary until he and several of his men came to what was clearly the border road.

After a few minutes of "international liaison," Miller was fairly ready to be back in his truck and out of range when he nearly overplayed his hand by asking why they were carrying so much gear, referring to the duffel bags. The captain missed a beat, staring at Miller as if he suddenly did not understand him, but then brushed off the inquiry, stating that they always carry a lot of equipment. They said goodbye, and Miller tried not to walk too fast back to his vehicle, but it wasn't easy. He remembers feeling a knot in his chest like indigestion as he started his truck and a prickly heat washing over him as he was forced to make a two-point turn with the rear of his Bronco facing the narco-traffickers. A matter of seconds would have been all that was needed for two or three of them to run up behind him and spray his vehicle with bullets.

Since that time, Miller has heard many other stories involving armed encounters with suspected Mexican military personnel (or darn-good impersonators), often related to narcotics smuggling events. He still considers himself fortunate to have survived the encounter and thanks God that he was able to learn from the experience. That incident occurred ten years ago, and the border is a more dangerous place now than it's ever been.[1]

In the Mexican-American War in the mid-1800s, almost 1,200 Americans were killed in action. In 1941, almost 2,900 people were killed in the attack on Pearl Harbor. On 9/11, almost three thousand people were killed in the terrorist attacks on the World Trade Center, the Pentagon, and United Flight 93. All those attacks on US sovereignty and security were met with a swift and overwhelming response.

Between December 2006 and April 2011, more than thirty-four thousand people were killed in drug-related murders in neighboring Mexico, and approximately seventeen thousand Americans die annually from using drugs—most of which are brought into the United States by Mexican cartels. They are selling poison to Americans, taking their money, buying their guns, and kidnapping their citizens—all on American soil and often in America's heartland, far from the border. The drug war has officially arrived on US soil, but it seems like no one has noticed.

Americans who read about current events and foreign affairs tend to do so out of professional interest or personal curiosity. Most US citizens feel completely unaffected by border skirmishes in Kashmir, incursions by terrorist groups from Colombia into Venezuela, or territorial disputes in Ossetia and Abkhazia. And for people who live in Montana, or Kentucky, or Rhode Island, it's possible they couldn't care less about the drug war in Mexico; violence along the southwest border is likely low on their totem pole of concerns.

By the end of this book, readers will have a clear understanding of what Mexico's drug war means for Americans. Why? Because no matter where they live in the United States, chances are this war has arrived in their city, their town, and possibly their neighborhood. And that is something worth getting smart about sooner rather than later.

The Mexican drug trade has infected the United States. In 2008, over 14 percent of Americans over the age of twelve had used some sort of illegal drug. Almost twenty-six million people in the United States over the age of twelve had used marijuana in 2007. Despite the best efforts of governments and parents to educate adults and children about the dangers of using illegal drugs, almost three million Americans tried an illegal drug, or a prescription drug for a nonprescription purpose, for the first time in 2008. That's over eight thousand first-timers per day.

There are several ways that illegal drugs make their way from Mexico into the United States. Drug traffickers use hidden compartments in cars and trucks to bring them across the border at checkpoints, as well as backpackers who hike them across in remote areas between official border crossings. Less often, smugglers will use speedboats, drug submarines, freight trains, and even ultralight aircraft. One of their more enterprising feats is the creation of border tunnels—drug smuggling underground corridors that often run the length of a football field from Mexico into the United States. Sometimes these tunnels even have concrete walls and floors, fluorescent lighting, and air-conditioning. Illegal drugs are coming into America literally right under people's feet, and often no one can even detect them.

Once illegal drugs make their way in from Mexico, they spread to every city, town, and rural hamlet by way of the vast highway network. Major cities like Houston, Denver, Atlanta, New York, Detroit, and Miami serve as drug distribution hubs, and the drugs keep moving from there. Mexican cartels have a physical presence in over 270 US cities and towns, from Washington state to Florida and from California to Maine.

Worse yet, some drugs don't even need to be brought in from Mexico because they're produced right here. Huge marijuana farms, known as "grows," can be found in dozens of US states, and they're fiercely protected by dangerous men wielding powerful weapons against any unsuspecting person who might stumble across one. Methamphetamine, the second-most-common drug smuggled by Mexican cartels, is also produced here in the United States. There's a meth lab in every state, and many of them are run by Mexican cartels. One of the largest meth labs ever discovered by US law enforcement was actually just outside of Atlanta—not exactly a border community. In 2004, Iowa—as pure Midwest USA as it gets—was considered the "meth capital of the world."

Both the Mexican and US governments are attempting to battle the effects of drug violence in their respective countries through a variety of agencies and strategies. The Mexican government resorted to the use of its army in 2006 because it could no longer trust its extensively corrupted local police forces. It is also relying more heavily on its federal law enforcement agencies, whose agents are usually better trained and better paid than local cops—and therefore *slightly* less vulnerable to intimidation and bribery. The US government relies on a host of federal, state, and local law enforcement agencies along the border to interdict northbound drug shipments and prevent the southbound flow of guns and money.

If there's any kind of constant in the drug trade, it's change. Mexican cartels are run like profit-seeking corporations; so when the market makes a move, so do they. Over the years, they have shown an amazing ability to adjust to both changing drug-consumer tastes and increasing law enforcement initiatives. For example, cocaine was really popular—and really expensive—in the 1980s. The big Colombian cartels that provided that cocaine eventually went down, as did the social acceptability and overall use of cocaine in the United States. Mexican cartels took over cocaine distribution for the Colombians, but demand for marijuana and methamphetamine—both easily produced in Mexico—had started to grow. They're much cheaper and more easily supplied than cocaine, so the Mexican cartels took advantage of these changes.

To this day, these cartels keep a constant finger on the pulse of US demand for drugs in order to keep their biggest customer happy. When pseudoephedrine (a major component of meth) was restricted by law, they started making meth with alternative chemicals. When demand for cocaine would go up or down, they'd make appropriate arrangements with their South American suppliers to immediately compensate for that.

Mexican cartels extract thousands of guns and billions of dollars in drug profits from their US host to wreak brutal havoc well within Mexico and along the US border. In 2006, Mexican and Colombian cartels were thought to earn between $8 and $35 *billion annually* from drug sales to US customers. To protect themselves, their people use a method called "straw purchasing" to buy guns legally in the United States and smuggle them illegally into Mexico. There, cartel enforcers use them to murder rivals, snitches, cops, and politicians. Guns that seem common enough to Americans who are remotely familiar with firearms—9mm Berettas, .38 Specials, and Bushmaster XM15 rifles—are among the weapons of choice for Mexican cartels. They are taking advantage of US laws by buying these guns in shops and at gun shows in states across the country—not just in the four southwest border states. Cartels also use intimidation, bribery, and kidnappings on both sides of the border to bend police, government officials, and the public to their will. Kidnappings, which in the past almost exclusively involved people somehow involved in the drug trade, are now increasingly involving innocent bystanders. They are also occurring more frequently in the United States, sometimes in places well away from the border.

In late March 2010, a lifelong rancher in Arizona—a US citizen—was shot and killed on his property by an unidentified individual. The circumstances of the shooting led to speculation that the killer might have been a scared illegal immigrant or even a professional cartel hit man seeking retaliation. Regardless, the rancher's murder acted as a catalyst to intensify the debate over illegal immigration and actual-versus-potential border-violence "spillover." The four border states made it clear that enough was enough and that it was time for the government to finally start paying *real* attention to the drug war at its doorstep. For years, they had been asking for deployments (in some cases, redeployment) of National Guard troops to the border, and those requests had been categorically denied. Finally, in late May 2010, President Obama decided to send 1,200 National Guard troops to various locations along the southwest border and to seek additional funding for border security initiatives.

But will the US government's efforts, and those of the Mexican government, be enough to stop, or at least slow down, the cartel "virus" that has infected the country? After all, the United States is such a comfortable environment for the drug trade: high demand for drugs, a sophisticated transportation network, a variety of places where drugs can be grown or manufactured, a vulnerable southwest border, and a population that is mostly unaware of the extent of the infestation.

CHAPTER 1

THE WAR INSIDE MEXICO

THERE ISN'T TOO MUCH THAT stands out about La Tuna de Badiraguato. This tiny town of 200 people in the Mexican mountains is a quiet place with few prospects for people born there. Poppy fields cover the land as far as the eye can see. It's the kind of place that Americans would call a one-stoplight town, and even that might be too expansive. Basic utilities that we take for granted like clean running water and a sewage system are nonexistent, as are basic facilities like hospitals and schools. Children are taught by traveling teachers until maybe the age of twelve. After that, a life of hard and mostly unrewarding work begins.[1]

In Badiraguato, that work is likely connected to the drug trade. Most people who are born there never leave. Instead, they work the poppy fields in the foothills of the Sierra Madre Occidental, often until they grow old, can't work anymore, and die. This was the sad life that Joaquin Guzmán Loera was born into. However, it was a life he wouldn't tolerate for long.

Joaquin, given the common Sinaloan nickname of "El Chapo" because he was short and stocky, had a childhood typical for La Tuna. He worked day and night in the poppy fields, was beaten regularly by his father, and received no decent education to speak of. Joaquin wanted out. His exit from La Tuna and into bigger and better things was courtesy of his uncle, Pedro Avilés Pérez. Luckily for Joaquin, Uncle Pedro was the pioneer of Mexican drug trafficking.[2]

In his early twenties, Joaquin entered the drug trade under the wing of this expert trafficker, in a part of Mexico known for its "Wild West" character of lawlessness and violence. He started out as just another *narco,* working with the brothers who would eventually form the Beltrán Leyva Organization (BLO). But he was ambitious, in more ways than one. He was anxious to show his bosses what he could do, both in the movement of drugs north and in the punishment of rivals and incompetents. He quickly moved up in the ranks and soon was working directly for Miguel Ángel Félix Gallardo, known as "El Padrino" (The Godfather) because of his role as the leader of drug trafficking operations in Mexico.

Despite his growing responsibilities and wealth, Joaquin lived a pretty mellow life. He got married—twice—and had kids. He preferred to spend time with friends and family when he wasn't working. It didn't take long for his hard work and brutal business practices to pay off. In the late 1980s, Félix Gallardo divided up his drug trafficking empire, and Joaquin was given control of the Tecate *plaza,* or drug smuggling corridor. He was finally in charge, and he has never looked back.[3]

In the twenty-three years since El Chapo assumed his first command, so to speak, he's made quite a name for himself in Mexico. He runs the largest, wealthiest, and most powerful drug trafficking organization in Mexico—the Sinaloa Federation. His empire stretches into Central and South America, where contacts supply him with the cocaine he so expertly moves into the United States. In his home state of Sinaloa, he oversees large swaths of marijuana- and heroin-producing territory in or near the Sierra

Madre Occidental, as well as overseeing the "superlabs" that produce huge volumes of highly addictive methamphetamine.

El Chapo has also inadvertently become the international face of Mexican drug trafficking. In March 2009, *Forbes* magazine ranked him #701 in their list of the world's top 1,000 billionaires.[4] Later that year, *Forbes* ranked him #41 in their list of the world's most powerful people.[5] This kind of publicity ascribed to a career criminal and murderer infuriated a lot of people on both sides of the US-Mexico border; they felt that that kind of recognition should be reserved for people who earned their riches and power through more legitimate means.

Despite his extreme success in the drug world, El Chapo doesn't really seek out the spotlight; that's bad for business. He doesn't usually exhibit the status symbols that other *capos,* or drug lords, enjoy. He's a "jeans and baseball cap" kind of guy and doesn't care for expensive suits or flashy jewelry. Of course, he surrounds himself with ample protection via armed bodyguards and armored vehicles and convoys, and he stays eternally mobile. Yet, for the stressful lifestyle he leads of a man who's always looking over his shoulder—he's the most wanted man in Mexico, and the US government has a $5-million reward offer for him—El Chapo always has a calm demeanor and is in control of his emotions. He is a long way from La Tuna de Badiraguato, and the only way he's likely to return there is in a coffin.[6]

THE EVOLUTION OF MEXICAN DRUG TRAFFICKING ORGANIZATIONS

When Félix Gallardo divided up his drug empire into smaller pieces, he might not have been able to imagine the carnage that would result in two decades' time. He was the only major player in Mexican drug trafficking at the time, so he called all the shots. He was actually trained as a federal police agent and later became a bodyguard for the governor of Sinaloa before entering the illegal drug trade. In addition to creating the foundations of El Chapo's Federation, Félix Gallardo assigned territory to the Arellano Felix family, the Carrillo Fuentes family, and Juan García Abrego. They would be in charge of what would become the powerful Tijuana, Juárez, and Gulf cartels, respectively. Over the years, the composition and influence of the major cartels in Mexico would fluctuate, but Félix Gallardo's core organizations persist to this day.

This isn't to say that they get along now like they did back in the late 1980s. Things in the Mexican drug trade worked differently back then. The drug lords could get together and make arrangements to split drug profits from shared *plazas*. They could also arrange for cease-fires if some rogue lieutenants got out of hand. The major cartels had the luxury of operating in a country run by a political party that was more or less happy to stay out of the *capos'* way in exchange for relative peace. This is how it went, until the untimely death of Amado Carrillo Fuentes.

In the late 1990s, Amado, known as "The Lord of the Skies" for the fleet of jets he used to transport drugs, was arguably the most powerful man in the Mexican drug world. He was wanted by both Mexican and US authorities, and he soon found it extremely difficult to travel or operate with any degree of anonymity or safety. He decided, as some *capos* do, to undergo major plastic surgery to radically alter his appearance. During the long procedure, Carrillo Fuentes died from complications related either to medication or to a malfunctioning respirator. Two of his bodyguards were in the surgical suite with him, and to this day, conspiracy theories abound about whether his death was an accident or perpetrated by the doctor or his bodyguards.

Regardless, the absence of Carrillo Fuentes created a huge power vacuum in the Mexican drug world, and former allies and new rivals were eager to fill it. Everyone assumed the rival Arellano Felix brothers would be the first to come in for the kill, seeing that El Chapo (their primary competition) was in a maximum-security Mexican prison at the time. Things in Ciudad Juárez did heat up as the turf war began, but it was only a sneak preview of what was to come.

In 2001, El Chapo escaped from that "maximum-security Mexican prison" (which many would say is a contradiction in terms). The official story from the Mexican government was that he befriended a prison maintenance worker named Javier Camberos. El Chapo told the guards (whom he had enlisted onto his own payroll) that Camberos was going to be smuggling some gold out of the prison in a laundry cart and that they were not to search the cart. But on the night of January 19, 2001, El Chapo himself hid in the cart as Camberos wheeled him out of the prison. Unofficially, many Mexicans believe that prison officials just let him walk out. We'll never know because surveillance tapes for that night were conveniently erased.[7]

After El Chapo came back onto the *narco* scene in full force, it was "game on" for control of the lucrative Juárez *plaza*. He was actually surrounded on both sides by rivals: the Vicente Carrillo Fuentes Organization (VCFO) and the Gulf cartel to the east, and the Arellano Felix Organization (AFO) to the west. As the years progressed, El Chapo and his rivals engaged in a bloody battle, unprecedented in Mexican history, for slowly shrinking territory and drug revenue.

Mexico's major cartels continue to evolve, partly of their own doing and partly because of arrests or killings by Mexican government forces. Alliances that seemed ironclad just a few years back can dissolve as a result of a single incident, whether actual or perceived. On the flip side, cartels that have been bitter rivals for years can join forces to wage war against a mutual—and usually more powerful—enemy. For example, the BLO was a big part of El Chapo's Sinaloa Federation for many years. However, the BLO split off from the Federation after the arrest of its then-leader Alfredo Beltrán Leyva at a Culiacán safe house in January 2008. The brothers blamed El Chapo for Alfredo's arrest, saying he tipped authorities off to Alfredo's location. They retaliated by forming their own organization and aligning with the Gulf cartel. Their coup de grâce was the assassination of Édgar Guzmán López, El Chapo's son, a few months later.

After the split, the BLO became one of the most powerful cartels in Mexico, capable of smuggling narcotics, battling rivals, and demonstrating a willingness to order the assassination of high-ranking government officials. However, it suffered a serious setback in December 2009 when Arturo Beltrán Leyva, Alfredo's brother and one of the cartel's top bosses, was killed by Mexican navy commandos in a raid. The Mexican government has said it ascertained Arturo's location through the use of good intelligence and diligent police work, but there are many who believe El Chapo tipped off the commandos to his location in order to eliminate a competitor.

Héctor, Arturo's brother, was the natural selection to fill the power vacuum left by Arturo. In 2010, the BLO itself underwent a split, between Héctor's main faction and one run by Edgar "La Barbie" Valdez Villarreal, the head of the BLO's enforcement group. Héctor decided to rename his faction, and the old BLO became the new Cartel Pacifico del Sur (South Pacific Cartel), although it's also known as "El H" and "La Empresa." Héctor also still maintains a friendship with his old allies, Los Zetas, and is using this alliance to do battle against La Familia Michoacana (LFM) and the Federation in Guerrero state.

La Barbie, meanwhile, was arrested in late 2010 by Mexican authorities, and his faction of the former BLO is assumed to be almost completely disintegrated. Based on the fact that his capture by Mexican authorities was completely uneventful, the current assumption is that he made a deal to turn himself in and receive favorable treatment in exchange for providing intelligence on his rivals. In November 2010, the Mexican government agreed to extradite La Barbie to the United States.

One would think that the Sinaloa Federation and the Gulf cartel, which formed the biggest cartel rivalry in Mexico at the time, could never form a truce, let alone an alliance of any sort. However, just that very thing happened in the spring of 2010. The Gulf cartel had been getting hit hard by Mexican forces in the previous few years and had lost much of its power and territory. Its former enforcement arm, Los Zetas, had split off two years before and become one of the more powerful—and vicious—new cartels in Mexico. Los Zetas are a group of former Mexican-army Special Forces troops who have grown into a well-trained, well-armed, and well-funded cartel engaged in assassinations, mass killings of migrants, kidnappings for ransom, and extortion. They have grown to become probably the biggest threat to El Chapo's operations that he's seen since he first sat down on the Federation's throne.

Not one to sit by idly while events unfold around him, El Chapo did the unthinkable: he entered into an alliance with the Gulf cartel and the up-and-coming LFM cartel to wage war against Los Zetas. This arrangement was called the New Federation, and they wasted no time in starting a public relations campaign. In March 2010, they posted a video message for the Mexican people on YouTube, which included the following:

> Without the "Z" you will live without fear. . . . If you are a Zeta, run because the MONSTER is coming . . . the new alliance have raised their weapons to f**k the Zetas because they have undermined the drug trafficking business with their kidnappings, extortions, etc. To sum it up, they don't give a s**t about the freedom and tranquility of the Mexican people.[8]

It's hard to say for sure what the drug trafficking landscape will look like in a year or in five years' or ten years' time. By the time a reader picks up this book, the New Federation might have dissolved and El Chapo might be at war again with the Gulf cartel. It's also possible that El Chapo might finally be captured (although this is unlikely) or that new and smaller cartels might form to fill power vacuums left by other jailed or dead *capos*. The one thing that will always remain constant in the evolution of Mexican drug cartels is change.

THE BATTLE FOR TERRITORY AND DRUG PROFITS

Over thirty-four thousand people have been killed through April 2011 in drug-related violence in Mexico since President Calderón's war against organized crime began in earnest in 2006. These killings run the gamut from conventional murder by handgun to the more creative—having the victims' remains intentionally picked off by vultures, for example. The violence is also directed against a wide variety of targets: government officials and miscellaneous politicians, law enforcement agents, rival cartel members, low-level drug dealers, prominent businessmen, witnesses, and informants. It happens in downtown areas of major cities, often in broad daylight and in full view of many witnesses. It also occurs in rural areas in the middle of nowhere, along isolated stretches of seldom-traveled roads, and in the punishing desert. Most worrisome to many Mexicans, the violence visits them in middle- to upper-class neighborhoods that often have gates and alarms and security cameras, all of which provide a false sense of security.

Drug-related violence in Mexico generally falls into three categories: violence directed against the authorities, against other cartels, and against the general public. It's important to look at examples of incidents in each of these categories to fully understand how incredibly out of hand the violence in Mexico has become. Because some of this violence has occurred on US soil—albeit on a much smaller scale—it's crucial to realize the brutality that Mexican *narcos* are capable of, in case they ever decide to bring more of it across the border.

Cartel enforcers use a variety of violent tactics and can easily adapt plans based on the target, environment, and general situation. Cartel-orchestrated assassinations usually target Mexican law enforcement or members of the local government, although civilians connected to the Mexican drug trade are often targeted as well. Cartel enforcers target police chiefs, mayors, and other mid- to senior-level government individuals, often with a high rate of success. As many as one or two dozen assassinations occur throughout Mexico in any given week. Cartels and other criminal groups have used grenades, homemade bombs, and other explosive devices against Mexican police, soldiers, and even American diplomatic facilities. They also routinely use grisly executions to intimidate their rivals, the government, and the public.[9]

Kidnappings in Mexico jumped almost 40 percent between 2004 and 2007, according to official statistics. Police say there were 751 kidnappings in Mexico in 2007, but the independent Citizens' Institute of Security Studies (ICESI) says the real number could be above seven thousand. This gap is pretty typical, because the majority of kidnappings in Mexico (and anyplace where kidnapping is a problem, for that matter) go unreported for fear the kidnappers will harm the hostages. In 2008, Tijuana suffered more kidnappings than almost any other city outside of Baghdad.[10]

Between May 2004 and May 2005, there were thirty-five reported abductions of Americans in the southwest border area. Much larger numbers of Mexican citizens have been abducted along the border. From January to mid-August 2005, 202 kidnappings occurred in the Mexican state of Tamaulipas, the main battleground for Los Zetas and the Gulf cartel. Thirty-four of these abductions occurred in Nuevo Laredo and involved US citizens who had crossed the border. Twenty-three victims were released by their captors, nine victims remain missing, and two were confirmed dead. Kidnappings in the Phoenix area are occurring so regularly that the city's police department has created a task force with the sole purpose of investigating them. Police suspect many of these abductions have led to killings in which bound and bullet-riddled bodies have been found dumped in the desert. Phoenix officials claimed that more than 340 such kidnappings occurred in 2008,[11] but police said the real number is higher.[12]

The drug traffickers' weapons of choice include variants of the AK-47 and AR-15, .50-caliber sniper rifles, and a Belgian-made pistol called the "cop killer" or *mata policia* because of its ability to pierce a bulletproof vest with certain ammunition. Arms traffickers have left Mexico awash in assault rifles, pistols, telescope sighting devices, grenades, grenade launchers, and high-powered ammunition.[13]

Fear as a result of drug-related violence has spread like wildfire throughout Mexico. Wealthy Mexicans ride in bulletproof vehicles, wear protective clothing, and hire bodyguards. Businessmen and casual diners alike avoid eating at certain restaurants that are known to be popular with cartel members. Many Mexicans take special care not to wear anything that might attract attention from cartel enforcers—certain clothing, hats, jewelry, and the like. People avoid eye contact if a Hummer or other large SUV pulls alongside them at a stoplight. Police checkpoints are a cause for concern because the people dressed as police officers could be real police, or they could be cartel enforcers disguised as police. Women are careful when dealing with unwanted male attention for fear that the men might be carrying weapons they are very willing to use. Men are careful about the women they look at for fear they might be a wife or girlfriend of someone also willing to use a weapon. Some Mexicans are even having microchips inserted in their forearms so they can be tracked in case they are kidnapped by drug traffickers.[14]

Banners known as *narcomantas* placed in public areas have become a common intimidation tool and are often used to threaten violence against individuals. Banners hung ostensibly by drug cartels in cities across Mexico in late August 2008 were noteworthy in that part of their message was directed toward civilians, assuring them that the cartels—not the government—control the level of violence in the country.[15] Oddly enough, these same public messages are sometimes created by the people in support of the cartels. In early December 2010, shortly after the death of LFM's founder Nazario Moreno González, cartel supporters hung a *manta* telling the cartel to "hit them hard" (in reference to the Mexican government) and to take care not to kill innocent people in the process.

Violent acts committed by drug trafficking organizations and their enforcers are currently viewed as criminal acts. Yet, most of those acts are identical in nature to acts committed by traditional terrorist groups like al-Qa'ida, the Revolutionary Armed Forces of Colombia (the FARC), and the Provisional Irish Republican Army (IRA)—and have similar intentions. Cartel hit men routinely use beheadings during executions of their rivals or enemies. Cartels engage in insurgent-style tactics against the Mexican military, Mexican and US law enforcement, and civilians alike, just as the FARC do in Colombia. Mexican cartels have successfully targeted government officials and law enforcement officers for assassination, just as the IRA did in the 1970s and 1980s. Most importantly, the intention of all these groups is the same—to intimidate the populace and change the behavior of a government. The motivations are clearly different for each group, but the effect on the people is the same.[16]

Violence Against Government Forces

Most Mexicans will say that life was far from perfect and peaceful before President Calderón came into office in December 2006, but it was definitely less bloody. The aggressive stance Calderón has taken against organized crime since his inauguration is largely blamed for the huge surge in drug-related violence over the last several years.

His administration and many Mexicans were hoping that his unprecedented deployment of tens of thousands of soldiers to hot spots around the country would at least keep the situation under control for a year or two until he could come up with a more sustainable strategy—ideally one that would involve less corrupt and more effective federal and local police forces. While that process is still ongoing, the cartels are fighting back much harder and more viciously every day against every soldier and cop that Calderón can throw at them.

In June 2010, along a highway in Michoacán, gunmen sealed off the road with buses they had set on fire, boxing in a convoy of federal police trucks. They launched an armed assault from high ground, killing twelve officers. That same month, an ambush of army soldiers by armed men camouflaged with foliage in Tepalcatepec left two soldiers wounded and three gunmen dead.

Three hundred and twenty-four police officers were killed in clashes with organized crime groups between January and June 2010, compared with 511 in all of 2009. In August 2010, the Mexican government revealed for the first time that 191 soldiers had been killed in the drug war during the time between Calderón's inauguration in December 2006 and August 1, 2010. Also, it announced that 2,076 police officers had been killed in the same time span.

Media reports say that this wave of violence against soldiers and cops began on July 11, 2009, when LFM launched fifteen coordinated attacks over two days on police stations and patrols in eight cities across three Mexican states. There were twelve similar ambushes in the following year. In Reynosa, gunmen hijacked sixteen vehicles, including buses and tractor-trailers, to block streets around a military garrison. They then launched an attack on soldiers leaving the base. The soldiers managed to repel the attack, and the gunmen fled. In Ciudad Juárez, a street vendor flagged down a police convoy. When it stopped, three vehicles blocked the convoy and assailants opened fire, killing six federal police officers, a city policeman, and a civilian.

In Guerrero, ten gunmen armed with assault rifles surrounded three police officers carrying out an arrest warrant. The gunmen killed them in a hail of 450 bullets. Near the western Michoacán town of Maravatío, gunmen fired from an overpass and both sides of a highway as a federal police convoy passed. Five officers were killed and seven wounded.

The use of hand grenades against police, military, and even media targets seems to be a favorite tactic of crime organizations these days. From July 2009 to July 2010, there were seventy-two grenade attacks by cartels against various targets. Between December 2006 and July 2010, there were 101 grenade attacks against government buildings.[17] Assailants have rolled grenades into brothels in the border city of Reynosa, hurled one at the US consulate in Nuevo Laredo, and tossed them at a military barracks in Tampico and in front of television stations in Nayarit and Tamaulipas. Grenades haven't caused as many casualties as the use of assault weapons by *narcos,* but the psychological factor of the explosion itself is often more damaging than gunfire.

Violence Between Cartels

It's tough to gauge who is spilling more blood in Mexico: cartels fighting the authorities or fighting each other. Violence initiated by one cartel against another always has a purpose, and it invariably sends a very strong message. Killings are usually served up as a form of revenge or punishment, and the level of brutality has escalated over time so that they retain their shock factor. Examples of assassinations, decapitations, and other killings of rival cartel members number in the thousands, so only some of the more disturbing incidents are described here.

In June 2010, Mexican police discovered six bodies in an underground cave on the outskirts of Cancún, a popular tourist destination in the Yucatán peninsula. This wouldn't have been anything out of the ordinary, except three of the victims had their hearts cut out of their bodies. All of the victims—four men and two women—showed signs of torture, and two had the letter Z carved into their bodies, ostensibly the mark of Los Zetas.[18]

In September 2006, masked armed men possibly linked to drug smugglers stormed into a bar in Uruapan and threw five human heads onto a crowded dance floor. Police believed it was an apparent warning aimed at a rival drug gang. Along with the heads, the men threw down a note saying the act was "divine justice" carried out on behalf of "the family." That translates to "La Familia Michoacana," which was just getting off the ground in 2006 but has grown into one of the most vicious—and unusual—organized crime groups in Mexico.

Nazario Moreno González, founder of LFM, probably didn't think he'd end up being viewed as a messiah by so many people in his home state of Michoacán. It's difficult to find any details on Moreno's upbringing, but it's likely that religion played a huge role in his life. As an adult, he preached to the poor in his hometown of Apatzingán, and he always had a Bible handy. Soon, Moreno won the hearts and minds of the locals—but more important, he won their loyalty. This came in handy when Moreno decided to form a sort of vigilante organization in 2004. He used the religious principles he had been preaching to form a then-unnamed group that would be dedicated to the eradication of methamphetamine and other narcotics, kidnappings, extortion, murder for hire, highway assaults, and robberies.

LFM might have begun as vigilantes determined to thwart the manufacture and transport of meth by the Michoacán-based Milenio cartel, an ally of El Chapo and his Sinaloa Federation. It's also possible Moreno created the group to prevent the violent Zetas from entering Michoacán.[19] Regardless, he started making his intentions clear through a series of messages, or *narcomensajes,* left next to bodies or decapitated heads. Known by then as "La Familia Michoacana," the group even started taking out full-page advertisements in local papers, posting its manifesto and claiming they were an anticrime organization. In one of the greatest ironies in Mexico's drug world, LFM has become one of the biggest meth traffickers in the country.

Violent acts committed by one cartel against another are rarely without some sort of drama, and it's often personal. For example, in January 2010, members of the AFO kidnapped the sister of Raydel "El Muletas" López Uriarte, the number-two guy in a breakaway faction of the AFO that was loyal to the Sinaloa Federation. In response, López had several of AFO leader Fernando Sanchez Arellano's relatives kidnapped and killed. López's sister was eventually released, but not before the captors killed her boyfriend. Several of Sanchez's relatives were also released.

The psychological factors at play between organizations fighting to the death for drug profits cannot be discounted. When new recruits come into an organization known for its brutality, like the AFO or Los Zetas, they have to show they're up to the task. Then, the killing gets going pretty quickly. The violence also serves to show domination and is an intimidation tool for rivals who dare encroach upon a cartel's turf. And the level has to be ratcheted up every so often. Just like video games and broadcast television, the tolerance for certain things—like beheadings, tongues cut out, and similar brutalities—increases, so the narcos have to get more creative. This is why, over time, drug-related murders are occurring more frequently in some places and are becoming more grisly.

While many other cities along Mexico's northern border have experienced major crime waves and spikes in drug-related violence over the last few years, none compare to the bloodshed witnessed by residents of Ciudad Juárez in Mexico's Chihuahua state. It's a large city, with a population of roughly 1.5 million people, and is situated directly across the border from El Paso, Texas. Juárez is also a major industrial city, home to approximately 300 *maquiladoras,* or assembly plants. The city is rapidly growing and is a very busy place, which explains why it has four international crossings. In 2008, almost twenty-three million people passed through those ports of entry.

This also explains why Juárez is the most contested piece of real estate among Mexican drug traffickers. It is the most lucrative *plaza* along the US-Mexico border. Over the last five years or so, competition between the Sinaloa Federation and the Vicente Carrillo Fuentes Organization for control of the city has resulted in a record-high body count. The death toll in 2007 was relatively modest with only 320 murders.[20] Then, in 2008, it shot up to 1,623, only to climb to 2,754 in 2009. The year 2010 saw 3,111 people murdered in Juárez, making it another record year for the violence-plagued city.[21] This means that roughly one out of every four murders in all of Mexico happens in Ciudad Juárez. No wonder the US State Department travel warnings for the city keep getting renewed every six months.

In July 2010, unidentified drug traffickers in the city filled a car with twenty pounds of explosives and parked it outside a federal police station. Media reports claimed that before detonating the bomb with a cell phone, the assailants had dumped an injured man dressed as a municipal police officer on the sidewalk as bait to lure police and emergency paramedics closer to the vehicle. The well-planned explosion killed four people, including a doctor and a police officer.[22]

To make a bad situation worse, a message left at the scene implicated the VCFO and claimed they still had more car bombs. It also threatened further attacks, and as a result, the US Consulate in Juárez immediately shut down for a "security review." Fortunately, the anticipated follow-up bombing never occurred.

The border city also seems to be a magnet for decapitated bodies. There are too many news stories of the discovery of decapitated bodies in Ciudad Juárez. Hundreds each year are found in piles, in mass graves, in pieces inside garbage bags, hanging from overpasses, in cars—and many with notes attached. Those *narcomensajes* from cartel members usually say something to the tune of "If you mess with us, this is what will happen to you," or "This is what happens to people who work for [insert rival cartel leader's name here]."

This isn't to say that these gruesome things happen only in Juárez. They're certainly happening in relatively large numbers in Acapulco and Nuevo Laredo. However, no other city in Mexico is feeling the effects of the drug war as strongly as Juárez.

INNOCENTS CAUGHT IN THE CROSSFIRE

Traditionally and historically, Mexican organized crime groups have shied away from targeting innocent bystanders and have tried to limit the amount of collateral damage they inflict during attacks on police, soldiers, or rivals. They operated very much in the same way that the Italian Mafia did in America: family members were strictly off limits, and they didn't mark anyone for death unless they had a plausibly good reason. Unfortunately, several incidents in the last two years or so demonstrate how that mindset is changing.

Probably the most dramatic incident in the last few years to have a major impact on the public's sense of security occurred in September 2008 on Mexico's day of independence. Hundreds of people gathered that Monday night in the city of Morelia's central square when explosions shocked everyone. Witnesses said a bulky man in black threw a grenade-like object into the crowd and then apologized to people next to him. A second blast struck moments after the first. The attack claimed the lives of eight people and injured over a hundred, and some Mexican government officials labeled the incident a terrorist attack. Speculation about the culprits focused on LFM and Los Zetas, but ultimately, no one was prosecuted.

While most major tourist areas in Mexico, such as Cancún, Cozumel, and Los Cabos, haven't seen much action by way of daylight shootings and grenade attacks, this doesn't mean they're completely immune. In April 2010, a big gun fight took place in Acapulco's main tourist area. Similar gun battles had occurred previously near the popular vacation destination—but always in the outskirts and away from the tourist hotels, restaurants, and shopping areas. This one in particular happened in broad daylight and left six people dead, including a mother and her eight-year-old child, a taxi driver, and a police officer. News reports said several motorists crashed their cars and ran over medians in an attempt to escape the gunfire, which left at least a dozen cars filled with bullet holes. Authorities said they had never before seen anything so brazen in Acapulco.[23]

Some cartel hits target rivals or snitches but occur in places where innocents are placed in great danger, and the attack itself spreads fear among the general public. For instance, 2009 and 2010 saw a rash of violent attacks in Mexican drug rehabilitation centers. In June 2010, at least thirty armed men marched into a drug treatment facility in Chihuahua state, killed nineteen people, and wounded four others.[24] An attack in a Juárez facility in September 2009 left seventeen dead and two wounded, ten dead in a second Juárez center that same month, and twenty dead in a third facility the previous March.

Authorities blame drug gangs for the rehab center killings, and the victims were probably members of rival groups. While innocents aren't usually targeted in these treatment facility attacks, the increased tolerance for collateral damage in the public sphere means not every innocent can escape the spray of bullets in such incidents.

Parties or other festive gatherings have increasingly become sites of armed attacks by cartel enforcers. On July 19, 2010, gunmen stormed a party in the city of Torreon in northern Mexico and massacred seventeen people, wounding eighteen others. The attackers showed up at the party in several cars and started shooting without any warning or conversation.[25] In January 2010, gunmen barged into a private party in Ciudad Juárez and killed fifteen people, many of them high school or university students. Relatives said the attack was a case of mistaken identity, while state officials claimed someone at the party was targeted.

Nothing represents the innocent bystander better than a small child, so there's a particular brand of fear when it comes to kids being affected by drug violence. Schools across Mexico are teaching students to dive to the floor and cover their heads because of the drug-related violence.[26] At least nine shootouts have erupted in school zones since mid-October 2009, three of them in June 2010 alone. On June 15, soldiers and gunmen battled for an hour just sixty feet from a preschool in the central town of Taxco. Another shootout erupted near public schools on June 18 in the western town of Bellavista and on June 24 in the northern city of Apodaca, where police evacuated two elementary schools and a preschool.[27] While drug traffickers aren't targeting schools or children for violent acts, teachers are now warning students not to take videos or photos of the gun battles and post them to social networking sites for fear that that might put them in danger.

Speaking of teachers, they started becoming new targets for cartel violence in late 2010. Shortly before Christmas, painted threats scrawled outside numerous public schools demanded that teachers hand over their

Christmas bonuses or face the possibility of an armed attack on the teach-ers—and even the children. The week before the threats appeared, car-tel members set fire to a preschool in the San Antonio district of Ciudad Juárez. The reason for the fire was clearly scribbled on a nearby wall: "For not paying." Parents started pulling their kids out of school, and three schools actually shut down as a result of the threats sent to a dozen or so schools. Parents also wanted the police to start posting at least one patrol car at each school, but police departments responded that they just didn't have the resources to do that.[28]

THE NARCOS MOVING NORTH

While Mexican drug cartels have an extensive and established presence here in the United States, the violence they've inflicted on US soil has fortu-nately not reached anywhere near the levels perpetrated in parts of Mexico. However, that doesn't mean they're not engaging in violent activity in the southwest border states and beyond.

Mexican drug cartels are heavily invested in growing marijuana on US public lands. Because the plants have such high value—$4,000 per plant in some cases—the men who run those grows defend them with heavy fire-power against any encroachment by law enforcement. In June 2009, police officers in Lassen County, California, encountered three suspected mari-juana growers. One engaged the officers in a gun battle using an AK-47 rifle. The two sheriff's deputies were wounded, but the shooter was killed when officers returned fire. In July 2010—also in California—a man was shot and killed by Santa Clara County sheriff's deputies after he pointed a rifle at them in a remote area where twenty thousand marijuana plants were being grown.

In August 2010 in Oregon, Jackson County SWAT and marijuana eradication teams were investigating an outdoor marijuana grow in a Bu-reau of Land Management area when they spotted a man armed with a shotgun. Two deputies opened fire and shot him—then spotted a second man who fled on foot. Investigators had reason to believe the marijuana grow was operated by a Mexican drug cartel.

US law enforcement agencies have known for some time that Mexican crime groups often hire US-based gangs and ad-hoc assassins to do their dirty work north of the border. In 2006, a gunman tried to kill the head of a Mexican cartel cell in a Houston restaurant but got the wrong guy. Pedro Cárdenas Guillen, nephew of the former Gulf cartel kingpin Osiel Cárdenas Guillen, was shot in the head and left in a ditch near Fort Bend County, Texas.[29]

In October 2010, the body of Martin Alejandro Cota-Monroy was found in his apartment in Chandler, Arizona, about twenty-five miles outside of Phoenix and 160 miles north of the border. And technically, it was only his body, as his severed head was found lying on the floor a few feet away. Investigators thought it was likely that the man's murder was the work of Mexican cartels working in Arizona and that Cota-Monroy's killing was punishment for stealing drugs.[30]

In 2006, an innocent used-car dealer was kidnapped and severely beaten while being held for ransom. He was rescued by Houston police, but not before he was punched, kicked, and thrown across a room so forcefully that his face was unrecognizable. Authorities said the kidnappers were low-ranking thugs working for a Mexican cartel cell. In July 2009, a ranking cartel member who was working as an informant for US authorities was shot eight times at close range in El Paso, literally right down the street from the city's police chief's home.

Safe houses—locations owned by cartels where kidnapping victims are held and tortured—aren't found only in the border states. In April 2009, the Associated Press published an article describing the discovery of a grisly stash house and several corpses in a wealthy Alabama county. The local sheriff was stunned by the find, given that he works in a place where they might discover five dead bodies in an entire year. Furthermore, some of the men showed signs of torture. News stories described

THE WAR INSIDE MEXICO   33

the victims: "burns seared into their earlobes revealed where modified jumper cables had been clamped as an improvised electrocution device. Adhesive from duct tape used to bind the victims still clung to wrists and faces, from mouths to noses. As a final touch, throats were slashed open, post mortem." Authorities soon discovered this was a retaliation hit over drug money with ties to the Gulf cartel.[31]

In May 2009, seventeen members of the Mexican drug trafficking group "Los Palillos" were indicted in San Diego for the drug-related murders of nine people within the city limits—including two whose bodies were dissolved in vats of acid.[32] This practice of getting rid of bodies in an acid mixture nicknamed *pozole* is more common in Mexico, but it happens here in the United States, too. Lye is often used along with the acid, and the only evidence that a body was ever put in the vat is the teeth that fall out when the mixture is poured into the sewer. The Los Palillos victims, who had been walking down the streets or in their driveways, were abducted by men dressed in police uniforms and wearing badges, held in rented homes, and sometimes killed, authorities said. Los Palillos collected thousands of dollars in ransom payments from kidnappings they conducted on US soil.[33]

Street gangs on both sides of the border are heavily involved in the distribution of Mexican cartel–supplied drugs, and some are even involved in enforcement activities on behalf of certain syndicates. For example, the Aztecas—known as "Barrio Azteca" in the United States—work for the VCFO and are suspected of being involved in the shooting of three US Consulate employees in Ciudad Juárez in March 2010. Prison gangs like the Mexican Mafia, Texas Syndicate, and Hermanos de Pistoleros Latinos are also involved in such activities. The Mara Salvatrucha, more commonly known as MS-13, is arguably the most notorious of these gangs and is even more dangerous because of its widespread presence in six countries and thirty-three (or more, by now) US states.

In January 2009, an unidentified man threw a live grenade into a strip club in Pharr, Texas, where the clientele included several off-duty police officers. The grenade didn't explode because the pin wasn't removed properly, so there were no injuries. But the subsequent investigation was challenging because there were so many potential culprits and motivations. It was never made clear if the cops or the gang members in the bar were the ultimate target, and with several gangs operating in the area, nailing one as the primary suspect was tough. What was revealed was that the grenade used in the Pharr incident came from the same lot as South Korean grenades used in an attack against the US Consulate in Monterrey, Mexico, and those found in a Mexican warehouse belonging to Los Zetas. Authorities never discovered how that grenade made its way from Mexico into the hands of a Texas gang or whether the person who threw it was acting solely on gang orders or on orders from Los Zetas.[34] The use of a grenade—a typical Mexican drug cartel tactic—within the United States by gangs with possible ties to Mexico is unsettling.

One particular border incident has done more to ignite a firestorm of debate over both border security and illegal immigration than any other incident in recent memory. In late March 2010, longtime rancher Robert Krentz was gunned down on his 35,000-acre property just northeast of Douglas, Arizona, a stone's throw away from the US-Mexico border and essentially a sister town to Agua Prieta on the Mexican side. Because that area is isolated from major cities in either country, it serves as a busy smuggling corridor for both drugs and people and has experienced an increasing number of burglaries. Media accounts say that on March 26, Krentz's brother reported drug smuggling activity to the US Border Patrol, which led to the seizure of 290 pounds of marijuana and the arrest of eight people on the ranch. Krentz's murder happened the next night.[35]

The public frenzy started after initial reports indicated that investigators found one set of footprints leading away from the crime scene to the border, leading many to believe that the murderer was an illegal immigrant. These claims were later put into doubt, and speculation began that Krentz's murder was a targeted, professional hit ordered in retaliation for his brother's going to the authorities. To date, no one knows exactly what happened to Krentz that night, other than the fact that he was shot in cold blood.

One of the more disturbing tactics being used by Mexican cartels in the United States to reclaim lost drugs and money is the home invasion by heavily armed hit men dressed up like US law enforcement officers. In June 2008, several men wearing Phoenix Police Department uniforms forced their way into a Phoenix home using the same breaching and clearing methods as a professional tactical team. The real local police happened to be in the area and heard shots fired from the vicinity of the home. By the time they arrived, the armed men were gone but had left behind a corpse and a house riddled with fifty to a hundred bullets.

This isn't the only instance where men associated with Mexican cartels have impersonated American police officers and broken into homes, demanding drugs, money, or other valuables. In most cases, they forcibly break in and announce in both English and Spanish that they're law enforcement officers. They usually threaten the victims and often tie them up. Fortunately, their victims are usually left alive, and most incidents are reported to local agencies. They obtain the tactical gear and badges by either breaking into police vehicles and stealing them or using imitation badges and gear manufactured for their use or purchased as "souvenir" items online.

Traditionally, Mexican cartels have used their own people in enforcement activities—the term "enforcement" meaning intimidation, assaults, kidnappings, and murders. These hit men, known as *sicarios,* are usually well trained, experienced with weapons and assassination tactics, overall quite professional, and good at what they do. The involvement of gangs in enforcement activities has caused the level of professionalism in these hits to decline significantly in some areas—most notably Tijuana.

That comes across with a strange tone of disappointment. It used to be that, no matter how public an assassination attempt was, the target would be taken out quickly and efficiently with no collateral damage. Most experienced *sicarios* take pride in their work and know that they need to get in, take care of the job, and get out. But when cartels start hiring gangbangers to do their dirty work for them, it can get messy. And messy means that innocent bystanders in the wrong place at the wrong time are getting caught in the crossfire with more regularity.

With the AFO in rapid decline and splintering into several pieces, a number of criminal gangs are operating in the Tijuana area and to a lesser extent in San Diego County to the north of the border. Tijuana residents are hearing more reports of hit men walking into a fast food restaurant or bar or auto parts store and spraying the place with bullets. Ostensibly, this is so they'll be sure to get their target (and their paycheck), but those kinds of hits display an obvious lack of concern for collateral damage. Unfortunately, with many smaller drug trafficking organizations in decline and unable to either afford or acquire quality *sicarios,* gang members are the new—and more indiscriminately brutal—solution to their enforcement problems.

One example of the havoc that younger, inexperienced *sicarios* can wreak is the case of David and Tiffany Hartley. In late September 2010, the married couple was riding on Jet Skis on Falcon Lake, a huge reservoir that straddles the US border with Mexico in southern Texas. They were interested in going to see a popular landmark, a submerged old church on the Mexican side of the lake. When the Hartleys crossed into Mexican waters, they might not have realized that the area was swarming with violent drug traffickers and under the control of the violent Los Zetas cartel.

In the process of turning around to head back to the US side, the Hartleys saw several armed individuals on motorboats heading quickly in their direction. The Hartleys assumed they were pirates of some kind, so they sped off on their Jet Skis toward Texas. Unfortunately, David Hartley never made it. The men on the boats started firing off rounds, and David was shot in the head and killed. Tiffany went back to try to pull his large body onto her Jet Ski, but she didn't have the strength to do it. With the men still circling and pointing their guns at her, she felt she had no choice but to leave David's body in the water and attempt to reach safety on the Texas side of the lake. She made it and was able to contact authorities once she reached the shore.

The Hartley story was scrutinized by law enforcement agencies on both sides of the border, as well as the media. The running theory became that the men who shot David Hartley were "Zetitas," or very young hit men working for the cartel. It was likely that these young killers mistook the Hartleys for scouts from a rival cartel, and their itchy trigger fingers got the best of them. It's likely that no one will ever find out what really happened or who killed David Hartley because his body was never found and the lead investigator in the case was killed and decapitated a few weeks after taking on the case.

A story that really shocked both the media and the general public was the capture of a fourteen-year-old alleged hit man named Edgar Jimenez in December 2010. Nicknamed "El Ponchis," Jimenez claimed he was forcibly recruited by the Pacific cartel (a division of the Sinaloa Federation) and drugged before being ordered to kill people. The real kicker is that he was born in the United States and was actually caught trying to board a plane from Morelos to Tijuana with his sister; they were planning to continue on to San Diego to see their mother. The Mexican daily *La Razon* claimed he was paid $3,000 per hit, and there are a few videos on YouTube of Jimenez with his victims. Because the Mexican justice system isn't really equipped to try murderers this young under adult statutes, Jimenez was to be tried as a juvenile, with a maximum sentence of three years.

This trend of recruiting younger people into cartel ranks is extending into America. An eighty-six-page indictment unsealed in July 2010 alleged that the AFO was renting apartments in the United States under a franchise scheme aimed at recruiting Americans into their illegal activities. This scheme also coordinated drug trafficking operations as well as kidnapping and extortion on both sides of the southwest border. The criminal complaint states, "Mexican drug cartels are recruiting young Americans in an effort to keep their drug trafficking operations under the radar, including using young women as drug mules to cross from Mexico into the United States." The San Diego group was also recruiting members of US-based Latino street gangs, both illegal immigrants and US citizens, and former Mexican police officers.[36]

In light of all these stories regarding the movement of narco activity north of the border, one might be inclined to think that the country is being overrun by drug traffickers and that border violence spillover is indisputable. Well, some statistics and government officials say otherwise.

Opinion is pretty polarized regarding the occurrence of Mexican drug-related violence in America. On one side are mayors and police chiefs in certain border cities who loudly proclaim theirs is one of the safest cities in the country. Looking strictly at crime statistics, they'd be right. Crime levels in San Diego have remained steady or dropped over the last six years, which is roughly when the dramatic crime spike in Tijuana started. In late January 2010, the *San Diego Union-Tribune* published an article stating that the border city's overall crime rate had plunged 18 percent in 2009, with a decrease of 25.5 percent in homicides and 15.4 percent in rapes.[37] In November 2009, CQ Press ranked El Paso as the second-safest city in the United States, based on 2008 crime statistics. FBI reports and statistics provided by police agencies showed that crime rates in Nogales, Douglas, Yuma, and other Arizona border towns have remained essentially flat for the past decade.[38]

It can be very difficult to reconcile those crime statistics with firsthand accounts of violent acts north of the border and hard to accept statements by Department of Homeland Security (DHS) officials who say that the border has never been more secure. If that's the case, one has to wonder why 1,200 National Guard troops were redeployed to the southwest border in the summer of 2010 to augment Customs and Border Protection (CBP) agents and why more resources are being diverted to border security. El Paso might have only a handful of murders each year, but ranchers in Arizona whose homes are regularly being burglarized by drug traffickers and border crossers don't care about big city crime statistics—only about the safety and sanctity of their private property. As drug traffickers and human smugglers get more desperate to move their cargo north, their actions will betray that desperation and likely become more brazen. Today, some cartels operating on both sides of the border are already facing desperate times, putting more lives in danger than ever before, and threatening the security of the United States.

CHAPTER 2

DRUG TRAFFICKING IN THE TWENTY-FIRST CENTURY

THE LAST THING SONIA ever expected to be doing to earn money was transporting illegal drugs across America. She migrated to the United States as a teenager and attended high school like any other girl her age. She got married, had kids, and moved to California to start her own little business. But things began to go downhill quickly. Her husband became an absentee father, and her mother—whom she had brought up from Mexico to help care for her kids—became very sick. Between her mother's medical bills and the cost of raising three children, Sonia was strapped for cash in a big way.

To get away from the stress of her daily life, Sonia often partied with a girlfriend, Patricia. It was obvious to anyone that Patricia and her husband had money, and they definitely lived "the good life." Sonia enjoyed spending time with them because she felt it was a much-needed escape from her job, her kids, and her debts. During one of Sonia's visits, Patricia asked her if she was doing OK. Sonia told Patricia about her money troubles, her husband essentially leaving her without any financial support, and her lack of options. Patricia confided in her that she had some "connections" that might be able to help her. All she'd have to do was make a few trips in her car across the country with some packages. She'd be paid well for being a courier of sorts. Sonia couldn't say no.

For the next several years, Sonia moved packages containing various kinds of illegal drugs in her car across the country. She kind of knew that Patricia and her husband were connected to the Sinaloa Federation, but she didn't really care. She was paid well, and that allowed her to pay her bills. Sometimes she was paid with drugs instead of cash, which was problematic because Sonia didn't use drugs. Fortunately for her, she had her own connections in her home state of Michoacán. Sonia made arrangements to sell the drugs to people associated with La Familia Michoacana. She also sometimes moved drugs for them from Mexico into Southern California via Tijuana.

Unfortunately for Sonia, the convenient arrangement didn't last. One night, while she was waiting in her car in a parking lot to make a drug delivery, she was busted by the DEA (US Drug Enforcement Administration). Even though she was a legal US resident, Sonia had committed a felony, which meant she would likely be sent back to Mexico after serving jail time in the United States. She would be separated from her children, who had grown up as Americans and might not want to go to Mexico after her release from prison. Her prospects were grim. She had known in both her head and her heart that what she was doing was wrong, but the lure of easy money was just too tempting to ignore. Not everyone who gets involved in drug trafficking has Sonia's noble intentions. But they all share the same glimmer in their eyes when they see that dangling carrot: big and easy money.

Mexican drug cartels exist solely because of the enormous profits to be made from the trafficking of illegal drugs into the United States. In

2009 alone, over 1,665 tons of illegal drugs were seized along the south-west border. That's roughly equivalent to the weight of a small US Navy frigate. Marijuana, the drug most commonly smuggled across the border, accounted for over 98 percent of the seizures. Cocaine, methamphetamine, heroin, and a small amount of MDMA—more commonly known as Ecstasy—accounted for the rest. The profits generated by Mexican drug cartels are truly mind boggling: in 2006, the National Drug Intelligence Center (NDIC) estimated that Mexican and Colombian drug trafficking organizations annually generate between $8.3 and $24.9 billion in wholesale drug earnings in the United States. The low end of that range is the equivalent of what the US government spent on the Iraq war in a typical month.[1]

Before those drugs ever make it to America, they have to get into certain parts of Mexico. For marijuana, methamphetamine, and heroin, that's the easy part because they're all produced domestically. Opium poppies grow extremely well in the central mountains of Mexico, known as the Sierra Madre Occidental. Sinaloa state, the cradle of the Federation cartel, is also home to vast marijuana fields. Mexican meth superlabs are becoming the norm, now that heavy restrictions on the sale of ephedrine have been imposed in the United States. One Mexican superlab can produce the same amount of methamphetamine as twenty standard meth labs in America.

Cocaine supply lines in Mexico are considerably more complicated because cocaine must be brought in from outside sources. The largest of these sources is Colombia, and the FARC supplies roughly 90 percent of the cocaine moved throughout Mexico. The rest of it comes from Peru, Bolivia, and a few other places. This is where the Central and South American supply lines established by expanding cartels, like the Federation and Los Zetas, come into play.

Finding people to move drugs from Mexico into the United States is the easy part. In many parts of Mexico, there are few economic prospects for young people and adults alike. As it was for Sonia, the lure of quick and easy money can be irresistible for those looking to escape a dead-end life in a Mexican backwater. The glamour of the narco lifestyle is also tough to resist, especially for teenagers who hear about the exploits of *capos* in songs called *narcocorridos*. If there aren't enough people who volunteer to smuggle drugs, cartels sometimes forcibly recruit drug mules. This type of enslavement is often a form of punishment meted out to people who haven't paid "taxes" to the cartels or who somehow did something to upset them.

Drug and human smuggling outfits in Arizona are targeting young people in Phoenix bars for recruitment into their ranks. The state has a high unemployment rate and thus many US citizens who are desperate for money and employment and who can blend in with the general population going about its business. Recruiters for the cartels often flash large amounts of cash at the potential new hires who are targeted to bring drugs, guns, and people to various locations along the US-Mexico border.[2]

Getting the drugs across the border is the hard part. Fortunately for the traffickers—and unfortunately for the United States—there are several means of drug transport at smugglers' disposal. Some are considerably more common than others, and as law enforcement efforts along the border and within Mexico intensify, the cartels quickly adapt and either move elsewhere or develop new smuggling methods. Here are some of the most prevalent cross-border drug smuggling methods.

LAND TRANSPORT

For those who have never been to the US-Mexico border by road or highway, it can be hard to envision the sheer volume of vehicle traffic that passes across the southwest border on a daily basis. Both pedestrians and vehicles—private and commercial—pass through border stations called "ports of entry," which are controlled by CBP. There are currently twenty-five land ports of entry along the border; some are for both pedestrians and vehicles, and some are designated for commercial traffic only.

In 2009, over 4.3 million trucks crossed from Mexico into the United States through southwest-border ports of entry, according to the US Bureau of Transportation, and over 41.3 million pedestrians and 70.3 million private vehicles.[3] The estimated wait times for reaching the primary inspection booth, the first point of contact with CBP when crossing the border, can be two hours or longer at the busier ports of entry during peak hours.[4]

Trucks and cars pose a huge challenge for CBP inspectors because there are so many places to hide drugs: hidden compartments inside the seats, the tires, and the gas tank, just to name a few. The technology used in drug detection has vastly improved, but sometimes the best help comes from a good drug dog or several pairs of hands ripping a car apart from the inside out. And getting so destructive is often the only way to access some of these compartments, which can be mind boggling in their sophistication.

In February 2009, police in New Bedford, Massachusetts, discovered a hidden compartment behind the speedometer in a 2002 Volkswagen Jetta. The compartment "could only be opened by triggering an exact sequence of switches, such as setting the radio to a particular station, then flipping a turn signal and stepping on the emergency brake. This would then flip open the gauge cluster and reveal a compartment large enough to hold drugs, guns, and cash," according to media reports. One can imagine the level of expertise it takes to construct such a compartment. The local police said the people involved would have had to take out the entire engine block to do it, at a cost of $10,000 to $15,000. "There is a specialty group of people out there with the skills to do this," said New Bedford police spokesman Lt. Jeffrey P. Silva. "People who do this are known throughout the criminal underground."[5]

Smugglers often bring drugs across the border the old-fashioned way—on foot through unguarded territory—when drug trafficking organizations don't want to run the risk of being caught at a port of entry. There are several downsides to this method. First, smugglers are limited by the amount of weight they can successfully carry across often-forbidding terrain. The landscape along the 2,000-mile-long border can vary dramatically, from sandblasted and scorched desert to rugged hills and rocky outcroppings. Temperatures can soar to over 120 degrees in some places and plummet to 50 degrees when the sun goes down, so having the right clothing for the season is crucial to survival. Natural clean water sources are often hard to come by, so smugglers usually have to take as much water as they can carry, in addition to their drug load. Second, to increase the overall load size, they have to increase the number of hikers in a smuggling group, and this makes them easier to detect. However, the advantage to smuggling drugs by foot is the fact that there are hundreds of miles along the border without either a border fence or the possibility of a rapid response by Border Patrol agents.

When more traditional overland methods of drug smuggling don't seem feasible in a particular place, cartels have been known to go underground—literally. Over seventy-five border tunnels have been discovered along the US-Mexico border since 2006.[6] Some of these tunnels are small and crudely dug, but others are absolute marvels of construction, taking into account what they're used for and the clandestine circumstances under which they're built. A few have had wooden support beams throughout, concrete flooring, extensive lighting, and ventilation systems. Some even have rails for moving carts filled with narcotics headed north into the United States—or conversely, bundles of money heading south into Mexico.

One of the more sophisticated border tunnels was discovered in January 2006 in a fruit distribution center in Otay Mesa, California. The tunnel went eighty-five feet underground and emerged a half mile away in Tijuana, where it was used by the AFO to smuggle drugs into the United States.[7] Typically, tunnels are discovered when somebody tips off authorities to signs of suspicious work like digging sounds, activity at odd hours, or numerous trucks. Although several tunnel-detection methods are currently in use by border officials—including ground-penetrating radar and sonic equipment—investigation and good observation methods tend to supersede the benefits of modern technology. Border Patrol agents know that sometimes the best way they have to find border tunnels is to accidentally run over the entrance to one with a truck.

However, tunnel-detection technology is improving. In mid-2009, the Department of Homeland Security began working with Lockheed Martin to develop a ground-penetrating radar system specifically designed to detect border tunnels by using much lower frequencies and new imaging technology. A prototype device developed by Idaho National Laboratories is called the Look-Ahead Sensor (LAS); it transmits acoustic waves into the earth. An onboard motion detector measures how the waves shake the dirt and rock through which they pass. The LAS then sends the measurements generated by the waves to a laptop computer, where special software can graph and analyze them to determine if a tunnel possibly exists below the sensor.

In 2003, Immigration and Customs Enforcement (ICE) formed the San Diego Tunnel Task Force—the only formally established group of its kind, although Nogales, Arizona, has a more informal one with the same mission. The task force is a multi-agency effort—including the Border Patrol, DEA, US Department of Justice (USDOJ), and US Navy personnel—to conduct investigations that eventually lead to the discovery of tunnels used to smuggle large quantities of drugs into the United States. The task force actually recently discovered two tunnels in the Otay Mesa, California, area; they were found only three weeks apart. One of those discoveries led to a seizure of twenty tons of marijuana. The tunnel had two entrances on the US side, roughly eight hundred feet apart in two different warehouses, and ran ninety feet deep. Inside, one tunnel's walls were fortified with wood and cinderblock supports, and the passageway was equipped with advanced rail, electrical, and ventilation systems.

Tunnels rarely last more than a couple of months before they are unearthed. Once they're discovered, they're filled with concrete, often at great expense. One Otay Mesa tunnel cost $700,000 to fill. Despite the short-lived nature of these tunnels, drug smugglers keep digging and human smugglers keep moving people in this often dangerous manner.

MARITIME TRANSPORT

A frequent sight off the coast of Miami is a fifty-foot cigarette boat propelling through ocean waves at a clip of sixty knots. The ability to cut through rough ocean waters at high speeds, combined with a decent amount of storage capacity, makes these competition-grade power boats—also known as "go-fast boats," for obvious reasons—the ideal method of maritime transport for drug smugglers. Go-fasts are difficult to detect using conventional radar, particularly in calm seas, and the US Coast Guard has limited resources with which to chase these boats if intercepted at sea. However, the "Coasties" do have helicopters equipped with weapons capable of disabling the powerful motors of go-fasts.

While speed is almost always the most desirable trait in a seagoing smuggling vessel, sometimes the ability to blend in can be even more important. Smugglers have been known to use larger yachts and luxury vessels to slip larger loads into waters just off the US coast. Those loads are usually off-loaded onto motorized rafts or other small boats that can slip onto a deserted stretch of beach along the California or Texas coast. The Coast Guard does have some capability to detect suspicious vessels from shore, but it's a difficult task at best in places like San Diego and the offshore Coronado Islands, where hundreds of pleasure boats and larger yachts cruise along on any given weekend.

Speed is also sometimes trumped by sheer load capacity. The newest craze in maritime smuggling started in the 1990s with the use of self-propelled semi-submersible submarines, more commonly known as "drug submarines." They're usually bare-bones affairs, with small diesel-type engines and exhaust pipes, which plug along at the tortoise pace of six knots or so. Some drug subs actually look like they're held together with cardboard, duct tape, and PVC pipe, although some industrially constructed million-dollar models have been seized in Colombia.

In July 2010, Ecuadorean counter-drug and military authorities, with the assistance of the DEA, seized a fully operational submarine built for the primary purpose of transporting multi-ton quantities of cocaine. The twin-screw, diesel electric-powered submarine was about ninety-five feet long and about nine feet high from the deck plates to the ceiling. The sophisticated vessel also had a conning tower, a periscope, and an air-conditioning system—in stark contrast to the usual bare-bones drug subs that have been seized to date. The submarine was constructed in a remote part of the jungle in an effort to avoid detection by the authorities, and it was located near a small waterway close to the Ecuador-Colombia border. As a result of DEA intelligence, Ecuadorean authorities were able to seize the vessel before it was able to make its first smuggling trip. This was the first seizure of a secretly built, fully operational submarine made specifically for maritime drug trafficking.[8]

The advantages that drug subs have are their sheer capacity to haul drugs—up to eight tons, in some cases—and the smugglers' ability to purposely flood and sink them within a minute or two. They're also virtually undetectable visually or by radar, and many of those that have been captured at sea were found by pure luck. Drug subs are increasingly being used to move cocaine from Colombia into southern parts of Mexico, where the drug loads are then moved overland. However, some have been detected more recently in waters closer to the US coastline.

Drug smugglers are still using commercial vessels and their onboard containers to stash drug loads, although this isn't their preferred method. Those who use them are typically Dominican or South American traffickers trying to smuggle drugs into the eastern United States through Caribbean routes. Mexican cartels have the benefit of a direct land route to transport drugs, so using commercial vessels is likely more trouble than it's worth for them. The main benefit, however, is that drugs can easily be hidden alongside legitimate cargo, and few cargo containers are physically inspected upon arrival at US ports. Current seizure statistics show that container ships with Caribbean points of origin are the ones most likely to be carrying contraband; commercial vessel seizures of drugs smuggled by Mexican cartels account for only 1 percent of all southwest border drug seizures.

Despite this statistic, some of the most creative ways smugglers have transported drugs have involved maritime methods. In June 2009, the Mexican navy was inspecting some freight containers in the Yucatán port of Progreso when they came across something that looked suspicious. They brought in x-ray equipment and sniffer dogs to inspect one container in particular, and what they found inside threw them for a loop. Inside the container was more than a ton of cocaine stuffed inside the carcasses of more than twenty frozen sharks.[9] Also in June 2009, US Border Patrol agents arrested two Mexican surfers for trying to smuggle 141 pounds of marijuana. The bales were attached to a third board with black duct tape, and the two men were towing the loaded board behind them about 200 yards offshore from Imperial Beach, California.[10]

AIR TRANSPORT

Amado Carrillo Fuentes, the drug lord known as "The Lord of the Skies," who died during plastic surgery in 1997, pioneered the use of air transport to smuggle drugs. At one time, he had a fleet of at least twenty-two private Boeing 727 airplanes he used to transport Colombian cocaine to both municipal airports and dirt airstrips around Mexico.[11]

One interesting trend that US border agencies are seeing is the increased use of ultralight aircraft to transport loads of marijuana across the border. Depending on the ultralight model, they can carry more than 250 pounds of cargo, in addition to the pilot. Most models don't have a long range, so they have to take off relatively close to the border in Mexico and have another method of transportation ready to go at a pre-arranged location in the United States. Usually that will take the form of an ATV or truck that can carry the pilot and the drug load to their ultimate destination.

In just the six months between October 2009 and mid-April 2010, the CBP Air and Marine Operation Center (AMOC) in Riverside, California, detected 193 suspected incursions and 135 confirmed incursions by ultralights. In May 2010, the North American Aerospace Defense Command scrambled two F-16 jet fighters to intercept an ultralight aircraft crossing into Arizona and followed it for about thirty minutes before it flew back into Mexico. Some ultralights have been detected as far as 200 miles inside the US-Mexico border.[12] And they're hard to catch because drug smugglers using them don't follow Federal Aviation Administration rules regarding the use of lights, specific altitudes, or flight paths. Both legal and humanitarian considerations prevent US law enforcement from trying to down them while in flight, making them even harder to catch.

While flight is currently the least common method that drug trafficking organizations use to smuggle drugs into the United States, South American suppliers are flying cocaine and heroin into Mexico instead, where they're then moved overland across the border. Air interdiction efforts in Colombia have also increased, which is why we're seeing fewer and fewer drugs coming in by air.

DISTRIBUTION WITHIN THE UNITED STATES

Once illegal drugs make their way from Mexico into the United States, the hardest part is done. When drugs are brought across the border, they are generally stored in warehouses or safe houses in some of the region's principal metropolitan areas, including Dallas, El Paso, Houston, Los Angeles, Phoenix, San Antonio, and San Diego.[13] The drugs are divided into separate packages for shipment to various parts of America. Some of the busiest drug transit routes in the Southwest used for this purpose include highway I-5, which runs north from San Diego, California, to the

Canadian border north of Seattle; I-8, which runs east from San Diego through Yuma, Arizona, and connects with I-10 just south of Phoenix; I-15, which runs north from San Diego into Los Angeles, then northeast through Las Vegas; I-10, which runs east from Los Angeles all the way to Jacksonville and conveniently passes through cities like Phoenix, Tucson, El Paso, and San Antonio; and I-35, which runs northeast from Laredo, Texas, through Austin and Dallas, then on into the Midwest.

Distribution within cities and towns depends on the composition of criminal elements in each location. In most urban areas, gangs are largely responsible for drug dealing. Some are more closely involved with the Mexican cartels themselves than others are, but there is ample evidence that the cartels are keeping a close eye on their product once it enters the United States. Current USDOJ estimates indicate that Mexican drug trafficking organizations have an established presence in one form or another in over 270 US cities, and that doesn't even include all the smaller towns and rural communities where Mexican-grown and -manufactured drugs are being sold to American consumers.

In some cases, it's the average American who could be involved in moving the drugs. In November 2010, thirty-five people were named in an indictment alleging they were transporting drugs within the United States for the Sinaloa Federation. Of those arrested, twenty-three were in Colorado, two in El Paso, one in Illinois, one in Alabama, and one in Nevada. They included street gang members, a retired Denver firefighter, and an assistant baseball coach at Regis University. The US attorney for the case said his reaction to the variety of people arrested was "beyond surprise."[14]

Once illegal drugs make their way across the border, they keep going into the rest of the country. For people living in or near a decent-sized metropolitan area, chances are pretty high that their hometown is infested with drugs being managed by one of the Mexican cartels. The National Drug Intelligence Center (NDIC) identifies seven cities that are most frequently used as points of origin or destination for drug shipments that come from Mexico:

Chicago, Denver, Detroit, Houston, Miami, New York, and Tucson. Notice that only two out of the seven are anywhere near the southwest border.[15]

Mexican drug cartels are "hiding in plain sight" in different parts of the United States. Atlanta's changing demographics have led it to become one of the nation's busiest drug distribution hubs. Suburban Gwinnett County, about thirty miles northeast of Atlanta, is the "epicenter" of the region's drug activity. Gwinnett's Hispanic population surged from 8,470 in 1990 to 64,137 in 2000. Currently, 17 percent of the county's 776,000 people are Hispanic. "You see Mexican drug-trafficking operations deploying representatives to hide within these communities in plain sight," said Rodney Benson, the DEA's Atlanta chief. "They were attempting to blend into the same communities as those who were hard-working, law-abiding people."[16] In fiscal year 2008, federal drug authorities seized more drug-related cash in Atlanta—about $70 million—than in any other region in the country. "The same folks who are rolling heads in the streets of Ciudad Juárez are operating in Atlanta. Here, they are just better behaved," says Jack Killorin, who heads a federal task force for the Office of National Drug Control Policy (ONDCP) in Atlanta.[17] Typical Mexican drug gang members in the United States work very hard to maintain a low profile. It's easier for them to distribute drugs when the police don't know who they are and where they are. If they're successful at this, it means that the general population tends to not know who they are, either.

Depending on the part of the country, methamphetamine might be a community's biggest drug threat. Sometimes known as "ice" (crystal methamphetamine) or "crank" (homemade, moonshine-type meth), this highly addictive and insidious drug is easily made with a variety of interchangeable chemicals. Not only is it one of the Mexican drug cartels' biggest drug exports, but it's also being made *everywhere* in the United States, often in labs far away from the border but run by Mexican personnel.

Meth labs are funny things. They're easy to hide because they don't require a lot of equipment, yet they're also easily detectable because of the distinctive smell they produce and the sometimes careless ways that chemical containers are disposed of. They are also incredibly common throughout America, and it's disturbing to see how many have been discovered in recent years. For example, in Florida between 2004 and 2010, over 560 clandestine drug laboratories were found by law enforcement agencies. In Utah, only about sixty labs were found during the same period, and in Maine, only nine. Then there are states like California, with over 770 meth labs discovered, Kansas with over 370, and Michigan with over 700.[18]

To demonstrate how deeply into America's heartland the Mexican cartels have infiltrated, take a look at Iowa. In 2004, when roughly twenty clandestine drug laboratories *per month* were being found there, Iowa was officially dubbed "the meth capital of the world." This number decreased dramatically after the sale of pseudoephedrine was banned in Iowa in 2005. In 2008, thirty-five labs were discovered across the state of Iowa. Although domestic production in the state declined, it was quickly replaced by the influx of Mexican-made crystal meth.

In South Dakota, officials boasted in 2006 that their law restricting pseudoephedrine had resulted in a faster reduction in the number of meth labs than in any other state. Still, 74 percent of the local police said that the law had not changed the *demand* for meth at all, and 61 percent said that *supply* had remained steady or increased.[19]

In October 2009, authorities busted a meth lab that was run by LFM in the middle-class Atlanta suburb of Lawrenceville. It was one of the largest US meth labs authorities had ever seen; they seized 174 pounds of the illegal drug and arrested several members of the cartel. LFM members used flammable chemicals to crystallize a liquid solution of methamphetamine that had been manufactured in Mexico.[20] All this was unfolding in a typical suburban neighborhood in Georgia where kids play on the street every day.

The methods used by Mexican cartels to smuggle illegal drugs into the United States have had to adapt over the years because of law enforcement efforts north of the border, which are making some strides in drug seizures and drug interdiction. However, the cartels always seem to stay one step ahead. It also doesn't help that US demand for marijuana, cocaine, heroin, and methamphetamine has changed very little in the last few decades. Until it does, drug trafficking from Mexico into America will continue relatively unabated.

CHAPTER 3

FROM MEXICO TO MAIN STREET

AN ILLEGAL DRUG'S JOURNEY INTO AMERICA

IT'S GOING TO BE ANOTHER long, hot day in the poppy fields for Ernesto. His life in the Mexican state of Guerrero is hard, even brutal at times. But he does what he has to do in order to support his wife and three children, who will likely have few opportunities of their own. He thinks about this as he gears up at sunrise to begin the laborious process of harvesting the now-mature opium poppies nearby.

Ernesto had to wait for the poppy flowers' petals to fall off. After that, he makes a few slices in the capsules that remain on the stalks. Over the course of a day, raw opium will ooze through these cuts. After the capsules are done oozing, he'll scrape off the opium gum and collect it in paper bags. The average poppy field has thousands of poppy plants, so Ernesto has much work to do, for which he hopes to receive good compensation.

Finally, he'll cut off the capsules and open them up so he can scrape out the seeds that will be used for next year's crop.

After he's done collecting all the opium gum he can, Ernesto will lay out the gum to dry and then bundle it up in a banana leaf or plastic. It lasts for a long time, so Ernesto can wait for the right buyer with the right price to visit his village in Guerrero and make a good offer. These days, Ernesto can make between US $700 and $1,200 for each pound of opium gum,[1] and this is only the first harvest. If the weather cooperates, he might be able to get two more before the end of the season.

Almost 1,900 miles away in the busy city of Chicago, Michael needs to get well, and fast. He's a heroin addict, and the last hit he took was diluted so much that the drug's effect lasted for what felt like only seconds. Fortunately for Michael, he lives in a city where heroin is easy to find and relatively inexpensive.

After finding his dealer, he quickly pays $50 for his fix. It's more than he would normally pay, but his tolerance is starting to build up. He needs to start paying more for the higher-purity heroin that isn't cut with lots of other chemicals. After he gets settled at home and the drug enters his system, he's transported far away from his pain, his troubles, and his miserable life in Chicago's North Side. He can't even begin to fathom how far removed he is from Ernesto, 1,900 miles away in a Mexican village.

But as far apart as Ernesto and Michael seem to be geographically, they are at the ends of a long "rope" that stretches from Mexico to Middle America that used to be called the "Heroin Highway." Now, countless ropes connect marijuana, methamphetamine, and heroin producers in Mexico to drug users in the United States. Sadly, those ropes aren't easily cut, and even when they become frayed, they're often easily repaired. There's also a lot that happens between the two ends, and having a better understanding of how illegal drugs go from their fundamental sources to their ultimate users is the first step in developing a strategy to cut those ropes.

BETWEEN BEGINNINGS AND THE BORDER

Once an opium gum buyer has the basic materials that he needs from harvesters like Ernesto, the real work begins. Raw opium has to go through several complex chemical steps to become the heroin that Michael will eventually inject or inhale. First, the gum has to go to a refinery, where it is converted into morphine through boiling and filtering. Next, the morphine is pressed into bricks, and then it must go through a complex chemical process to convert it into heroin, which can reach purity levels above 90 percent. However, by the time it reaches the end user, Mexican heroin can be diluted down to as little as 5 percent pure, although some varieties are considerably more potent—and often more expensive on the street. Black tar heroin, which is a more concentrated version than the more common brown powder Mexican heroin, can reach purity levels between 50 and 80 percent, but it can be sold as cheaply as $10 for a small baggie.[2] The more pure a heroin sample is at the beginning, the more it can be diluted along the way into larger—and more profitable—volumes of sellable product.

Carlos is one of the first people to get his hands on several almost-pure repackaged bricks of heroin from a hidden Mexican refinery. He's been ordered by his bosses in the Vicente Carrillo Fuentes Organization—also known as the Juárez cartel—to transport the bricks to a warehouse in Ciudad Juárez for holding and further processing. Once Carlos's load arrives at the warehouse, other Juárez cartel employees get to work on "cutting" the heroin. This is a method by which certain substances that look similar to heroin are added in order to increase the overall sellable volume. Some cutting substances include caffeine, lactose, antimalarial drugs, painkillers, and an acid or base indicator.

These sound like strange things to be using to dilute a potent illegal drug, but they actually serve a purpose. Caffeine, for example, causes heroin to vaporize at a lower temperature, which might be seen by heroin users who smoke or inhale heroin as a practical benefit of mixing the two substances. Chloroquine, a well-known antimalarial drug, does not alter the effects of heroin or influence the way in which it is consumed, but its widespread availability, low price, color, and crystalline structure are probably why it's used. Acetaminophen, known by brand names like Tylenol, is easy to purchase and relatively cheap, and its mild pain-reducing properties and bitter taste might disguise heroin of poor quality.[3] The main idea with cutting agents is to find something that is relatively nontoxic, looks like the drug it's being used with, and has similar properties, like water solubility.

Once the heroin in the Juárez cartel's warehouse is cut according to instructions, it has to be packaged for transportation across the border. Each cartel has its own way of packing its drugs, but generally they're wrapped tightly in foil or plastic—the latter to make the package waterproof. The packages also usually take the form of a brick for easier packing into vehicles, backpacks, and generally tight spaces. Many times, the bricks are stamped with a symbol that clearly identifies which cartel the drugs belong to.

Next, couriers are selected by cartel leadership to bring the bricks across the border.[4] Chapter 2 presented the various ways that illegal drugs are brought into the United States from Mexico. For this example, ten people are selected to bring five bricks each through one of the four ports of entry open to vehicles between Juárez and El Paso, Texas. Those couriers are selected, by the way, through coordination between the source cartel and other Mexican criminal organizations that specialize in drug transport. According to the National Drug Intelligence Center, Mexican cartels commonly employ independent transportation brokers to facilitate the movement of drug shipments across the US-Mexico border and into and through West Texas.[5] These brokers help to further insulate cartels from law enforcement and are generally well worth the money they're paid by the cartels to do that job.

Optimistically, perhaps three of the ten cars are stopped and thoroughly searched by US Customs and Border Protection at the vehicle crossing, those drivers' five bricks are seized, and the drivers themselves are taken into custody for prosecution, removal, or both. The drivers had hidden their drugs pretty well in the false bottoms of luggage and in hidden compartments, but they don't fool the drug dogs on duty that day. That's bad news for those drivers, but the other seven make it through into El Paso, and their thirty-five bricks are untouched. They are lucky to have better hiding compartments in their vehicles, which include four SUVs with huge gas tanks perfect for hiding drugs. They are also lucky that no canine units are scanning their lanes when they cross.

ON THE ROAD AGAIN

Now that those thirty-five bricks of heroin are in El Paso, they'll go into a local warehouse or some other staging area, like an apartment or a rented house owned and controlled by the Juárez cartel. But they won't stay there for long. Workers selected by the VCFO open the bricks, possibly dilute the heroin further, and repackage specific amounts for wholesale distribution. Then it becomes a matter of which direction to take the heroin, depending on where the demand is. It also depends on which highways have fewer checkpoints. In this case, a shipment of heroin is going by vehicle to the Chicago area, and that shipment will include a few of these bricks.

Antonio is the driver for this shipment. Growing up in a lower-middle-class neighborhood in El Paso, he didn't exactly aspire to being a drug courier. His parents brought him to Texas from Mexico when he was six years old, and while they were able to find work, they still weren't exactly living the best life. Antonio made friends, but they weren't in the good-kids crowd. He made some money here and there, with some jobs being legit and others, not so much. But he had a clean record, and more importantly, a reliable pickup truck.

After Antonio graduated from high school, attending college wasn't anywhere on his priority list. His parents couldn't afford to send him, and his grades weren't scholarship material. After a couple of years of scraping by, a friend of a friend approached him at a party. This new acquaintance had a quick and easy way for Antonio to make some money, and all it would involve was long-distance driving and no questions asked. He wasn't stupid; Antonio had a good idea of what he'd be transporting, but he agreed that the fewer details he knew—like the fact that the friend of a friend worked for the Juárez cartel—the better. After a couple of weeks, he got a phone call and was asked to do his first courier job. He'd be heading the next morning to Chicago after picking up his load. He'd never see it, as his car would be packed in El Paso and unloaded in Chicago by someone else. He would be paid handsomely upon his safe return to El Paso.

Chicago is only one of those 270 US cities across the country where Mexican drug cartels have a major presence,[6] but "Chi-town" has a strong history of ties to Mexican heroin. In the 1980s, Amado Carrillo Fuentes— then head of the Juárez cartel—had been working on deals with Colombian producers to bring cocaine into Mexico. However, the Colombians were interested in entering the heroin business, so Carrillo Fuentes set up arrangements between Colombian producers and the Herrera Family in Durango, Mexico. The Herrera family had been in the heroin business for a long time and provided the trafficking opportunities the Colombians were looking for.[7] As far back as 1957, the Herrera organization ran a "farm-to-the-arm" heroin operation that cultivated opium poppy plants, processed and packaged heroin in Mexico, and transported it to Chicago—via the Heroin Highway. There, it was either sold locally or distributed to other US cities. This group was extremely difficult to penetrate because family members controlled the entire heroin process from top to bottom.[8] The Herrera family was pretty much put out of business by the DEA in the late 1980s with arrests of its top leaders, but heroin trafficking in Chicago continued.

The quickest way out of El Paso to Chicago is via Interstate 10. There is a Border Patrol checkpoint just west of Sierra Blanca, but Antonio was able to avoid it by taking a slightly longer route around it. The drive between the two cities takes roughly twenty-four hours, so Antonio would have to stop at some point to rest. He couldn't take the risk of staying in a hotel, so he'd catnap in his truck for a couple of hours at rest stops. The afternoon after his departure from El Paso, he arrived in Chicago, thankful not to have been pulled over for anything. Antonio headed straight for the address given to him by his new acquaintance and called the cell phone number to announce his arrival.

After a couple of minutes, two men emerged from the small warehouse and told him to unlock the tonneau cover of his truck bed. Whatever was in there, the men had it out and in the warehouse in less than two minutes. Antonio was free to go. It seemed anticlimactic after all the stress of driving so carefully and wondering what was in his truck bed. But the money he was paid when he got back to El Paso made Antonio forget all about the stress, the long drive, the uncomfortable naps, the men at the warehouse, and the mysterious contents of his truck. He'd be ready for the next haul when the call came.

TAKING IT TO THE STREETS

Back at the warehouse, the two men Antonio saw, as well as other people, were busy with his load and others. Some of his bricks would be given to other couriers just like him for transportation to places like New York and Miami.[9] Others would be opened and divided up into baggies for local distribution. According to the National Drug Intelligence Center, Mexican cartels operating in Chicago supply high-ranking, local street gang members with drugs for this purpose. These cartels—the Juárez cartel included—generally store large quantities of cocaine and marijuana and smaller quantities of heroin and ice methamphetamine in stash houses located in Chicago and surrounding suburban communities, for subsequent distribution. Twenty of these heroin baggies supplied by Juárez cartel employees made it into Ramon's hands.

Ramon grew up on Chicago's North Side. He came from Mexico as a child with his parents, who split up shortly after they arrived. His mom had a hard time raising him and his three sisters, even though she was working two jobs and long hours. While he was still in high school, gang life seemed very attractive and held the promise of good money if he got involved with certain aspects of gang business. The Latin Kings are the largest gang in Chicago, so being recruited by them was almost inevitable for Ramon. The Chicago Police Department estimates that they have over twenty-five thousand members in Chicago alone and are very well structured and organized.[10]

Street gangs like the Latin Kings are typically supplied with wholesale quantities—larger amounts at lower prices to be resold in smaller amounts for higher prices—of illicit drugs by Mexican cartel members working in the local area. Some Hispanic gangs have long-standing drug supply sources in Mexico or along the southwest border. People hired by the cartels, and sometimes gang members themselves, have routine ways of transporting drugs from those supply sources to gangs in different parts of the United States. For example, the Chicago-based Latin Kings street gang has members in Midland, Texas, who purchase cocaine from Mexican traffickers for $16,000 to $18,000 per kilogram, compared with $25,000 to $35,000 per kilogram when purchasing from wholesale traffickers in Chicago. These cost savings "allow gangs with sources of supply closer to the southwest border to gain a distinct business advantage and to serve as suppliers to other street gangs in the region," per the NDIC.[11] As a result of these practices, the Latin Kings have a pretty good heroin business going on the city's North Side in Humboldt Park, which serves as Ramon's "office."

On this particular morning, Ramon is driving through the park with a few baggies of higher-purity Mexican brown powder heroin, which came from Antonio's load. The brick it was separated from was cut only once, so Ramon can charge more than the $10 he normally demands for a baggie. He scans the park, looking for people who might approach him for a buy, when he sees Michael. He's sold to Michael before, so he's able to notice that the addict isn't looking so good. This bodes well for a strong sale.

Michael walks up to Ramon's car and quickly asks for something stronger than the usual. He buys only two baggies of heroin at $25 apiece, which is disappointing for Ramon, but he knows Michael will be back. They always come back.

DIFFERENT DRUGS, SAME STORY

This hypothetical example shows how the drug business works from one end of the rope—Ernesto and his poppy fields in Guerrero—to the other—with Michael and his heroin-induced stupor in Chicago. But heroin is just one of the many drugs trafficked by Mexican cartels, Ernesto is just one of thousands of drug producers, and Michael is just one of millions of drug users. An almost endless number of combinations can also be put together for the production and movement of marijuana, cocaine, and methamphetamine from within and beyond Mexico to the ultimate user in any and every part of America.

Although the drugs themselves are different from heroin, the transportation and distribution methods are mostly the same. Mexican cartels get their cocaine from Colombia and occasionally from Peru or Bolivia, but they buy their marijuana from growers like Ernesto, and they produce their own methamphetamine in superlabs hidden across Mexico. The drugs are moved to stash houses and warehouses all along the border on the Mexican side and then prepped for the border crossing. Specialists are contracted out by cartel leadership to move those drugs across the border by car, truck, hiker, drug tunnel, speedboat, or ultralight. Then they go into holding at stash houses in Los Angeles, El Paso, Houston, Tucson, and elsewhere. From there, the drugs are either distributed locally or moved by courier to dozens of major US cities like Denver, New York, Chicago, and Miami that serve as drug distribution hubs. In those cities and hundreds of suburbs and smaller communities beyond, Hispanic gangs in league with Mexican cartels take over the distribution and put those drugs into the hands of users.

So it becomes clear where many of the challenges are for those attempting to break the cycle. They can stop some drug producers, but not all. They can catch some drugs at the border, but not all. They can catch some cross-country couriers through checkpoints or traffic stops, but not all. They can arrest some gang members involved in selling drugs, but not all. And they can help some drug addicts, but not all. Unless something eliminates all of the Ernestos in Mexico or all of the Michaels in America, this drug transportation and distribution pattern from Mexico to the United States will be repeated endlessly.

CHAPTER 4

THE BIGGEST ARMED FORCE SOUTH OF THE BORDER

RAUL WAS SWEATING BULLETS, and it wasn't because of the weather; it was actually unseasonably cool for a September morning in Houston. He was getting ready to walk into a gun shop and make some purchases. Normally, this wouldn't be a big deal for Raul. After all, he was a US citizen, had never committed a crime (at least not one he had ever been caught committing), and was merely exercising his Second Amendment rights. He knew exactly what to buy and what questions to ask. He knew how to fill out the forms and that his quick background check would come up clean. There was only one little snag: Raul was buying these guns for a Mexican cartel, and he knew in the back of his mind that they would probably be used to kill Mexican cops or drug dealers.

But Raul couldn't think about that right then. He stood to pocket over $500 for a couple of hours of his time, if he could just pull this off. He wiped his brow with an old red bandanna and then purposefully strode into the gun shop. He looked around for the rifles and found the ones he was looking for. Raul saw a young shop employee and decided he might be less likely to get suspicious. *Can I see a Bushmaster XM15 rifle when you get a chance?* The employee was happy to help and brought one of the rifles over to Raul to inspect. Raul held it up, felt the weight, checked the sights—pretty much everything people would do if they were buying such a rifle for themselves. *OK, I'd like to buy four.* Unfortunately, the shop only had three in stock. This might pose a problem with Raul's broker, but he said he'd take the three.

It was time to move on to the pistols. *Do you have any FN FiveSeven pistols in stock?* Raul was in luck, as the shop had five. Raul inspected those and asked for three of them. He browsed through a few more handguns and asked to buy a .38-caliber revolver and a 9mm semi-automatic. To finish up his shopping list, he asked for as much ammunition as he could get without raising any suspicion—about two hundred rounds total.

Then for the hard part: Raul started filling out the standard ATF Form 4473—the Firearms Transaction Record that everyone has to fill out when buying or transferring ownership of a gun—while the shop employee made a copy of his Texas driver's license. He flinched ever so slightly when he got to question 11.a.: *Are you the actual transferee/buyer of the firearm(s) listed on this form?* It was actually the warning that came after that question that made Raul uneasy: *You are not the actual buyer if you are acquiring the firearm(s) on behalf of another person. If you are not the actual buyer, the dealer cannot transfer the firearm(s) to you.* But, like he was supposed to, he checked the "Yes" box and finished filling out the form. Within the hour, the shop employee had finished his background check (which, as expected, came back clean), boxed up the purchases, and sent Raul on his way.

With the required firearms in his possession (minus the one XM15 the store didn't have in stock), Raul had to pass them off to his broker, who also happened to be his cousin. Raul knew his cousin Manny was involved in some shady dealings, but he wasn't sure of the exact nature of Manny's "business." He also knew that Manny had been arrested for theft and a few other things—but nothing serious. When Manny had called Raul and offered the opportunity to make some quick and easy money, Raul was already wary of what that opportunity would involve. But when Manny explained that all Raul had to do was buy a few guns in a couple of different shops, it seemed pretty straightforward and easy to do. After all, it wasn't as if he was using a fake ID or anything. And if the feds came looking for him, he could just say he sold the guns to some friends of friends and didn't write up any documentation for the sales.

The next day, Raul and his guns made the three-hour drive to San Antonio to meet up with Manny. He assured his cousin that everything went well and that he was fairly certain that he didn't raise any suspicion while in the shop. Manny was happy about this because it meant that Raul would be able to buy more guns at that shop at a later date. After some chitchat and catching up, Manny took the guns out of the trunk of Raul's car. He was disappointed that Raul couldn't get that fourth XM15, but it would be OK. He counted all the guns and ammunition, took a wad of cash out of his pocket that made Raul's eyes pop, and peeled off five $100 bills. *It's $100 for each rifle, $50 for the handguns, and $50 for the ammo,* Manny told him. Raul just nodded his head silently and pocketed the cash. One could get used to this kind of money for so little time and work. With that, Raul bid his cousin farewell, got back in his car, and headed home to Houston.

Then it was time for Manny the Broker to get to work. He had several men like Raul working for him and had accumulated enough firearms to start prepping them for the trip south to Mexico. Over the course of a week, Manny divided the guns among a dozen or so people who would stash them in hidden compartments in their cars. The drivers would spread out over several Texas ports of entry: Brownsville, McAllen, Laredo, and Eagle Pass. He wasn't too concerned that the cars would be inspected because Mexican customs agents had proven to be mostly useless. Even though the US Department of Homeland Security had said several months prior that it would start inspecting 10 percent of southbound vehicles at the border, that was still only 10 percent. The odds were in Manny's favor.

Luckily for Manny, none of his drivers got checked on their way into Mexico. Once in the country, they all went their separate ways, depending on which *capo* needed what guns and where. The driver of the car with an XM15, an AK-47, an FN FiveSeven pistol, and 300 rounds of ammunition hidden inside made his way to a stash house in Reynosa, a short while after crossing the border. His cargo was added to a veritable arsenal that had been accumulating there for a few weeks. He was paid $800, which was pennies in comparison to what he could be making if he were moving more guns and moving them much farther south, but he took it without question.

A few days later, some Gulf cartel enforcers arrived at the stash house to load up. After grabbing several rifles, handguns, a few grenades, and plenty of ammunition, the enforcers headed out to find their targets. However, they didn't expect trouble; they didn't know that some police officers seemed to have developed a conscience in recent days and weren't cooperating with the terms of their "agreement" with the cartel. The next day, headlines mentioned a big firefight between police and Gulf cartel members in Reynosa. Three police officers and two cartel members were killed. Police were able to seize five firearms, 150 rounds of ammunition, two grenades, and $5,000 in cash. Of the five firearms, four had intact serial numbers, so the Mexican police provided them to their ATF liaison in the United States for tracing. Three of them were successfully traced to gun shops in the United States—one in Arizona and two in Texas. One of the two Texas-origin firearms—the Bushmaster XM15 that Raul bought a couple of weeks before—was used to kill the Mexican cops.

While this scenario is hypothetical, it's completely based on the actual way southbound weapons trafficking from America to Mexico works— a system that works quite well. The subject has raised the ire of groups and governments on both sides of the border. The Mexican government is incredibly unhappy with the gun laws in some states that allow this to happen, and only recently has the US government formally acknowledged the role it plays in arming Mexican cartels. Most American and Mexican government studies and statistics claim that roughly 80 to 90 percent of firearms used by cartels in Mexico come from the United States. But pro-gun groups like the National Rifle Association (NRA) and other smaller, state-based organizations think those figures are extremely flawed and are the basis for a conspiracy by a left-wing government to reinstate the assault weapons ban.

Regardless of the polarized and heated opinions, there is a clear and definable problem here: Mexican cartels are using US citizens to buy assault weapons, rifles, and pistols and are then smuggling them across the border into Mexico for their use. Attempting to stop it is a task that is difficult at best.

GUN LAWS IN MEXICO AND THE US SOUTHWEST BORDER STATES

Some people might be surprised to learn that private ownership of a firearm in Mexico is not easily accomplished. With all the reports of daily shootings and assassinations in Acapulco, Ciudad Juárez, Reynosa, and other narco hot spots, it would seem that guns in Mexico are readily accessible, especially since the Mexican constitution has its own version of the Second Amendment. But while Mexican citizens are guaranteed the right to own firearms, the country's gun control laws are arguably some of the strictest in the world.

It wasn't always that way. Mexican gun laws were relatively lax until the late 1960s, when civil disturbances led to stricter gun control measures. Now, an aspiring gun owner in Mexico must fill out a mountain of paperwork and provide five character references, can only buy a small-caliber handgun in a specially designated store and not from another person, and must then comply with a lengthy list of restrictions on carrying and concealing the gun (these restrictions would fill up several pages). Criminal elements in Mexico find all this bureaucratic red tape too much to deal with, especially when they can easily get their hands on almost any weapons they want, just across the border.

In three of the four southwest border states, the situation is just the opposite. In Arizona, you don't need a state permit to buy a rifle, shotgun, or handgun.[1] Arizona firearms dealers conduct all background checks on potential buyers through a state-based system and a national database called the National Instant Check System (NICS). There is no state-mandated waiting period to purchase a firearm.[2] Similarly in New Mexico, there's no need for a state permit to buy a rifle, shotgun, or handgun. Residents of neighboring states can drive over and buy guns in New Mexico, and conversely, residents of New Mexico can buy guns in neighboring states. Like in Arizona, there is no state-mandated waiting period to purchase a firearm. Firearms dealers must also use the NICS to conduct criminal background checks on all firearm purchasers.[3]

Texas is probably the most gun-friendly state of all. A Texas resident can buy rifles and shotguns, ammunition, reloading components, or firearms accessories both in Texas and in neighboring states. It is, however, illegal in Texas to sell, rent, lend, or give a gun to any person if it is known that the person intends to use it unlawfully. Like Arizona and New Mexico, no state license is required to possess a rifle, shotgun, or handgun.[4] Texas relies solely on the NICS when conducting a background check on a prospective gun buyer. There is no state-mandated waiting period to purchase a firearm.[5]

In contrast to Texas, as well as the other two border states, California's gun laws are some of the most restrictive in the country, which explains why many of the weapons illegally transported into Mexico are not purchased there. In California, it is illegal to sell, own, or transport short-barreled shotguns or rifles, camouflaged firearms,[6] machine guns,[7] assault weapons or .50 BMG rifles,[8] armor-piercing bullets,[9] and certain other high-powered and special-use weapons. An individual in California can't buy more than one handgun within a thirty-day period,[10] and every handgun sold must be of a make and model that has passed required safety and functionality tests and is approved for publication in the California Department of Justice's official list of handguns that are certified as safe for sale in California. Also, no firearms dealer in California can sell a handgun unless the buyer presents solid paperwork showing that he or she is a California resident.[11] California firearms dealers conduct all background checks on potential buyers through a state-based system, which includes checking the NICS database.[12]

There is no question that significant numbers of firearms are flowing south from the United States into Mexico, largely resulting from the lack of serious restrictions in some states' gun laws. But the two questions so many people want answered are, "Exactly *how many* guns are going into Mexico, and exactly *where* are they coming from?" No one really knows, and of course no one will ever know with absolute certainty.

This is very frustrating for many, including the Mexican and US governments, the NRA, the antigun activists, and countless law enforcement officials trying to stem the southbound flow of guns. Seizure and trace statistics are funny things, in that they can be—and have routinely been—manipulated to fit almost any group's agenda. For instance, the "90 percent" figure estimating *successful* traces has been the source of much debate and controversy.[13]

The debate is heated because it's hard to identify the origin of the thousands of guns seized by the Mexican government each year that are *not successfully* traced.[14] Pro-gun lobby groups argue the 90-percent figure constantly, and they work hard to convince the public—and key members of Congress—that the number of firearms that Mexican cartels purchase in the United States represents only a small percentage of the overall number of weapons used in Mexico. They say that cartel members get most of their weapons from Central America, Asia, Eastern Europe, and third-world countries, in addition to getting them directly from Mexican military stocks through corrupt sources. This explanation completely throws common business sense out the window—specifically, that it's much cheaper, quicker, and easier for cartels to use the straw-purchasing method in the United States than it is for them to obtain their firearms from those other sources. Remember, cartels are business operations, and they will always do things the cheapest, quickest, and easiest way.

People who buy guns in the United States on behalf of Mexican cartels—as well as on behalf of any other criminal or organization—are called "straw purchasers," or simply "straw men." These individuals have no criminal histories and are US residents or citizens—meaning that they will easily pass a background check at a US gun shop, gun show, or pawnshop. When straw men buy guns within the United States for drug traffickers, they lie on the mandatory forms they must fill out, stating that the guns they are purchasing are for personal use and will not be provided to anybody else. If the gun seller notices suspicious behavior from the buyer, he or she can report the buyer to the ATF. However, the seller then risks losing a sale—possibly a big one that could be legitimate. Few gun sellers are prosecuted for selling guns to straw men because it's extremely difficult to prove the seller knew for certain how the guns were going to be used. It's also extremely difficult for the ATF and other law enforcement agencies to identify straw men because the purchases themselves are designed to look legitimate and to fall within the law (apart from the outright lying on purchase forms).

An ATF supervisor, who wished not to be named, compared the silliness of the debate over the exact percentage of Mexican guns that come from American sources to the northbound flow of illegal drugs. "Nobody blinks an eye when we talk about the amount of drugs coming into the United States from Mexico. You don't see a debate over exactly how many tons of Mexican-source marijuana are coming across the border. We hear that roughly 50 percent of drugs from Mexico come through Arizona, and people say that sounds about right. But then someone says that Arizona is the number-two source of guns for Mexican cartels, and people say, 'Oh, that can't be true.'"

Several thousands of guns seized in Mexico are never submitted for tracing because their serial numbers have been obliterated—rendered unreadable by one method or another. Until recently, only a small percentage of US-origin guns in Mexico had had their serial numbers obliterated; that number has increased significantly—from roughly 5 to 20 percent. This renders those guns untraceable to the actual buyer, although the ATF can still determine other things about them. Other guns are stolen or "misplaced" by corrupt law enforcement officials, either for personal use or for passing on to Mexican drug trafficking cartels. Some are never submitted for tracing because corrupt officials are attempting to protect the cartel-sponsored purchasers. And finally, some are simply destroyed without being traced in any fashion.[15]

Many guns, grenades, and other high-powered weapons that are used by Mexican drug trafficking organizations come from Central America, South Korea, and former–Eastern Bloc countries. Some are remnants from civil wars and other conflicts in Latin America, and some are sold to cartels on the black market. This is not to discount these sources for weapons in Mexico because it is important to note that the United States is definitely not the only source of those guns. However, America remains the cheapest and easiest way to obtain the drug traffickers' weapons of choice—namely, pistols, rifles, and assault-style firearms. This is because the cartels have mastered the art of using US weapons laws in ways that reduce US security.

HOW THE CARTELS BUY GUNS IN THE UNITED STATES

George Iknadosian looks like a pretty unassuming guy. With his salt-and-pepper hair, full beard, receding hairline, and glasses, he doesn't seem like the kind of person who would want to contribute to murder and mayhem a few hundred miles away. He had been the owner of the X-Caliber gun shop in Phoenix, Arizona, for several years, and business seemed to be good enough to keep the shop's doors open. Then in May 2008, Iknadosian was arrested and accused of knowingly selling more than 650 AK-47 assault-type weapons to at least two straw purchasers from Mexico. He also allegedly gave the two smugglers tips on how to evade the police, according to the ATF case supervisor. One of the guns traced back to Iknadosian—a Colt .38-caliber pistol—was actually found tucked into the waistband of BLO boss Alfredo Beltrán Leyva when he was arrested by Mexican authorities in January 2008.[16] In Nogales, Mexico, also in 2008, the chief of the Sonora state antidrug unit, Juan Manuel Pavón, was murdered by cartel hit men, just hours after attending a US seminar on how to resist the tide of American firearms surging into Mexico. Several weapons linked to the crime were traced back to X-Caliber Guns.[17]

What seemed like a successful, open-and-shut case for the ATF didn't turn out as prosecutors expected. In March 2009, an Arizona court dismissed the case after the judge ruled that the evidence prosecutors presented wasn't "material" and therefore didn't support charges against the defendant. Because the straw-man buying process involves people with clean backgrounds, the prosecution failed to prove that the guns sold by Iknadosian to the straw buyers ended up in the hands of someone who wasn't supposed to have them. This was despite the fact that several additional guns found at crime scenes in Mexico and in the possession of cartel members were traced back to Iknadosian and several straw buyers testified against Iknadosian in the case as part of a plea deal. "There is no proof whatsoever that any prohibited possessor ended up with the firearm," the judge said.[18] What made legal matters more difficult was the difference between federal law and Arizona state law regarding straw purchasing: Arizona has no statutes against it.

Federal agents and prosecutors worked for eleven months of extensive undercover operations and investigative activity to put this case together, only to have it dismissed. This case serves as a prime example of not only how difficult it is to detect straw purchases, but also how challenging it is to successfully prosecute such cases in court in an attempt to stem the southbound flow of weapons.

In an ironic twist, Iknadosian filed a lawsuit in March 2010 against the state of Arizona, the city of Phoenix, and Arizona Attorney General Terry Goddard for malicious prosecution, saying the arrest and trial devastated him emotionally and financially. He also accused a Phoenix police officer of conspiring with ATF agents to make a wrongful arrest and conduct a wrongful search of his property.[19]

MOVING GUNS SOUTH

Once the guns are successfully purchased, they are sent south through a method called "ant trafficking." Often no more than four guns (because getting caught with four is a misdemeanor and with five is a felony) are placed in dozens of southbound vehicles all along the US-Mexico border. Very few of these vehicles are checked at the twenty-five border crossings into Mexico, despite a new agreement between the US and Mexican governments to begin inspecting 10 percent of southbound vehicles. Even if some of those guns are seized, most make it into Mexico because of the trafficking system being used.

Fortunately, it's a bit easier to catch and successfully prosecute the straw buyers involved in ant trafficking. In December 2008, Tijuana resident Jonnatan Weiss fraudulently obtained a Nevada identification card under the pretense that he resided at an address in North Las Vegas, according to an ATF press release. Later that same day, Weiss attempted to purchase a .45-caliber pistol from a licensed firearms dealer in Las Vegas but was disapproved after government authorities found out that he made false statements on the gun purchase paperwork about his criminal history. A week later, Jonnatan's brother William fraudulently obtained a Nevada driver's license using the same North Las Vegas address (he was a California resident).[20]

Over the next six months, the Weiss brothers traveled from Mexico and California to Nevada as weapons traffickers. William was the main buyer and used his Nevada driver's license to circumvent restrictions on the sale of firearms to nonresidents. During this time, the brothers either bought or tried to buy at least nineteen pistols and three rifles, including one .50-caliber rifle. Many of the firearms were civilian versions or replicas of tactical or military firearms. They then moved the firearms to California, and thereafter to Mexico for resale to drug cartels.[21]

In February 2009, the ATF caught on and opened a case after a gun shop owner reported William was trying to buy several guns—including an assault rifle—worth $6,000 with $20 bills and was driving a car with California plates instead of Nevada plates. In November 2009, the two men pleaded guilty to "conspiracy to receive, transport, and deal in firearms and to the federal charge of transporting firearms into their state of residency." Jonnatan was sentenced to five years in federal prison, and William to two years. Despite the fact that this was a successful prosecution, the relatively short sentences remain a source of frustration for federal agents, district attorneys, and the federal government.

Examples abound of guns bought by straw men in America and later used by the cartels to kill people in Mexico. In March 2008 in Ciudad Juárez, gunmen used a .50-caliber Browning machine gun (BMG) to shoot Francisco Ledesma Salazar, the head of local police operations. In this particular case, a Juárez cartel member bought the firearm in Phoenix, Arizona.[22] In a bold attack on the military in Tijuana in October 2008, a Mexican Special Forces soldier was shot in the head as his unit drove into a neighborhood where a drug lord owned a home. After a two-hour standoff, police found a Barrett .50-caliber BMG sniper rifle, a .223-caliber assault rifle, and three .308-caliber rifles.[23] US District Court documents allegedly showed that all the guns used in the attack were bought in Las Vegas, Nevada.[24] In late 2006 in the tiny Sinaloan town of Zazalpa, sixty drug traffickers looking for rival cartel members rounded up all the town's residents and destroyed it, spraying buildings with bullets fired from US-purchased AR-15s.[25]

TRACING US-ORIGIN GUNS AND WHY THERE'S NO STOPPING THE FLOW

Here's how the firearms tracing process works: Someone (including a Mexican government agent) seizes a gun at a crime scene. Either it has a serial number or it doesn't (i.e., the number was obliterated). If there's no serial number, it can't be traced to the person who originally purchased the firearm. ATF agents focus on the guns that have an intact serial number and therefore *can* be traced to actual people. Once Mexican authorities provide a gun from a crime scene to the ATF, the agency has a few courses of action.

First, it can find out where the gun was manufactured and go to that company. Sometimes the company will allow the ATF direct access to their computer database of firearms they've manufactured, which includes the serial numbers. The company can then say to which wholesaler or dealer they sold that gun. The ATF can then go to that dealer and ask to whom they sold that gun. Luck is on the ATF's side if that person is the end of the trail and the ATF can find him. However, in places where individual-to-individual firearm sales are easy (e.g., Texas and Arizona), that gun could have been sold many times over at a gun show, at a pawnshop, or in someone's driveway, with no records kept. Responsible gun owners will always keep records of gun sales in order to clear their own names in such situations. Still, proving complicity would be difficult at best without a clear trail from that person to the gun's recovery in Mexico.

It's relatively easy to see why the southbound flow of weapons has gotten to this point and why the US government hasn't been able to stop it. There's a high demand for certain kinds of firearms by Mexican cartels, and

America is definitely not short on supply. Gun laws vary from state to state, of course, but cartels will always recruit straw buyers in states with the most lax laws, regardless of how far from the border they are.

Because of the Second Amendment, guns will always be for sale in the United States. No matter how US gun laws might be modified, Mexican cartels will always find a way to work within them or around them, simply because America will still be the closest and cheapest source of firearms. It's unlikely that the United States can stop the southbound weapons flow with laws alone. That leaves the imperative of enforcing—effectively—existing laws (and potential new ones).

North of the border, there are approximately 6,700 gun shops in relatively close proximity to the US-Mexico boundary. The ATF has four field offices in the region—in Houston, Phoenix, Dallas, and Los Angeles. In March 2009, the ATF reported to Congress that it had "148 agents dedicated to investigating firearms-trafficking full-time (about 6 percent of ATF's total agents) and fifty-nine Industry Operations Investigators (about 5 percent of ATF's total) responsible for conducting regulatory inspections of the 6,700 gun dealers along the two-thousand-mile-long southwest border."[26] Based on current staffing (which hasn't increased in a long time), the ATF is able to inspect these gun dealers roughly once a decade. In 2009, the agency inspected "a scant 10 percent of all gun dealers in the United States."[27]

South of the border, Mexican customs authorities have made a conscious decision to not inspect most southbound traffic. This seems like an illogical decision in light of the thousands of firearms that enter Mexico every month. To prevent drugs from coming into the United States, officers question or inspect pretty much everyone trying to come in to make sure they don't bring any drugs with them. Unfortunately, Mexican customs inspectors have the reputation of being just as corrupt as police officers are; so even if they were conducting regular vehicle inspections at ports of entry, it's likely that many firearms discovered by inspectors would wind up being diverted back to the cartels anyway. The Mexican government just doesn't have nearly enough trained, reliable customs inspectors to place at the many ports of entry along the border.

By this point in the book, the challenges of stopping southbound weapons trafficking are clear to readers. It's not so much that the US and Mexican governments are powerless to stop it; they just haven't applied their power in the right places. Arguments can continue about how many guns in Mexico were or were not sold to straw men in America or whether new US laws would make a difference. The fact remains that guns are tools of the trade in the drug world. US consumers demand the drugs, and the Mexican cartels supply them. The Mexican cartels demand firearms, and US gun sales supply them. It's unlikely that small measures will do anything to disrupt this mutually beneficial business arrangement.

CHAPTER 5

THE SECOND-BIGGEST MONEYMAKER FOR CARTELS: KIDNAPPING

IT'S 7:15 IN THE MORNING on a bright fall day in Las Vegas. Six-year-old Cole Puffinburger is up and dressed, ready for another day at Stanford Elementary School. Cole's mom and her fiancé are up and about, getting ready for work. It's just a routine morning like any other, until there's an unexpected knock at the door. A man outside claims to be a police officer and orders them to open up. Once the door is opened, three Hispanic men burst into Cole's home with guns and demand money. Terrified, Cole's mom and her fiancé insist that they don't have any, and the men quickly tie them up with zip ties, gag them, and start searching the house. Little Cole sees all of this, but the worst is yet to come for him. After the men tear apart the house and don't find what they're looking for, one of them holds a gun to Cole's head and drags the little boy outside to their car. And just like that, Cole is gone.[1]

Fortunately, this true story from October 2008 had a happy ending. After a frantic four-day search by police, a bus driver spotted Cole walking by himself on a street near the Las Vegas strip. It was 10:30 P.M. on the Saturday after Cole was kidnapped from his home, and luckily the bus driver recognized him from one of the "missing persons" flyers prominently posted.[2]

As scary as the experience was for the boy, the circumstances surrounding his disappearance have ominous implications for all of America. It turns out that Cole was kidnapped by men associated with a Mexican drug cartel. Cole's grandfather, Clemons Tinnemeyer, was allegedly involved in "significant drug dealing," which included methamphetamine. According to police, Tinnemeyer had made the poor decision to steal millions of dollars from the cartel; he had been in hiding for a month, and they wanted their money back. He was arrested the day before Cole was found,[3] and authorities declined to tell the media which Mexican drug cartel he was said to be working for.[4]

It's not just the cartels' illicit drugs that have infiltrated the United States well past the southwest border. Kidnappings conducted by or on behalf of Mexican cartels are happening here, too. While most kidnapping victims taken by the cartels are somehow involved in the drug trade and are criminals in their own right, innocent bystanders like Cole Puffinburger are increasingly targeted. But before considering kidnappings in the United States, it's important to start in Mexico, where they're infinitely more common and usually more brutal.

THE PROCESS OF CARTEL KIDNAPPINGS

While no two kidnappings in Mexico are identical, the process follows a generally accepted protocol when experienced kidnappers are involved.

An obviously significant step is selecting the target. Sometimes the kidnapping victim is an intentionally targeted person. This is usually the case when one cartel is seeking retribution against a rival cartel member or against a cartel employee who owes money or a drug load. These victims are followed so the kidnappers can determine their routines and consequently the best places to snatch them. Often, depending on in what city or town the kidnapping takes place, the victim is grabbed in broad daylight in front of his home or place of business, or on a busy sidewalk by thugs who pull alongside in a van. In these situations, the kidnappers have a plan in place to demand ransom or the return of stolen money or lost drugs.

In August 2009, seventeen members of a kidnapping-and-murder crew called "Los Palillos," or The Toothpicks, were indicted in San Diego for a string of brutal crimes. According to local news reports, nine of their murder victims were abducted or lured to houses rented by members of the group and held at those houses before eventually being killed. The bodies of two murder victims were dissolved in acid in May 2007 at a rented house. Los Palillos had a pretty good business going with these kidnappings because they had a system in place. Their system is mirrored by many criminal groups throughout Mexico.

After selecting their victim(s), the group would lure them to a set location, force them into a vehicle, and take them to a safe house. During their stay at the safe house, they would be interrogated and often tortured in an effort to obtain details about their financial situation, family members, and other pertinent information. The group would establish surveillance on the victim's home to verify the information given to interrogators as well as to be able to make good on any threats to harm family members. At this point, the kidnappers would use the victim's cell phone to send a "proof of life," a current image of the victim to prove he or she was alive. By using the victim's cell phone, the kidnappers could further convince family members that they had the victim with them. After providing the proof of life, kidnappers would tell family members to gather all the ransom money and follow all instructions but not to contact the police.

Then arrangements could be made for an exchange—or, at least, for what the victim and his or her family thought would be an exchange. Los Palillos would make all the plans for a money drop and establish surveillance at that site. Upon arrival, family members making the ransom drop would be told to get out of the car, leave the money, turn around, and get back in the car—and to not look back. After the ransom drop, kidnappers would make another proof-of-life call. Here, the kidnapping could go one of two ways. They could discuss the victim's release or thank the family for the down payment and request a second money drop. If the conversation took the former route, chances are the victim would go home, looking a little worse for wear. If it went the latter route, there's a greater chance the victim would be killed and his or her body would either be dumped somewhere or be dissolved in a vat of acid. Either way, Los Palillos would make money, just like cartel kidnappers in Mexico are doing right now.

Mexico is one of the worst countries in which to get kidnapped; there are no rules, and often no standard protocols are followed. Anything goes. Sometimes there's a simple exchange of ransom for the victim, but more often than not, there's bloodshed. In Colombia, kidnappers typically provide proof of life by sending family members a photo of the victim holding the front page of a very recently published newspaper. In Mexico, the preferred method is to send the family an amputated finger. Mexican kidnappers not only have little concern for their hostages' basic well-being; they'll often torture their victims just for fun. Sometimes their "fun" goes a little too far, and a hostage will die in a safe house from his or her wounds. For this and other reasons, one in seven kidnap victims in Mexico will not survive the experience.

KIDNAPPING CARTEL MEMBERS

Many people believe that tourists, journalists, and government officials are more often kidnapped than the members of rival cartels—mainly because the media are unwilling to report the vast majority of kidnappings for fear of retaliation. Most drug trade–related kidnappings in Mexico and the United States are acts of retribution, punishment, or warning. Most kidnappings conducted by or on behalf of Mexican cartels target people with some connection to the drug trade: people who have lost drug loads, owe cartel bosses money, or have snitched to the authorities. However, many drug cartels have expanded into the kidnapping business as a source of new revenue in the face of diminishing drug income. Cartels are looking more toward the kidnapping of migrants, government officials, and businessmen for the ransom money they can supply.

Sometimes family members of people who have erred in the eyes of a cartel will be kidnapped as leverage to get the cartel's lost drugs or money back, but that's the exception rather than the rule. The problem with that style of kidnapping is that there's no guarantee that the victim will be released after the drugs are resupplied or the money is paid.

In Mexico, there are at least seven kidnappings that never appear in the media, and possibly more, out of every ten that actually occur. Occasionally news includes a random and sometimes vague report about a drug-related kidnapping. For example, in April 2010, an eighteen-year-old US citizen from San Diego and her Mexican boyfriend were kidnapped in Rosarito Beach near Tijuana. The woman, who was seven months pregnant, was held for three days and left for dead in a Rosarito Beach neighborhood after her abductors tried repeatedly to slit her throat. The abductors had demanded $300,000 from her family to release her, but they were never paid. Another US citizen who was detained based on the investigation allegedly confessed to slaying the pregnant woman's boyfriend and told investigators that he killed the boyfriend because he had failed to pay back a $400 drug debt.[5]

News accounts of these victims' fates are rare not only because most go unreported. It seems that the "good people" getting kidnapped or killed make for better headlines than the "bad people." Because it's been mostly the latter getting kidnapped until recently, many Mexicans and Americans alike have been apathetic to the widespread practice. But citizens of both countries cannot afford to be apathetic anymore, because innocents are increasingly in the cartels' crosshairs.

KIDNAPPING CIVILIANS

Migrants who use human smugglers, or coyotes, to get them across the border into the United States are often preyed upon by kidnappers. The narcos know that migrants paid their coyote a few thousand dollars to smuggle them across the border. They also know that migrants have relatives in the States and that those family members can probably come up with some ransom money. Migrants are also easy targets because they're very vulnerable, traveling in large groups without weapons. Even if their coyote is armed, he's no match for a large group of men with assault rifles.

Lupe Gonzalez[6] knows these facts all too well. Several years ago, Lupe illegally came to America from Mexico to find work and provide for her three children back home. Her husband left her when her children were very young, and when she came to the United States, she had to leave them in her parents' care. After several years of separation, Lupe couldn't stand to be away from her kids anymore. On top of the pain of being apart, she could no longer rely on her elderly parents, who were ailing and were having a harder time taking care of the children. So Lupe found a coyote and paid him to bring her three children across the border into Texas. Lupe's brother Mario agreed to accompany the kids until they reached the border.

The group hit a minor obstacle in a city just a few miles south of the border. They were stopped by the police, but that was no problem. The coyote was prepared for this, and as is the custom in Mexico, he paid off the officer. After a cursory glance into the car, the policeman let them go. The rest of the trip en route to the border was pretty uneventful, until their car was stopped again—this time by a group of armed men. The coyote, Mario, and the children were ordered out of the car at gunpoint. One of the men made a quick phone call, and within minutes, the police officers who had pulled them over a short while earlier arrived at the scene. The gunmen ordered the children to go with the police officers, who—obviously in on the kidnapping—told the coyote and Mario to leave immediately or be arrested. Lupe's brother was scared for the kids, but he also feared for his own life. They all did as they were told.

The next day Mario called Lupe to tell her what had happened. Why he didn't contact her immediately is unclear; maybe he was overwhelmed with guilt and just didn't know how to break the news. Out of her mind with worry, Lupe's fear factor shot up even higher when the kidnappers contacted her a few days later with a ransom demand of $3,000. They told Lupe that her kids were safe in Texas and let her talk to her daughter so she would know they were alive. Lupe had very little money of her own, but with help from family members, she was able to scrape together the ransom and make the payment. Unfortunately, the kidnappers did something very common in the kidnapping-and-ransom trade: they thanked her for the down payment and demanded $9,000 more—$3,000 for each child. They also moved the children to another Texas city. Lupe didn't have the money or any way to get it, as she and her family were totally tapped out after making the first ransom payment. Desperate, Lupe made a fateful decision: she called the US police.

Based on the information Lupe provided to the police, they were able to set up an operation to arrest the kidnappers at the ransom drop point. The good news is that several of the kidnappers were sent to prison, and Lupe's children were returned to her safely. The bad news is that Lupe and her children were immediately thrown into detention for being in the United States illegally, and the men she had helped put in jail were members of one of Mexico's deadliest cartels. As of June 2010, Lupe and her kids were being processed for removal by US immigration authorities and were awaiting a judge's determination whether they would qualify for asylum based on their credible fear claims. Because of Lupe's collaborative actions with US law enforcement and the cartel's knowledge of her and her kids' identities, Lupe and her children would surely be killed if they were returned to Mexico. As tragic as Lupe's story is, there is no way of knowing how many similar stories are out there, because the vast majority of kidnappings of this kind are never reported.

One of the more horrific examples of migrant kidnapping occurred in August 2010, roughly one hundred miles south of the border in Tamaulipas state. Seventy-two migrants from various Central and South American countries were en route to the border when they were stopped by a group of armed men who identified themselves as Zetas. The migrants were kidnapped and taken to a ranch in San Fernando, where the men told the migrants they would have to pay a ransom in order to be let go. When the migrants couldn't pay, the Zetas offered them the "opportunity" to work as foot soldiers for the cartel. When the migrants declined, they were executed at gunpoint. One man, an Ecuadorean, managed to escape and told authorities at a marines' checkpoint what had happened. The marines responded and killed three of the armed men at a ranch near where the migrants were intercepted. Authorities had no idea why Los Zetas resorted to such a display of brutality with these migrants.

In October 2010, twenty-two Mexican citizens were happily traveling in a four-car caravan from the city of Morelia, Michoacán state, to the resort city of Acapulco for a much-needed vacation. The men were all mechanics in the same area and spent the better part of every year saving for their annual trip. When they arrived in the city, they stopped at a store so a couple of the men could buy some refreshments before moving on to find a place to stay. When the two exited the store, their friends were gone. Witnesses said that armed men had kidnapped the group. Subsequent media reports claimed that the armed men might have targeted the group by mistake, as there was no evidence that any of them was involved in criminal activity.[7] The bodies of eighteen of the men were later found in a mass grave outside the Acapulco city limits. They were apparently targeted by people who worked for Edgar "La Barbie" Valdez Villarreal of the BLO and who mistakenly believed that the men were representatives of LFM intent on conducting assassinations in the area.

The biggest problem with tracking and investigating kidnappings of civilians in Mexico—whether intentional or accidental—is that everyone assumes that the victim or a family member is somehow involved in the drug trade. There's a statistical foundation for that assumption, but the negative consequence is that most kidnappings are never properly investigated. It is estimated that fewer than a quarter of these crimes are ever reported to authorities in Mexico. Of those that are reported, investigations are begun for only 13 percent of the cases, and in only 5 percent of these are the accused brought before a judge, according to Mexico's Citizen Institute for Research on Insecurity, or ICESI.[8] If the kidnapping of civilians for ransom continues to increase in Mexico, either the Mexican authorities need to step up their investigative work, or the cartels are just going to keep getting richer.

CARTEL KIDNAPPINGS IN THE UNITED STATES

There is growing concern among US authorities about the increase in drug-related kidnappings occurring on American soil. In March 2009, *Newsweek* briefly told the story of what had happened to a man named Manuel in Phoenix the month before. Manuel was coming out of a Radio Shack store with his family when seemingly out of nowhere a man came up to him and held a gun to his head, trying to force him into an SUV. Other men sitting in the SUV had shotguns trained on Manuel the whole time. Manuel got into the car, and after some shots were fired, Manuel's wife watched as he disappeared from view. All of this happened in a city of 1.3 million people, located a comfortable 180 miles away from Arizona's border with Mexico, in broad daylight outside a retail store. Apparently, Manuel owed someone a lot of drug money. The kidnappers demanded $1,000,000 and his Cadillac Escalade as ransom from his family. Two men reportedly affiliated with one of the major Mexican cartels were apprehended by US police while the men were driving off with his car. But Manuel was never seen or heard from again. "He's a drug dealer, and he lost a load," said Lt. Lauri Burgett of the Phoenix Police Department about Manuel's predicament. Authorities believe he was taken to Mexico and made to answer for his "transgression."[9]

In 2009, 318 kidnappings were reported in Phoenix; that compares to 117 in 2000 and is slightly lower than the 2008 total of 368.[10] The majority of those kidnappings, according to the Phoenix Police Department,[11] were related to either the Mexican drug trade or human smuggling rings. But those statistics do nothing to quell the fear among local residents. Many safe houses that serve as holding locations for kidnap victims are located in middle-class suburban residential neighborhoods. The same thugs who cross the border from Mexico into the United States to carry out kidnappings on behalf of the cartels are branching out into home invasions in those same neighborhoods.

As mentioned earlier, it's rare for unsuspecting, completely "clean" US citizens to become kidnap victims; but some evidence indicates that this is changing. Take the case of Raul Alvarado, a car salesman from Hidalgo, Texas. In late November 2009, Alvarado got a phone call from a friend and the friend's cousin, during which they asked him to meet them at a Starbucks in McAllen, Texas. When Alvarado showed up, it wasn't his friend and the cousin who were waiting for him but three men he didn't know. They forced him at gunpoint to get into their car and sped away toward the border, eventually ending up in Reynosa, Mexico. The kidnappers originally demanded $100,000 in ransom but lowered it when they realized their hostage and his family couldn't pay it. Instead, Alvarado attempted to buy his freedom by paying $30,000 and giving them two cars—all to no avail.

Then Alvarado got lucky. Something that rarely happens in Mexico somehow manifested in his favor: a suspicious neighbor called the Mexican police. The anonymous caller told the authorities that they believed someone was being held against his will in a Reynosa neighborhood house. The police went to check out the tip and found Alvarado in the house, handcuffed with his head covered and showing signs of abuse. Based on the ransom demand, the location in Texas where the kidnapping occurred (directly across the border from Gulf cartel–controlled territory), and other publicly available details about the case, it doesn't appear that Alvarado had anything to do with the drug trade or had any kind of affiliation with a Mexican cartel. Considering he attempted to pay partial ransom with cars, it appears that he was targeted just because he was a business owner.

In August 2008, Daniel Ramirez Jr. was minding his own business at his Country Village Store in Weslaco, Texas, when he was kidnapped by people working for the Gulf cartel. His only "crime" had been refusing an offer to work for them. Kidnappers took Ramirez to a safe house in Mission, Texas, about twenty-four miles west of Weslaco. There he was held before being taken to a ranch in Mexico where his body was "cooked"— which could mean anything from being dissolved in a vat of acid to literally being barbecued on a grill. Ramirez was killed even though his father had paid the Gulf cartel's enforcers $40,000 of the $100,000 ransom they had demanded.[12] According to FBI spokesman Jorge Cisneros, an increasing number of cross-border kidnappings in Texas have involved American victims with no ties to illegal activity.[13]

US law enforcement agencies, like the FBI and the Phoenix Police Department, are actively involved in the investigation of cross-border kidnappings that are occurring on US soil. They understand the negative impact that this kind of criminal activity can have on border (and nonborder) communities, no matter who the victim is. Unfortunately, the reason for the growing number of these kidnappings—the Mexican drug trade—is not going away, which means that the kidnappings occurring in the United States that are related to drug smuggling and human smuggling probably aren't going to go away any time soon, either.

CHAPTER 6

THE MEXICAN PEOPLE

SOMETHING SEEMS TO GET LOST in the mix of murders, shootings, narcos, and corruption: the people of Mexico who have nothing to do with the drug trade and must endure what the war is doing to their communities and their country. Many people will not talk to the police about illegal activity that they've witnessed or heard about because they're scared for their lives. And often, they're just as scared of the authorities as they are of the narcos. So why care about the Mexican people? "It's their problem and not ours," according to some Americans.

There are millions of Mexican-Americans living in the United States, many of whom are affected by the current situation in Mexico. Regardless of one's stance on the illegal immigration debate, it's important to acknowledge that most people in the United States who are Mexican-born or of Mexican descent are good people and contributing members of society and communities. Most of them have relatives still living in Mexico, often in places with high levels of violence. There's a pretty good chance that each reader knows someone—a friend, coworker, subordinate, supervisor, neighbor, or store employee—who is affected by the drug war because of family ties.

THE DRUG PROBLEM WITHIN

Over the past few years, several media reports have detailed the exploding domestic drug market in Mexico, as well as soaring drug-dependency rates. Fortunately, drug use in Mexico is still only a fraction of that in the United States. Officials estimate that 3.5 million Mexicans have used narcotics at least once and that nearly 600,000 have become dependent drug consumers. That compares to roughly twenty-two million regular drug consumers in America—but note that the number of Mexican addicts has doubled in the last five years.[1]

The new border fence and intensified patrols by both Mexican and US federal agents have made it harder for Mexican cartels to get drugs into the United States. As a result, more narcotics remain in Mexico, where they are sold to local consumers, said Marcela López Cabrera, director of Mexico City's Monte Fenix clinic, which trains drug counselors.[2] Another major factor that influences domestic drug use in Mexico is how incredibly cheap and readily available drugs are. Cocaine prices in Mexico have dropped so much that it's almost free. A gram of cocaine sells in central Mexico for about $19. Crack is $9.50 a rock and getting cheaper.[3]

In many areas—particularly the Tijuana and Acapulco areas—major drug cartels have become fractured. Former cartel members have gone independent and started their own drug businesses, resulting in small legions of drug dealers throughout the country. Many observers are calling this process the "atomization" of Mexico's cartels. The explosion of the domestic drug market and growing business of drug sellers mean more obstacles in Mexico's path toward reducing violence. There are signs that the street trade, known as *narcomenudeo,* is adding to overall drug violence. The well-armed gangs that have fought each other for control of key international drug smuggling routes are battling over the market in Mexico as well. Another side effect from this trend is the massive increase in the number of drug rehab centers and subsequently the number of Mexicans enrolled in drug treatment programs. Because many of those patients were also dealers at some point, rehab clinics and their patients have been the targets of brutal slayings as well as cartel recruitment efforts.[4]

There has been some good news on the domestic drug front. Mexican media reported in October 2009 that the availability of cocaine in Mexico had dropped by 60 percent in the previous six years, mainly due to bigger and more frequent seizures by Mexican and Colombian authorities. The report also indicated that the methamphetamine supply had been reduced as well, but rehab center and addiction statistics indicate that there's a long way to go in the battle to reduce the supply of all drugs in Mexico.

There are two major aspects of this problem that warrant attention: the violence and public health crises posed to the Mexican government, and the ethical and moral issues surrounding the successes of border enforcement efforts. The Calderón administration has taken some small steps toward treating the addiction problem as a public health issue by decriminalizing "personal use" amounts of various drugs. Individuals caught with greater amounts are relegated to treatment programs instead of jail, in an attempt to relieve pressure on jails, law enforcement, and the judicial system. However, some official statistics from Mexican sources say only 3 percent of Mexican addicts are currently receiving some form of treatment. That rehab centers are increasingly the targets of cartel attacks possibly reduces the motivation for some to seek treatment.

The second aspect is a more difficult one to grapple with. Mexico has historically blamed Americans' insatiable addiction to drugs for its own violence issues. There is plenty of truth to this line of thinking, as without a demand, there's no need for the supply. While US enforcement efforts don't affect the demand side, they are having an impact on the supply. That's good news for drug trade–related issues in the United States, but those efforts are obviously having a negative impact south of the border.

In some ways, this problem can be likened to the southbound weapons trafficking issue. Americans sell lots of guns, and many of those end up in Mexico, to be used by cartels in violent attacks against rivals or delinquent dealers. The US government has recently acknowledged some level of complicity in this problem and has vowed to step up efforts to interdict the southbound flow of weapons, ostensibly with the goal of reducing gun-related crime and overall violence in Mexico. But one has to ask if the US government should ever be apologetic for enforcement efforts that successfully reduce the quantities of drugs that enter the United States but cause dramatic increases in addiction within Mexico.

The United States has already acknowledged it has contributed greatly to drug trafficking via its demand and to weapons trafficking via its supply. This might be the limit of the mea culpa stance of the US government, especially given its pride in providing law enforcement efforts. The United States will likely continue to offer financial assistance to Mexico so it can try to tackle its domestic addiction problems, but the Mexican government will probably be on its own in figuring out how to reduce domestic consumption—just as the US government has been doing for decades.

DESTROYING THE MEXICAN WAY OF LIFE

Earlier chapters have touched on how bad the situation is in Ciudad Juárez. It appears that many of the city's residents aren't sticking around to find out if things are going to get better or worse. Over the last three years, 230,000 residents of Juárez—roughly 18 percent of the population—left the city to escape the violence. The primary destination for about half of those residents was El Paso, Texas, and most others moved to the neighboring Mexican states of Durango, Coahuila, and Veracruz. A poll of residents that was conducted by students and professors at the Autonomous University of Ciudad Juárez indicated that insecurity over the drug violence and the government's inability to protect them led to the mass exodus.[5]

Those who decided to stay in Juárez have made profound changes to their daily lives. For example, "83 percent of people said they stopped giving personal information over the phone, 75 percent do not talk to strangers, and a similar percentage stopped going out at night. More than half of respondents said they stopped carrying cash, don't allow their kids to walk the streets alone, and stopped attending public events."

Even the city government has acknowledged it can't do much to stop things from getting more out of control. In late August 2010, it canceled the traditional festivities surrounding Mexico's day of independence. On the eve of September 16, mayors in Mexico normally lead crowds at city hall esplanades in the traditional ceremony of *grito de independencia,* or call to independence. To celebrate, every year thousands of Juárez residents flock to city hall to attend the night festival, where mariachis, folk dancers, and singers perform on that evening. Sadly, 2010 was the first time in almost a century that the festivities were canceled—and all due to the narcos.[6]

Mexicans are not happy with this situation in their country. According to a Pew Research Center poll, almost 80 percent aren't satisfied with the way the drug war is going. As expected, 80 percent fully support the use of the army to fight the cartels, and 55 percent believe the military is making progress. But surprisingly, 78 percent of respondents support US assistance in training the Mexican military, 57 percent support American funds going toward Mexico's efforts, and 26 percent support the deployment of US troops to Mexico.[7] This is unexpected for a country that has historically had a great of deal of tension with the United States stemming from its interventions in Latin American affairs. For a country that abhors US involvement in domestic issues, the support of one out of every four Mexicans for a US military presence on their soil is a big deal, and it shows just how bad things have gotten there.

Residents of the Nuevo León city of Monterrey are altering their daily lives because they fear becoming inadvertent victims. Locals say they now host parties in the afternoon so that guests can avoid driving at night. Many residents say they won't travel to South Padre Island, a popular resort off the south Texas coast, for fear of passing through Reynosa, a battleground for Los Zetas and the Gulf cartel. In the summer of 2010, Monterrey's high-end Palacio de Hierro shopping mall was held up by gunmen for the third time that year.[8]

Monterrey is an interesting case study in the spread of narco fear in Mexico because of its high-end status as a business mecca for the rich. Drug violence hadn't really touched it until perhaps the spring of 2010, when rich narcos started gravitating toward the Monterrey lifestyle. Since then, the city's residents and business owners have become targets for theft, burglary, and kidnapping for ransom. They're also starting to see *narcobloqueos,* or roadblocks set up by cartels, more frequently. According to a *Wall Street Journal* article, during a *narcobloqueo,* "Members of a crime group commandeer buses, commercial trucks, or tractor-trailers. Then they block major highways with the vehicles and leave the scene, disrupting traffic for hours. Officials say the tactic is aimed at keeping police and the military from circulating through the city, though it is also used as a show of power."[9]

Mexico has been a democracy with relatively transparent elections for quite some time. However, the violence is starting to impact one of the fundamental tenets of democracy—a citizen's right and ability to vote on election day. In July 2010, hundreds of state and local elections were scheduled, but many people were too terrified to go to the polls. A sizable portion of the population also had no interest in voting because they had no faith in their government.

According to an article in the *El Paso Times,* the "null vote" has been a constant in recent Mexican elections in which voters decided not to give their vote to any of the parties. Instead, they crossed out the ballot completely as a sign of protest because of the lack of viable choices. Daily kill-ings in Ciudad Juárez and Chihuahua, as well as the bloody attacks on police forces, created such a sense of insecurity in the general population that people didn't want to expose themselves to waiting in a line to cast their votes.[10]

The regular sight of bloodstains on the street or decapitated bodies in public should be enough to scare the Mexican populace out of their minds, but some narcos disagree. It's almost as if they have to embark on a public relations campaign every so often through highly visible banners and other narcomensajes. These messages serve several purposes: Some-times they blame rivals for a mass killing, and on other occasions they teach a lesson about what happens to people who get in their way. Cartels even delve into the territory of "psychological operations" when they post banners telling the Mexican people that their government can't protect them from the violence.

Some narcos have moved online to make their threats. YouTube vid-eos of cartel members committing atrocities against each other have be-come more common. Captives, many bloody from being beaten, are "tied up, blindfolded, and posed in front of a draped sheet in an anonymous setting. Surrounded by heavily armed captors in ski masks and guided by questioning from an off-camera voice, the captives are forced to confess allegiances to cartels or corrupt officials." Many are then murdered, on camera. The most explicit videos, when detected, are usually removed by major websites like YouTube but stay posted on narco blogs run by anonymous administrators.[11]

What frustrates many people is that no legal action results from these videos. The Mexican authorities can't do anything unless someone makes a complaint, and no one does—for obvious reasons. Since the video files are uploaded to the Internet by usually anonymous users, the authorities can't prove the videos are authentic (although most probably are). Organized crime groups have also delved into social media outlets like Facebook and

Twitter to spread their message of fear. But these tools are also being used against them by young Mexicans who want to fight back and want a way out of the violence.

Like terrorists, narcos don't have to go through with threatened acts of violence to make an impact. In June 2010, violence was escalating in the state of Nayarit, and rumors were heatedly circulating that cartels were going to attack their rivals' children while they were at school. Although the rumors were never substantiated, the fear of such attacks was enough to coax the governor into shutting all schools for three weeks.

THE REALITY FOR MEXICO'S YOUTH

There's a catchy tune in Mexico called "*El Señor de la Montaña*" ("The Man of the Mountain") that was very popular—particularly with young people—when it came out in 2006 and continues to be today. It's just one of the dozens of narcocorridos written by various groups that pay homage to Joaquin "El Chapo" Guzmán Loera. These songs evolved from the Mexican folk tradition of singing about revolutionary heroes and legends throughout history. Now, these narco ballads glorify the lives and exploits of drug traffickers, kidnappers, and killers. And Mexico's youth just love them.

Some of the songs written by younger musicians have hip-hop and rap influences, making them hugely popular—despite the fact that President Calderón has banned them from the airwaves. This probably increases their intrigue, as do the common social messages and government criticism that many contain in their lyrics. But songs glorifying drug lords are only one of many social factors sucking Mexico's youth—and economic future—into its deadly grasp.

Sadly, the prospects for many of Mexico's young people are grim. Mexico is an industrialized nation and an economic powerhouse, but often that doesn't translate into upward mobility for teenagers—especially those who live in rural areas. Earlier passages in this book described El Chapo's origins, and his story is not unique. There are millions of Mexican boys and girls just entering their teen years with few prospects for a truly productive life outside of the environment in which they grew up.

Both the American and Mexican media have published reports that the Mexican economy is recovering, albeit slowly, from the global economic recession and that American investment in Mexico is on the rise. New car manufacturing plants are being constructed that are supposed to employ several hundred Mexican workers. Tourism is rebounding from a lull caused by reports of violence near tourist towns, so hotels, airlines, and restaurants are recovering. But how does any of that translate to something meaningful for a fifteen-year-old boy with a fifth-grade education, who can barely read, living on a poppy farm in Guerrero?

Some of Mexico's youth do make it out and succeed. Their parents recognize that they're not going to accomplish much by staying put, so they try their best to get their kids educated and into the bigger cities where there are some job prospects. But there's a reason why millions of Mexican citizens try to cross into the United States illegally every year. Decent-paying jobs in Mexico are hard to come by, especially for unskilled workers and young people without a college education. Many Mexican teenagers are left with only two options: try to get into America and find a job without getting busted by immigration authorities, or join up with the drug trade. It's not hard to guess which one is easier and pays better.

Mexico is learning to deal with a generation of *ninis*—millions of Mexican teenagers who *ni trabajan, ni estudian* ("neither work nor study"). They wander the streets of Mexico with no real place to go, nothing to do, and no goals to achieve. Even if they do continue their schooling, they stay at home with their parents and never venture out into the world. When asked what they want to do or what they want to become, they only say that they're going to keep studying. And even if they can get work, many jobs come without medical insurance or are under contract for only a short time.[12]

Current estimates place the population of *ninis* around seven million in all of Mexico, but the government claims there are only a few hundred thousand. According to a recent report, one of the largest populations of ninis is in Ciudad Juárez: 120,000 Juárez residents between the ages of thirteen and twenty-four—or 45 percent of the population—were "in neither formal work nor school. Cartels will now pay a young person $1,000 per trip if he or she smuggles drugs over the border; the youths say the drug gangs will fork over as little as $100 for someone to carry out an assassination."[13] The sad reality is that, yes, children in Mexico are the future . . . the future of the drug war.

JOURNALISTS ON THE FRONT LINES

When many people picture journalists reporting from a war zone, they imagine the ones embedded with military units during the 2003 United States entry into Iraq, or others in the middle of civil unrest in Myanmar, or still others with bombs exploding behind them in Afghanistan. Yet, in recent years, Mexico has become one of the world's most dangerous countries to work in as a journalist—even though it's considered a stable democracy with only a high crime rate. Reporters Without Borders, an international organization that champions freedom of the press, has called Mexico "the Western Hemisphere's deadliest country for the media."[14]

While the exact number varies from source to source, it's said that approximately seventy journalists, photographers, editors, and news media producers have been killed in the last decade in Mexico. That's half the number of similar workers killed in Iraq since 2003; however, there are big differences between the incidents. In Iraq, the number of dead journalists has steadily dropped every year, with a tally of only four in 2009. Also, those killed were usually involved in sporadic crossfire or became random victims of homemade bombs. In Mexico, victims in the media business are specifically targeted because of what they do—or in many cases, don't do.

According to US media reports, Mexican drug lords "meticulously select journalists for execution, and the method is often very personal. Journalists have had their throats slashed and their bodies dissolved in acid; they've been dismembered and tortured by having messages carved into their bodies; they've been set on fire, and they've been buried alive, head first." In November 2009, the body of reporter José Bladimir Antuna García had a note attached to it that read: "This happened to me for giving information to the military and writing what I shouldn't have. Check the texts of your articles well before publishing them. Yours faithfully, Bladimir." He was a crime correspondent for the Mexican daily *El Tiempo* and was found stabbed to death behind a hospital in Durango.[15]

Threats by Mexican cartels against reporters aren't limited to Mexico, either. *El Paso Times* reporter Diana Washington Valdez routinely visited Ciudad Juárez but had to stop going because she felt her life would be in danger if she returned. In April 2010, she had received a message from a narco saying she should stop writing about drug trafficking.

As a result of these threats, which the media are taking very seriously at all levels, journalists are engaging in a practice called "autocensorship." Anxious to remain among the living and breathing, reporters are often careful not to publish details in their stories that would either make the local cartel look bad or subject it to adverse actions either by rivals or by law enforcement. And sadly enough, threats against journalists in Mexico aren't just coming from the narcos. Sixty-five percent of the 244 assaults on journalists that have occurred in the country were directed by public officials.[16] These are most likely officials who are collaborating with cartels—either voluntarily or under threat of death—and are just as interested in making sure, through the use of violence, that certain details are either included in or left out of news reports.

Mexico is the most dangerous country in the Americas for journalists, and it's only getting worse. Already, parts of Mexico sometimes experience news blackouts. In the latter part of 2010, the northeast border cities of

Reynosa and Matamoros had almost no drug-related news coming from traditional news sources, and residents and observers alike had to rely on social media like Twitter for information. At the behest of a cartel, all news outlets in the local area—often the site of major confrontations between cartels and the police—had ceased to report any news of drug-related violence. This is extremely frustrating for governments, law enforcement agencies, and people on both sides of the border who have relatives living in the affected area. There is no true freedom of the press in Mexico these days—not because the government won't allow it, but because organized crime has taken it away.

THE MEXICAN DIASPORA

Jose is a Mexican-American who grew up in Mexicali, Mexico (right across the border from Calexico, California). After he graduated from college in 2002, he moved to San Francisco to take a corporate job. Since then, he has lived in Los Angeles and San Diego, where he currently resides. Jose still has family in Mexicali, and his father lives in Rosarito (near Tijuana). In December 2008, his father was kidnapped for ransom. Despite the fact that the two men were estranged, it brought out an intense emotional response from Jose and also from his sister and his mother. During the kidnapping, Jose learned about several other friends who had gone through similar situations with their families, including a close friend whose brother-in-law, recently kidnapped, was widely known due to his prominence in Tijuana's society.[17]

Jose's father was able to pay his own way out of captivity, after losing a finger and receiving several severe beatings. Jose saw him twice after his ordeal, the mental side effects of which had left his father unable to speak. His father appeared to play it off as no big deal, but in doing so he overcompensated from being a survivor of such a traumatic event. All of his emotions were excessive, and it was obvious that there was more to it. After seeing him that second time, Jose decided to break all ties with him; his sister maintained contact. She last told Jose that their father was doing better.[18]

Sonia is a second-generation Mexican-American who has homes in California, Texas, and Mexico. She has led a rather nomadic existence and had dreams of making the world a better place. This led her into nonprofit work, which she has enjoyed for several years. She had some money and decided to start a family charity foundation with a friend in Coahuila state. Her vision was essentially to help disabled students, but she extended the mission to other schools as well.[19]

Despite her hard and positive work, Sonia made the mistake of being too high-profile in Mexico. Her foundation started receiving a lot of publicity. She was honored in a surprise ceremony in Mexico City in 2009, and coverage of the event made the front page of a major Mexican newspaper. Unfortunately, her new assistant, in her enthusiasm for the foundation and for Sonia's work, let it slip that all funding for the foundation came from family money. This immediately and unintentionally painted a huge red circle on Sonia as a potentially lucrative kidnapping target. She has completely altered the way she does business in Mexico now, never driving to Monterrey or Saltillo and only flying in, and working hard to keep her face and name out of the media.

Sonia is dumbfounded by the attitudes that many of her Mexican friends and colleagues have about the drug war. She says that no one ever brings it up in conversations, and if she mentions it, her friends get nervous and uneasy, like it's a taboo subject that no one is supposed to talk about, even though it's everywhere. She says she's been bold enough to ask them about the corruption and the cartel associations of the beloved politicians they work so hard to put in office. They usually respond that they know full well about those associations, but they have no choice.

Mexican-Americans traveling back to Mexico to visit family are also at risk for kidnapping and extortion by cartels. Nearly two million Mexicans living in the United States return to Mexico during the holiday season in December. Those who travel by car are often extorted by federal agents and state and municipal governments at checkpoints along the way, where they're required to pay between $50 and $100. A report said that over the course of the holiday season, these returning migrants will be forced to pay up to $150 million to extortionists. In addition to bringing roughly $5 billion in cash and gifts for family along with them, they have to plan to bring a little extra to cover the cost of bribes.[20]

VIGILANTISM ON THE RISE

So what can the Mexican people do? Unfortunately, they can't do much without putting their lives at risk. However, there are a few—and some would say crazy—souls who are willing both to talk and to do something about the violence. In June 2010, a mother in Reynosa, whose son was killed in crossfire when narcos attacked a police patrol as he drove home around midnight, publicly stated that the cops were on the Gulf cartel's payroll and blamed them and the government authorities. She knew that that might bring her a death sentence but claimed that when they killed her son, they killed her as well.[21]

An aggressive brand of vigilantism is growing in some parts of Mexico as a result of the increasing violence. The Mexican government discourages any such activity, but growing desperation is leading people to take matters into their own hands. In July 2009, reports started emerging about a group called the "Mata Zetas." The Mexican daily *El Universal* reported that the bodies of three men were found inside an abandoned truck in a residential neighborhood in Cancún. The men had been handcuffed and had bags placed over their heads. Together with the remains was a note that read, "We are the new group Mata Zetas and we are against kidnapping and extortion, and we will fight them in all states for a cleaner Mexico."[22] Another Mexican daily reported that a YouTube video had confirmed the existence of a group of hit men dedicated to the capture and killing of members of organized crime groups. The group called itself "Mata Zetas" and had previously denounced a series of crimes by leaders and members of Los Zetas.[23]

Exactly who comprised this group remained shady, but that didn't stop Mexican citizens from forming other loosely organized vigilante groups. Some resorted to nonlethal revenge tactics, like tying up alleged thieves and kidnappers, stripping them naked, and savagely beating them. An October 2009 video of five burglars being tortured and sexually abused by vigilantes for their crimes was posted on YouTube. It wasn't pretty, but they were left alive. Some targets of vigilantes aren't so lucky. Other alleged kidnappers and car thieves have been abducted and murdered and had their corpses dumped in public places along with threatening notes.[24]

In a brutal display of solidarity, townspeople and soldiers in the rural town of Ascension banded together to free a kidnapping victim in September 2010, with rather gruesome results. A group of men had kidnapped a seventeen-year-old girl who worked at a local seafood restaurant. When the locals discovered what had happened, they searched for and found the five young men who had abducted the girl and detained them, after successfully freeing her. Hundreds of angry residents beat two of the detained teenagers and blocked police from rescuing the suspects, who were later pronounced dead. In a standoff that lasted throughout the day, Ascension residents prevented two federal police helicopters from landing and blockaded roads to prevent military reinforcements from arriving. Armed with picks, shovels, and machetes, enraged residents shouted at "corrupt" soldiers and police, demanding that they leave. Although the town is in a rural area, its people had suffered numerous kidnappings and killings in recent years.[25]

The divisions in Mexican society over how vigilante groups should be regarded reflect a certain level of tolerance by some. Government officials, of course, stand behind the need for the rule of law. Nayarit's Governor Ney Gonzalez Sanchez says that no one has the right to take justice into their own hands. But comments sent to *El Universal* in response to the YouTube-posted torture video say differently. "Let's be honest. The majority of us are happy with what happened to these rotten kids," one said. "We must guard our houses and be prepared." Another said, "I'm not pleased with this, nor do I applaud it, but these kids were up to no good. They only reaped what they themselves sowed."[26]

There's no doubt that the Mexican people have had enough of the violence ripping their country apart. The truly scary part is that the narcos are basically correct when they say that the government can't protect civilians. So it becomes a "fight or flight" situation: leave for other Mexican states or the United States, as so many Juárez residents have done, or take matters into their own hands if they decide to stay and fight. Unfortunately, this is yet another opportunity for violence levels to spiral upward across the country.

There is a growing contingent of Mexicans who are more subtle in their ways of fighting the narcos. Social media outlets like Facebook, MySpace, YouTube, and Twitter are allowing Mexicans to communicate information about the drug war—for better or worse—anonymously, so they don't have to worry about reprisals from the cartels. One of the more popular feeds on Twitter is called "#reynosafollow." Because of the cartel-enforced frequent media blackouts there, Reynosa citizens post tweets about shootings, explosions, blockades, or general violence on Twitter with that hashtag so fellow residents, journalists, and other observers can find out what's going on in real time.

The online blogosphere is also exploding with drug war–related blogs that contain raw information, photos, and analyses from professionals and amateurs alike. Many are posted by anonymous blog owners for security reasons, but others are owned by professional writers who want to inform the world about the many aspects of violence in Mexico. These blogs also allow the Mexican people to tell their stories to the world in a safer manner.

Whether they still live in Mexico or now live in the United States or elsewhere in the world, Mexicans love their country and are incredibly saddened by what's happening to it. Some blame the narcos, and others, the Mexican government. Some point to their culture of corruption, and others revile the United States and its greedy love of drugs. But most are sad or angry that they feel powerless to do anything to return their country to a state of relative calm.

CHAPTER 7

FELIPE CALDERÓN'S PLAN TO SAVE MEXICO

FELIPE CALDERÓN DIDN'T EXACTLY come into the Mexican presidency with a clear mandate. A serious, soft-spoken man with gray hair, a receding hairline, and eyeglasses, he could easily pass for anyone's *tio*—uncle, that is. He's not what one would call a highly charismatic man. However, when talking in interviews or giving a speech on television, he gets a steely look in his eyes and speaks with quiet fire. It quickly becomes obvious that this is a man who is committed—to his country, to this drug war, and to the people of Mexico. As a poker player would say, President Calderón is "all in," and his administration is past the point of no return with the cartels.

A BRIEF HISTORY OF CORRUPTION AND COLLUSION IN MEXICO

Drug trafficking didn't start in Mexico yesterday or even five years ago. Cartels have been moving drugs through Mexico for decades, but they were largely overshadowed by the Colombian organizations until recently. As the major suppliers of marijuana and heroin for the Colombians, the Mexican cartels developed widespread distribution networks and contacts. There certainly were violent incidents that occurred between cartel members during the 1980s and earlier—but nowhere near the current levels.

The Institutional Revolutionary Party (the PRI) had a stranglehold on political power in Mexico from 2000 back to 1929. For the most part, PRI politicians weren't exactly the cleanest, but they were pragmatic. They had several regional arrangements with the various Mexican cartels, largely ignoring drug trafficking activity in exchange for financial compensation. These arrangements maintained a peace, of sorts. They also had what could be called "gentlemen's agreements" with some of the cartels for territory and even for drug profits.

In 2000, the presidential election of Vicente Fox, a member of the National Action Party (PAN), was a victory that ended the long history of PRI domination. Fox made some attempts to crack down on cartel activity, including the deployment of soldiers to various locations. However, he was largely seen as soft on drug trafficking, though he was never portrayed as colluding directly with Mexican cartels.

A PROMISE TO THE PEOPLE

The 2006 presidential election in Mexico was unusual because Felipe Calderón won by only a 0.56 percent margin over his opponent, Andrés Manuel López Obrador. The latter refused to concede even several months after an electoral commission declared Calderón the victor, and at first he claimed he was going to set up a parallel government. So Calderón came into office in December 2006 knowing that half the country voted against him, à la George W. Bush after the US election in 2000. Calderón also knew the course he planned to take against the cartels. Drug-related violence had been on the rise along the northern border, and drug trafficking activity was increasing there and elsewhere in Mexico. His predecessor,

Vicente Fox, had not taken a very aggressive stance against the cartels, and Calderón was fighting decades of political complacency.

During his presidential campaign, Calderón would often hold out his open palms, which he said were untainted by corruption and were ready to take a tight grip on the country. "Clean hands, firm hands" was his message. He promised the Mexican people that he would take an iron-fist approach to crime—a stance that resonated with many.[1]

When he began his presidency, Calderón placed the reduction of drug trafficking activity, associated violence, and corruption among the top five priorities for his presidential term. He has kept his promise—for better or worse.

THE FIGHT TO END CORRUPTION IN THE ARMY AND BEYOND

One of the first things Calderón did upon entering office was to make the military the tip of the spear in his new strategy. His line of thinking was that Mexico's police forces couldn't be relied upon to dismantle crime groups because most of them were on the cartels' payrolls. While the army wasn't completely incorruptible, it was the cleanest group of people who could legally carry weapons. Vicente Fox had deployed a few thousand troops to certain areas of Mexico during his tenure, but Calderón shipped out roughly forty-five thousand troops at the beginning of his term.

Here are the benefits of this strategy: First, the Mexican military has sheer numbers and firepower that police forces don't have. They can deploy by the hundreds to places where they're needed the most, like Ciudad Juárez, Nuevo Laredo, and Reynosa. They have access to tactical gear, protected vehicles, and high-powered weapons. The military is also a single entity, compared to the over 2,200 separate police forces.

Moreover, the Mexican military has had more success in apprehending or killing major drug kingpins in the last few years than the police have had. In December 2009, Arturo Beltrán Leyva, then head of the BLO, died along with six of his henchmen after the marines surrounded an apartment in Cuernavaca, a holiday town south of Mexico City. In July 2010, over a hundred soldiers burst in on Ignacio "Nacho" Coronel—the number-two guy in the Sinaloa Federation—and shot him as he tried to escape. In May 2010, the Mexican army made a significant discovery in the northern state of Nuevo León: a Zetas cartel hideout complete with a firing range, a fleet of armored trucks, and hundreds of weapons. The army has arrested or killed dozens of lower-level cartel members, seized tons of illegal drugs, and confiscated thousands of firearms, rounds of ammunition, and grenades.

While this is all well and good, the problem remains that the Mexican military wasn't designed for this kind of war. The purpose of the Mexican army is not to be a fighting army but to participate in rescue efforts when a natural disaster strikes the country. Since the 1920s, Mexico's political system has deliberately ensured that the army's power is quite limited. There is a tremendous consensus in the country regarding this matter because the Mexican people don't want the army to overthrow their government. Mexico has not even had an attempted military coup since 1920, and only four occurred before that.[2]

Unfortunately, sending in a few hundred poorly trained and ill-prepared troops to do battle against seasoned killers who don't play by any rules can lead to unforeseen human rights abuses and a general fear and distrust of the military, a fundamental national institution. For instance, 400 soldiers were deployed to the small Mexican border town of Ojinaga, across the river from Presidio, Texas, in March 2010. According to the town's residents, the soldiers themselves turned violent, ransacking homes and torturing people. One resident said her family was awakened one night in May 2010 when soldiers with machine guns (but no warrant) broke down her door. They said an anonymous call had directed them to her house. Another resident said she came home in June 2010 to find eight masked soldiers rifling through her belongings.[3]

Roberto, a twenty-five-year-old man who didn't want his last name used for fear of retribution, said that he, five other men, and a teenage boy were recently returning from a nearby town when they were stopped by soldiers. They were "beaten, bound, blindfolded, and taken to a military camp. He said soldiers wrapped their heads in plastic bags, beat and kicked them, and hung some of the members of the group upside down. Soldiers also forced some of them—including Roberto's twenty-year-old cousin—to drop their pants and applied pliers to one man's testicles," Roberto said. "It was always the same question: 'Where did you hide the drugs? Where did you hide the drugs?' I told them, 'If I knew, I would say instead of suffering through all this.'" He said he and his friends were released without charge and then reported their detention to human rights officials.[4]

In July 2010, more than a thousand people marched through the streets of Ojinaga, holding signs pleading with President Calderón to protect them from military troops.

In Puerto Las Ollas, a mountain village of fifty people in the southern state of Guerrero, residents recounted how soldiers seeking information in June 2010 "stuck needles under the fingernails of a disabled thirty-seven-year-old farmer, jabbed a knife into the back of his thirteen-year-old nephew, fired on a pastor, and stole food, milk, clothing, and medication." In Tijuana, two dozen policemen who were arrested on drug charges in March 2010 alleged that, to extract confessions, soldiers "beat them, held plastic bags over their heads until some lost consciousness, strapped their feet to a ceiling while dunking their heads in water, and applied electric shocks."[5]

The Mexican people were initially optimistic about the military deployments to their narco-infested cities and towns, but that optimism has largely faded. A Mexican-American citizen wrote the following about the overall national sentiment in April 2010:

It's hard for people in the United States to understand the ambiguous feelings with which the people of Mexico view their armed forces. . . . In Latin America, the armed forces are answerable only to their own chain of command and in the best of times to the executive branch of government, so their actions are made with impunity to any form of civilian oversight. Ethical and criminal corruption within the military in Latin America has always been a problem. Training, especially within the officer and NCO levels, is usually insufficient within the sphere of law enforcement tactics and respect for human rights. . . . In all the areas where the Mexican army has been pitted against the drug cartels civilian casualties have soared and the rule of law, to the degree that it existed previously, has mostly disappeared. . . . Case after case of innocent civilians killed by the military and covered up as cartel casualties has been revealed by the public and leaders of civil society and even admitted to by the federal government but in none of these many cases has any soldier or officer been brought to justice.[6]

Spokesmen for the Mexican military say that these are isolated incidents and that all allegations are being appropriately investigated. The National Human Rights Commission has received over two thousand complaints about army soldiers and has documented more than six hundred cases of abuse, many of which involved torture—including asphyxiation and the application of electric shocks to the genitals of drug suspects. This has led to a dramatic reduction in support of the deployments by the Mexican people. A poll in late June 2010 found that only 18 percent of those living in Juárez completely approved of the army's presence. Two months earlier, the number had been 65 percent.

A big part of the problem is that in cases of human rights abuse allegations, although the federal government has attempted to involve civilian authorities, the Mexican military primarily investigates itself.[7] This has resulted in a drastic reduction in the military's credibility. For example, back in May 2010, there were two separate incidents during which innocent civilians—two small children and two university students—were allegedly shot by army soldiers. The results of the investigation declared that three of the four victims were, in fact, shot by drug traffickers and not army soldiers (the fourth victim's shooter was never identified). The families of the victims claim the investigations were "cover-ups filled with lies."

It doesn't help that some members of the international community feel that the militarization of Mexico's drug war was a huge mistake and that the Mexican government is putting a Band-Aid on the wound to try to restore some semblance of faith by the people in their military. In September 2010, the opposition PRI began promoting in earnest a law to establish a more complete record of the weapons used by the army and to regulate the use of force to avoid civilian deaths at checkpoints and in operations. The ultimate goal is to effectively match up each soldier with his weapon using a ballistic "fingerprint."[8] If it's actually enforced, soldiers who engage in questionable behavior with their weapons should more easily be held accountable.

REVAMPING MEXICO'S POLICE FORCES

Mexico's law enforcement apparatus is one of the country's biggest liabilities in the drug war. There are over 2,200 municipal departments, thirty-two state police agencies, and a handful of federal agencies that don't cooperate with one another. The capability and level of professionalism among these agencies and departments range from pretty good to the bottom end of the scale. Considering the corruption that has infiltrated every agency, it's clear that Calderón has quite a mess to clean up.

His strategy for revamping the country's police forces is basically a three-pronged approach. The first order of business is getting rid of dirty cops. Given how many corrupt cops there are in Mexico, Calderón might end up eliminating entire departments. He started by firing police officers who couldn't pass lie detector tests or psychological exams that would show a proclivity for accepting bribes and such. And the firings are happening at both the federal and the local levels.

The commissioner of the Mexican federal police force announced in late August 2010 that 3,200 officers—10 percent of the federal force—had been fired that year for corruption, incompetence, or links to criminals. An additional one thousand officers were facing disciplinary action and could lose their jobs. The commissioner said none of the dismissed officers "would be allowed to work in any law enforcement capacity in the future."[9]

Next in the strategy, after removing those thousands of officers from their jobs, is replacing the dirty cops with new ones who are vetted (or at least as well vetted as possible) and better trained. But finding good cops in Mexico is a serious challenge. According to reports, currently

> more than 400 municipalities in Mexico don't have any police force at all, and almost 1,800 have departments with less than one hundred employees. Sixty-two percent of the officers make less than 4,000 pesos (about US $315) per month, and 68 percent don't have a high school education. Forty-three percent of local cops are too old to effectively perform their basic duties, and 70 percent are considered overweight to obese—which translates into an inability to chase a suspect for more than 300 feet. Many officers still use old .38-caliber revolvers—obsolete for over a decade and seriously outmatched by AK-47s and .50-caliber rifles used by narcos.[10]

A 2010 report by the ICESI stated that most Mexican police officers "don't possess the basic knowledge and essential practical skills of self-defense, marksmanship, computer literacy, or making oral or written statements." It also said that the low pay that officers receive and the dangerous conditions under which they work are "conducive to job neglect, acts of corruption such as bribes and charging illegal fees, and at worst, collusion with criminals." And cops continue to be killed left and right by cartel enforcers.

Calderón has begun the process of hiring new police officers at federal, state, and local levels, but unfortunately that process doesn't seem to be going as well as he had hoped. Current data shows that only 22 percent of police forces at the three levels of government have taken the exams that were supposed to help weed out corrupt or incompetent police in the two years since the initiative was announced. While almost half of the 72,000 federal police and 34 percent of the 171,000 local police have taken the exams, only 8 percent of the 283,000 state police have done so. In six states—Hidalgo, Mexico state, Nayarit, San Luis Potosí, Tlaxcala, and Yucatán—less than 1 percent of police have taken the exams.[11]

Fortunately, the Mexican police aren't above asking for help from the outside. In August 2010, the Ministry of Public Security announced an agreement for 200 Mexican private security companies to provide forty thousand guards to augment federal police forces.[12] This is good because the corporate workers have better training, better intelligence, and better equipment that they can bring to the fight. This is bad because there's little to no federal oversight of how these companies operate. Still, any help these private guards can provide is welcomed.

The third prong in the strategy is the consolidation of the over 2,200 municipal departments into less than three dozen state-level agencies. In June 2010, Calderón and the state governors approved a plan to abolish municipal police agencies and create thirty-two state-level law enforcement agencies with only one overarching authority in each state. Integral to that process would be a revision of how the police operate. While this won't completely solve the problems of corruption and incompetence, it is the best way for police agencies to communicate with each other and to receive guidance from a standardized authority.[13]

Not everyone is happy with the plan. Several mayors of both small towns and larger cities don't like the thought of "giving up" their local cops to a larger state agency. They want to protect the social and political elements of the municipalities, and since they know the town better than anyone does, they know to what hot spots police should be sent.[14]

Many questions will be raised as this new police structure moves forward, including if it's even possible to restore the public's confidence in its law enforcement institutions. Since 1982, Mexican presidents have reorganized the federal law enforcement system five times and have created at least four elite forces in an attempt to form new units that are free of corruption.[15]

FIXING A BROKEN JUSTICE SYSTEM

Mexico is a democracy, but its justice system operates quite differently from that of the United States. It's also quite broken—some say irreparably. The US legal system is called a "common law" system, which means that when judges hand down decisions in court cases, they make those decisions partly based on decisions made by judges in previous related cases. Mexico is a "civil law" country, which means judges make their decisions based on a combination of their constitution, Roman law, and Napoleonic code. Judges are also actively involved in gathering evidence and developing cases. There are no jury trials or oral arguments and no cross-examination of witnesses; testimony is presented on paper. However, the most important difference between the Mexican and American justice systems is that in Mexico, the accused essentially is guilty until proven innocent.[16]

This system should work well when it comes to putting drug traffickers and cartel hit men in jail, but reality is just the opposite. Fewer than 25 percent of all crimes are reported in Mexico, and of those, fewer than 2 percent are successfully prosecuted, due to the system's inefficiency and lack of transparency.[17] Mexican cops lack access to basic forensic equipment, and Mexico lacks a comprehensive national fingerprint database. Most police officers' job performance is evaluated on the number of arrests they make—not on whether they arrest the right person. The same goes for prosecutors.[18]

In 2009, President Calderón made a bold and controversial move by ordering the arrest of thirty-five mayors, prosecutors, police chiefs, and other officials in the state of Michoacán, his home state. They were later jailed and accused of taking bribes from a cartel. At first, it seemed like the Mexican government was finally cracking down on corrupt politicians across the board, especially since those arrested all belonged to different political parties. However, more than a year later, the judge rejected the validity of the evidence presented. Everyone except one suspect was sent home, and most of them returned to their desks shortly thereafter.[19]

The prosecutors definitely dropped the ball when it came to providing solid evidence, and the informants weren't much better. They were anonymous and paid, and the information they were providing to the court couldn't be verified. Some suspects were accused of accepting tens of thousands of dollars a month from LFM, but no one could say that investigators made a concerted effort to find proof of these financial exchanges by looking into their personal records. In affidavits, Mexican federal police described stakeouts in which they "watched alleged drug figures hand suitcases and envelopes to people whom the officers said they believed to be corrupt officials. As it turned out, investigators were not sure of the identities of the recipients, and the file contains no evidence that they ever determined what was in the bundles."[20]

Another case in March 2010 involved a four-year-old girl by the name of Paulette Gebara Farah who went missing from her family's apartment in Huixquilucan, an upscale suburb of Mexico City. Her parents were particularly concerned because little Paulette had trouble walking and talking and might not be able to escape captors or communicate her predicament to police. Her family initiated a huge public campaign to try to find her, placing billboards and hundreds of posters with her picture all over Mexico City. They also took advantage of social networking sites like Facebook and Twitter to try to get their little girl back.[21]

Nine days after Paulette went missing, police thought it would be a good idea to try to recreate events as they happened the night she disappeared. They didn't get very far after they started. Investigators found her body stuffed in a plastic bag and squeezed in between her bed's mattress and bed frame; she had suffocated the night she "disappeared." When police were asked how they could have overlooked something as important as the missing person's body, the regional attorney general at the time said the police had been focusing their search efforts outside the home. Paulette's mother quickly became the prime suspect, and the attorney general resigned shortly thereafter. A leader from the opposition political party in the state claimed that one hundred police officers and sniffer dogs searched everything within ten meters of Paulette's room and somehow missed the body. He called for an investigation into "what really happened."[22]

Even on the slight chance that a narco or some other major violent criminal makes it into the slammer, the odds are he won't be in it for long. The Mexican media has been rife with stories in the last few years of dramatic prison breaks. One of the more notable incidents occurred in May 2009 at a prison in Zacatecas. Video footage from security cameras showed a convoy of seventeen vehicles—with the convenient help of a helicopter patrolling overhead—pulling up to the Cieneguillas prison complex. About thirty armed men, some in police uniforms, got out and went inside toward the maximum-security area. They quickly rounded up the prisoners they were looking for, most of whom happened to be members of the Gulf cartel, loaded them into the convoy, and sped off without a shot being fired. Needless to say, it was an inside job; the prison warden and two top guards were arrested, and an additional forty guards were held for questioning. It was the third prison break in Zacatecas in recent years.[23]

In September 2010, eighty-five prisoners—again, mostly violent drug cartel members—escaped from a jail in Reynosa, which is right across the border from McAllen, Texas. Police arrested more than forty prison guards, but two guards were missing. Chances are they left town along with the prisoners.

Even if a cartel member does end up serving more than a couple of years, if he ranks high enough in his organization, he'll be treated like a king. He'll have enough money and power to throw around among prison guards and administrators and to buy things like gourmet food, wine, and liquor; unlimited conjugal visits with spouses and mistresses; extra cell space; and increased access to every privilege given in prison. More important, narcos can continue to conduct business from jail through virtually unlimited contact with their attorneys and associates.

Fortunately, the case of Mexico's broken justice system is one area of the drug war where the US government is trying to help. In late 2010, the US Attorney's Office in Arizona led training sessions for about 180 Mexican federal prosecutors, investigators, and forensic specialists on how to conduct oral trials and handle evidence. They also held workshops on how to better prosecute cases involving drug and firearms trafficking and money laundering. The program, expected to cost $500,000 to $700,000, will be funded at least in part by the Mérida Initiative. The rest of the money will come from US State Department funds given to the Justice Department for international assistance programs.[24]

In 2008, the Mexican government instituted a series of judicial reforms, including an oral trial procedure, but those changes aren't supposed to take full effect until 2016. This is a good first step, but reform in Mexico—and elsewhere in Latin America—is painfully slow, even slower than it is in Washington, DC. In a twisted sort of catch-22, the Mexican constitution required the government to go through its legal system in order to . . . reform its legal system. For example, the government first had to make significant changes to the constitution itself, like establishing the presumption of innocence and authorizing the detention of criminal suspects for a limited amount of time. Only after these changes (and there are more planned) can different Mexican states start implementing their own legal reforms.[25] One can see the inherent challenges to this process. But as the saying goes, a journey of a thousand miles starts with a single step. Let's hope the steps the Mexican government is taking to fix its broken justice system are pointing in the right direction.

DECRIMINALIZATION AND THE LEGALIZATION DEBATE

Calderón made a bold move in mid-2009 when he proposed—and received congressional approval for—the decriminalization of the possession of small amounts of marijuana, cocaine, methamphetamine, and other recreational drugs. His intention was to distinguish between small-time users and big-time dealers—the real criminals—while "retargeting major crime-fighting resources away from consumers and toward dealers and their drug-lord bosses." Calderón also wanted to start treating drug use in Mexico more as a public health issue rather than a criminal one.[26] Unfortunately, this decriminalization policy has accomplished absolutely nothing in the past year.

Calderón made another bold move in August 2010 by going on the record with a statement that the legalization debate should officially be put on the table, despite his own hesitations. He didn't say he was going to propose legalization of drugs or that it would necessarily be the best thing to do. After all, the decriminalization policy had met with controversy on an international scale and had not reduced levels of violence or drug dependency within Mexico. However, he felt that it was time for Mexico to at least take the issue seriously and do more homework on the potential effects of such a bold policy on drug trafficking and related violence.

Some in the United States argue that legalization won't reduce violence in Mexico or eliminate the black market because the cartels would continue to engage in other illicit activities including kidnapping, extortion, and theft. Unfortunately there's no way of knowing if legalization would be a net benefit or a net loss without actually taking the legislative steps to legalize certain drugs. Calderón, however, is realizing that desperate times call for desperate measures, and, for good or ill, seems to be ready to try anything.

That is how Calderón plans to proceed with the drug war until the end of his term in December 2012.

POLITICAL AND DIPLOMATIC CHALLENGES

Illegal immigration is a major hot-button issue in America these days, but it isn't the only political and diplomatic challenge facing the US and Mexican governments as they try to work together to combat drug and weapons trafficking, human smuggling, and money laundering. There are all sorts of complications in that complex relationship, and it's important to know at least a little bit about those challenges to see why attempting to implement certain strategies is considerably easier in theory than in reality.

The Border Fences

Yes, there will be two border fences. Unbeknownst to many Americans, Mexico has its own plans for a fence on its southern border with Guatemala. Before considering that hot political controversy, discussion of the northern border is in order.

The fence—or actually, the series of fences—along the US-Mexico border is a relatively recent project. The fence was proposed in 2005, and its construction was signed into law with the Secure Fence Act of 2006. The act called for over 700 miles of double-reinforced fencing to be built in parts of California, Arizona, New Mexico, and Texas in order to deter drug smugglers and illegal immigrants. It also authorized the installation of checkpoints, cameras, sensors, lighting, and vehicle barriers to achieve that same goal. In December 2007, the double-layer requirement for the fence was removed, and only thirty-four miles of that type were ever built. As of January 2009, almost 600 miles of some type of fencing were in place, but those sections varied—sometimes significantly—in length, height, and style.

The gaps between sections were supposed to be monitored by a "virtual fence," which included surveillance by high-tech sensors and cameras. However, construction of the virtual parts of the border fence was halted, and funding was redirected to other border security projects. In the spring of 2010, Border Patrol agents were relying on "cameras with unreliable signals, and the numbers of new defects identified with the virtual fence outpaced the numbers that were being fixed." Then–Customs and Border Protection Chief Alan Bersin dashed any hopes left for the virtual fence when he called it a "complete failure" during a Senate hearing in April 2010.[27]

In reality, the whole border fence has been a fiasco. Some agencies and American border cities and towns love the fence and say that illegal immigration and drug crimes have been dramatically reduced in their areas since the fence's construction. Others complain that the fence sections just divert drug traffickers and immigrants to areas where the fence is incomplete and drive up illegal crossings and crime rates in those places. Because the fence varies so much in construction style, there are some places where creative and well-equipped border crossers can just cut through it or climb over it with some help. As US Department of Homeland Security Secretary Janet Napolitano said, "You show me a 50-foot wall, and I'll show you a 51-foot ladder."

The fence has had other negative impacts on American border communities. The current and proposed locations of the fence divide three American Indian tribal lands. It would even divide the University of Texas at Brownsville in half if built there as planned. Because the winding Rio Grande determines the US-Mexico border to the east, it's too expensive to build a fence to follow it. Instead, the fence was built in a straight line to the north of the river, creating a big gap of land that's technically US territory between the river and the fence itself. Then there are the negative environmental impacts of the fence on things like water flow, vegetation growth, and animal migration. Natural resources are being affected by a fence that isn't really doing the job it was originally designed for. Despite all these drawbacks and failings, most Americans are still in favor of the border fence. A July 2010 Rasmussen Reports poll showed that 68 percent of survey participants supported the building of a southwest border fence.

Here's where things get knotty diplomatically between the United States and its neighbor. The Mexican government disapproves of the border fence. They believe that their citizens should be able to enter the United States in a safe and orderly manner (whether legally or not) and that the border fence endangers the lives of Mexican migrants. In November 2007, the Mexican government issued a 208-page report warning the US government of the potential fence-caused damage to the environment along the border. It also compared the fence to the Berlin Wall and the Great Wall of China. In December 2006, then-President Fox's foreign secretary, Luis Ernesto Derbez, said, "Mexico is not going to bear, it is not going to permit, and it will not allow a stupid thing like this wall."[28]

Maybe it's not allowed on the northern border, but Mexico hasn't had a problem quietly planning to erect its own fence on its southern border with Guatemala, where the Mexican government currently intends to build a wall. While the official purpose is to prevent the passage of contraband, it is also clearly intended to prevent the passage of illegal immigrants into Mexico. Of course, the Guatemalan government is none too happy. Guatemalan civil and governmental organizations have called the plan "senseless," saying a border fence will not prevent undocumented migrants from crossing the border on their way north.[29]

Other Controversial Immigration Issues

Nothing rocked the opposing immigration movements in 2010 more than Arizona's SB 1070, a law that would allow state authorities to enforce federal immigration laws. Public and private commentary on SB 1070 when it was first announced was extremely polarized, with proponents saying that it was about time the states started doing the job the federal government never got around to and opponents claiming the law would lead to racial profiling and immigrant abuses.

Stemming from the SB 1070 controversy was anger about the Mexican government's hypocrisy over the treatment of illegal immigrants. Calderón and other high-ranking political figures in the Mexican government very publicly stated their concern that SB 1070 would lead to the profiling, mistreatment, and abuse of Mexican immigrants seeking a better life in the United States. Mexico has historically called for a relaxation of US immigration laws because strict enforcement is causing immigrants to risk their lives by having to cross the border in increasingly dangerous areas. It seems that the Mexican government would probably be completely happy if America stopped enforcing immigration laws altogether. This is largely because of the millions (if not billions) of dollars in remittances that both legal and illegal Mexican migrants in the United States send back annually to their families in Mexico—dollars that get injected into the Mexican economy.

Taking into account this stance on immigration, it's interesting to look at how Mexican authorities regard those who enter Mexico illegally from Central America and beyond. According to Mexican laws, the Mexican government will bar foreigners if they upset "the equilibrium of the national demographics." If outsiders do not enhance the country's "economic or national interests" or are "not found to be physically or mentally healthy," they are not welcomed. Neither are those who show "contempt against national sovereignty or security." Law enforcement officials at all levels are required by national mandate to enforce Mexican immigration laws. Even the Mexican military is authorized to arrest illegal immigrants. Everyone in Mexico is required to carry a citizen's identification card, and visiting foreigners are tracked by the government. Unlike in the United States, illegal immigrants in Mexico can't complain because public political speeches by foreigners are banned.[30]

What's more, migrants seeking passage through Mexico have to worry about how they are treated by Mexican immigration authorities, known as "*la migra.*" The way *la migra* works in Mexico is considerably different from ICE or the Border Patrol in the United States. Immigration activists say that corrupt Mexican police freely engage in racial profiling and routinely harass Central American migrants. A *USA Today* article said that in one six-month period, from September 2008 through February 2009, "at least 9,758 migrants were kidnapped and held for ransom in Mexico—91 of them with the direct participation of Mexican police. Other migrants were routinely stopped and shaken down for bribes. A separate survey conducted during one month in 2008 at ten migrant shelters showed that Mexican authorities were behind migrant attacks in 35 of 240 cases, or 15 percent."[31]

THE EMBATTLED MÉRIDA INITIATIVE

In these times, international assistance is given during a crisis. Americans and foreigners alike either praise or criticize the United States for being the world's policeman. But America also provides more foreign aid than any other country in the world, in 2007 giving almost $42 billion, with most of it going to Africa and Asia.[32] The United States has sent military aircraft, troops, and supplies to the far reaches of the globe in a humanitarian capacity after hurricanes and floods. Its soldiers have deployed to conflicts where the national interest isn't always apparent, and it has poured billions of dollars into counterdrug programs throughout its own hemisphere. Yet the concept of America helping Mexico with its drug war remains incomprehensible for many.

Most resistance to the idea is rooted in the long and painful history of US interventions in Latin America. At the time in history when the United States was becoming an independent nation, Central and South America existed as a group of colonies. There were four primary European countries doing the colonizing: Spain, Portugal, France, and Great Britain. Political and economic events in Europe at the time were complicated, to say the least. An independence movement was sweeping through Latin America, and the European colonizers started to feel their lucrative territories slipping from their hands. In the early 1800s, they felt it was time to regain control over the colonies, but by then they had a different challenge to deal with: a brand-new and increasingly confident United States of America.

American leaders were anxious to prevent any further colonization efforts by these countries and to avoid interference by European powers in western hemispheric affairs. So, in December 1823, the US government introduced the Monroe Doctrine, which stated that further efforts by European countries to colonize land or interfere with states in the Americas would be viewed as acts of aggression requiring intervention. Great Britain, which had a huge commercial interest in Latin America, supported the doctrine, which most Latin American leaders also got behind. Little did these nascent countries know how they'd be cursing the doctrine in the future.

In the decades that followed, the US government used the Monroe Doctrine as a justification (or an excuse) for everything from westward expansion to the annexation of Hawaii. Under it, America entered the Spanish-American War, obtained Puerto Rico and the Philippines, and went into Cuba. President John F. Kennedy even cited it as a basis for confronting the Soviet Union during the Cuban Missile Crisis.

There was plenty of opportunity for the United States to get even more aggressive in Latin America. In 1904, President Theodore Roosevelt introduced the Roosevelt Corollary to the Monroe Doctrine, which asserted the US rights to intervene in Latin America in cases of "flagrant and chronic wrongdoing by a Latin American nation." The following century saw plenty of opportunity for US military intervention in the region, particularly during the Cold War. No longer was the United States concerned only about encroachment by European powers; the spread of communism had become the real scourge.

From 1890 to 2004, the United States sent troops into Latin America fifty-five times. Some of the more notable military operations that might sound familiar include deployments to Nicaragua in the 1920s and 1930s to battle Augusto Sandino, the Guatemalan Revolution in the mid-1950s, the 1961 Bay of Pigs invasion of Cuba, the ouster of Manuel Noriega from Panama, the Grenada invasion in the 1980s, and Aristide's ouster from the Haitian presidency in 2004.

Some of these interventions were welcomed by the governments and people of the countries involved, but many were not. Some of these operations have left a bitter taste in the mouths of local people. Making things worse is the historical perception by Latin American governments that the United States wasn't interested in minding its own business and instead felt responsible for ensuring military, political, and economic stability in the region. Both the Monroe Doctrine and the Roosevelt Corollary provided justification for doing whatever was necessary to make that happen.

Sending in the military isn't the only intervention by the United States in Latin America's business over the course of almost two centuries. Another is sending a lot of money, for a number of reasons. Financial aid usually takes one of two forms: economic assistance or counterdrug support. The former is the most politically complicated and has caused the most problems for relations between America and the benefactor countries. Bolivia is a good example. Usually competing with Honduras and Paraguay for the title of the poorest country in the western hemisphere, Bolivia's economy truly bottomed out in the early 1980s. The United States was willing to provide quite a bit of financial help, but there were strings attached. The Bolivian government had to enact several austerity measures and free-market policies in order to get its economy back on its feet. It worked for a little while, but the economy eventually collapsed.

Almost all the financial support the US government provides to Latin America, whether directly or through the World Bank or the International Monetary Fund, comes with strings attached. Those strings, like with Bolivia, almost always take the form of economic austerity measures and the implementation of neoliberal reforms. That basically means that the beneficiary government needs to start running its economy more like America's. So it comes as no surprise that many Latin American governments (and individuals) don't really care for the United States, its money, or the attached policies.

This brings up the current aid package to Mexico (and other Latin American countries), called the Mérida Initiative after the Mexican city where then-President George W. Bush and President Calderón met in 2007 to discuss expanded counterdrug efforts. The cooperative agreement provides roughly $1.7 billion in counterdrug support to Mexico, seven Central American countries, the Dominican Republic, and Haiti. Mexico is getting the lion's share of the funding, which is designated for training, equipment, and intelligence support designed to combat threats from drug trafficking, transnational crime, and money laundering.

The initiative is significant because it served as a formal acknowledgment that Mexico's drug war is a shared problem—and a shared responsibility. America has a huge stake in the success of the program because those threats clearly impact US citizens. The initiative has contributed to increasing the trust level between the two countries by acknowledging to Mexicans the US role in the problem. It is a sign of progress that Mexico has come around to admitting that it needs a helping hand and is willing to go to unprecedented lengths to cooperate.

Fortunately for US taxpayers, most of the money is being spent on military equipment manufactured in the United States or sold to the government by private contractors, which means those funds get pumped into our economy. That equipment includes helicopters, ion and x-ray scanners, canine units, secure telecommunications systems, and transport aircraft. The money also pays for US personnel to train the Mexican military and law enforcement agencies. None of it goes directly to the Mexican government or Mexican contractors, instead funding operational costs for the military and civilian agencies.

What good is the Mérida Initiative accomplishing? Cross-border communication between military and law enforcement agencies is better than it's ever been—which is not to say it's perfect, or even great; US agencies started with a very low level of trust with Mexican agencies because of the high potential for penetration by the cartels. But they had to start somewhere, and the best bilateral relationships usually start at the field level. The Mexican and US governments are also working on setting up a joint intelligence center, like those already in existence in Europe and Asia.

Unfortunately, the initiative got off to a very slow start, at a time when the support the money would have provided was sorely needed. The bureaucratic red tape in Congress slowed the release of funds to barely a trickle. By March 2010, only 9 percent of obligated funds had been spent. In addition to the red tape, there weren't enough people available to administer the programs for deploying the equipment. One problem is that the Mérida Initiative didn't really have concrete benchmarks by which to measure success—or failure. The plan also lacked a timeline for the delivery of equipment and the implementation of training programs.[33]

Finally, the US government decided it would withhold 15 percent of initiative funds until Mexico started cleaning up its human rights problems. That did not go over well in Mexico City. The Mexican government accused the US government of violating its sovereignty and interfering in its internal affairs. The language in the agreement was eventually softened, and some of that money was released, but it was a bitter reminder for the Mexican government.

THE CARTELS' RESPONSE

Obviously, Mexican cartels aren't planning to bend to the will of Calderón or the US government. They flout their power, wealth, and influence and continue to kill soldiers, police, and an increasing number of innocents with little concern for the value of human life. While not interested in taking the political reins themselves, cartels actively manipulate governments through bribery and intimidation. Notably, in the fall of 2010, cartel hit men went on a killing spree of over a dozen town mayors across the country. Because the mayors control the police in their towns, this was an easy way for cartels to publicly announce that they won't tolerate an officeholder who isn't interested in meeting their demands.

The cartels also routinely go on public relations binges, hanging those banners announcing that the government can't protect the people. In November 2010, LFM distributed thousands of flyers and posted banners offering to disband as a cartel if the government began providing real protection and opportunities for the Mexican people. There was a lot of debate at the time over the authenticity of the message, but one thing is clear: there are places in Mexico where the cartel response to Calderón's strategy is making it impossible for the government to provide that security and implement even modest strategies.

CHAPTER 8

THE FIGHT TO STOP CARTELS NORTH OF THE BORDER

THE FOLLOWING EVENT TOOK PLACE in 2003 in the rural eastern part of San Diego County. At the time, Border Patrol Agent Chris Moreno was the supervisor of a plainclothes operations unit. Moreno had a weakness for telling his father about the thrill of the chase and being outnumbered, and perhaps about enjoying a little bit of physical confrontation. He knew that their talks reminded his father of the cowboys and crime fighters of his youth, and the son felt a singular joy in being interrupted mid-story by the old man's questions and requests to start over. He worked harder when out on assignment, anticipating telling his father about it.

Because Moreno was a supervisor working in a plainclothes capacity, he had an unmarked vehicle that he was allowed to drive back and forth to work in the event that he was called out after hours. The vehicle itself, however, was a white Ford Crown Victoria and recognizable as a "cop car" by anyone who had spent half a minute growing up there and watching any sort of cop TV show. Fortunately, this description did not apply to the Border Patrol's illegal clientele. He would regularly spot groups barely concealed by the roadway, call them over, and convince them in his urgent "guero" Spanish to get in and lie down out of sight. Once they were packed in with no easy way to exit, Moreno would feign confusion and say in Español, "Oh, I forgot," pulling his badge out from where he kept it tucked on a chain inside his shirt. Usually this act would be received with chuckles and admissions that he had indeed fooled them well.

This particular morning, Moreno was making the fifty-minute drive up the winding rural highway past Tecate. He came swinging around a broad turn, passed under a small train trestle, and swept past a sheer wall of black rock that he knew dropped into a meadow just around the bend. He'd caught countless groups in this area, which wasn't surprising since the road he traveled on was a three-minute dash from the border, making it extremely attractive to smugglers of people and contraband. After dark, one could sneak up to a nearby hilltop with night-vision goggles and watch the groups gather in the brush, up to a hundred at a time, eating, commingling, and resting until their particular guide was ready to lead his designated chunk of humanity—by a surprising turn of events—into the waiting arms of the agents lying still as rocks in the meadow. One time, Moreno watched through an infrared scope as a group of twenty-five people spilled down a ravine from the gathering spot to the border road below. The last two stragglers unknowingly got within sixty feet of an adult mountain lion. He was forced to direct agents in with lights blazing and plenty of noise, or someone would definitely have come to a gruesome end. The lion disappeared like a flash into the brush at the first sight of the flashlights below, and the scattering aliens never knew how lucky they'd been that someone was watching.

At 7 A.M., however, nobody was watching, and as the sweeping cliff face gave way to the open meadow in his line of sight, he observed a brown sedan as it pulled onto the shoulder. Moreno sped past, noting the male driver staring straight ahead, hands gripping the steering wheel at ten and two o'clock. The barbed-wire fence there had long ago given up its straight, military lines for a more parabolic shape, the result of so many people going over and under it, and snagged bits of torn clothing were easily visible as markers, even at his speed. He proceeded without slowing for another half mile up the road and pulled into a semi-concealed driveway to watch for the vehicle to pass him. Adrenaline pumping, Moreno began calling his agents one by one and telling them that he had a good one that was about to load and to hurry and get their vehicles. Not two minutes later, the brown sedan passed him, and he pulled out.

It was quickly evident that the driver recognized Moreno, as after passing him, he accelerated away. Although he could see only the driver, Moreno felt certain that the car was loaded with something heavy, given the exaggerated bounce of its rear end as it passed over bumps and depressions in the roadway. As they continued east, the man was driving at the speed limit since he couldn't shake Moreno. He was also watching intently in his rearview mirror, causing his vehicle to drift back and forth in the lane. He's calculating his next move, Moreno thought, and he continued to update Border Patrol Dispatch and his agents on his location. Approximately seven miles later, the driver abruptly turned down a local road leading to the border, and Moreno prepared himself mentally for the off-road chase to the border that must be coming. Instead, the driver slowly turned right onto a wide opening to a dirt road leading to some local residences. Moreno mimicked his movements, staying a couple of car lengths back, and then slowed to a stop as the driver made an excruciatingly slow U-turn. So what would it be? Back out to the road to find a comfortable spot to run? He was OK with that since it gave his backup more time to respond.

But the vehicle didn't move. The two men sat there facing each other, staring, waiting for the other to make a move, their bumpers fifteen feet apart and not quite centered on each other. Moreno couldn't read the driver's face; it was totally blank. It seemed like the face of someone who was out of options, and Moreno decided to play his hand. He exited his vehicle, staying behind his door in case he had to jump back in a hurry, and started barking orders at the driver to "shut it down!" The driver didn't move a muscle; he just focused that cold stare on the agent. Moreno stepped around his door, pushing it closed behind him, and began walking toward the other car, arm outstretched and pointing like a lightning bolt might come out of it at any minute and extinguish his miserable existence if the driver did not heed his commands. *Shut it down, I said! Do not move! Do you understand me? DO NOT MOVE!* Moreno must have sensed that things were about to go wrong, because the background began fading and he was focused on the driver's face, his hands, and the sound of his own voice barking out commands. He was a couple of steps ahead of his bumper when he heard the sound of the driver's engine revving up.

Moreno thought the vehicle was actually moving backward at the moment that its tires grabbed the soft dirt and lurched forward toward him. In a split second, he calculated that he was going to be hit and probably pinned against his own vehicle as the driver drove straight at him. There was no more sound, only movement, only the vehicle bearing down on him and the unchanged look on the driver's face. His pistol was suddenly in both of his hands and pointing at that face. Moreno doesn't recall making the decision to draw it or the actual act of unsnapping his holster and pulling out the weapon.

The first round went off in a vacuum. He didn't hear it at all, and he didn't feel the gun move. The only indication that it had actually fired was that the driver's expression changed at that moment. Moreno was vaguely aware that he had made contact with his own vehicle behind him and was no longer moving backward. He adjusted his aim slightly to the left to compensate for the movement of the rapidly approaching vehicle. He focused on the only thing that he could see at that point, which was that face. As he pulled the trigger a second time, Moreno saw the driver duck down and away to his right, unconsciously pulling the steering wheel with him. This time he clearly saw the round exit the barrel of his weapon and strike the driver's side window where his head should have been, causing the glass to spiderweb and shatter.

In an instant, the vehicle was past him. Moreno had been spared by the driver's act of self-preservation, which caused the vehicle to jerk to the right and brush by him. He didn't fire again. The threat was gone. The vehicle swerved out onto the roadway and disappeared out of sight, speeding west into the morning. He immediately grabbed his vehicle radio and called out, *Shots fired! Shots fired!* A deluge of questions came next: where was the suspect, was he hit, did he need medical assistance, and so on. Moreno tried to sound composed because, of all things, the fear of embarrassment in front of his peers from screeching on the radio flooded his mind. Moreno didn't think he did such a good job of sounding calm, but he managed to put out a description and last-known route of travel to his responding agents before sinking into the resignation that he would have to hear about how he, an expert marksman, not only had obviously missed his target, but also had sounded like a frightened schoolgirl on the radio. His backup arrived and mercifully held back any taunts, and he listened intently for news of the suspect.

Twenty minutes later, he heard one of his agents, a large man of Puerto Rican descent, excitedly reporting that he was on the suspect's tail, heading right back to the area where the driver was first seen in his car. An unfortunate turn down a gated driveway was followed by an abbreviated attempt to flee on foot, during which Moreno's agent kicked the car door shut on the would-be escapee hard enough to fold him in half. The driver and three smuggled aliens were in custody.

Moreno was thinking: three smuggled aliens? That's what his life was worth to that guy? The agent had a baby on the way who was almost left fatherless along with an older sister. It was a depressing thought. There was no upwelling of anger, though, and no machismo telling him to boast that he wished he'd blown the guy's head off. There was just that shaky feeling of disbelief that someone would do that, just to get away. And to get away from a crime that he probably would not have been prosecuted for if he'd just pulled over and given up. Three aliens weren't worth the US Attorney's time. The courts were overflowing with border crime cases—more than they could handle and much more serious than transporting three smuggled migrants. The driver would have been home that afternoon, already booked and released. Moreno just couldn't understand it.

He found out later that his aim hadn't been too bad after all, considering he had a moving target. The first round had lodged in the A-pillar between the driver's window and the windshield. Had it been a higher-velocity round with more penetrating power, they might both be dead today—the driver aerated and Moreno squashed. The second round missed because the driver reacted and ducked. It entered the window, traveled through the passenger compartment, and lodged in the right-rear door of the sedan, just above the head of a female crouched on the floorboards. Moreno guessed they all had guardian angels watching them that day.

The other smuggled aliens, two males, were crammed in the trunk and very happy to be let out. The driver pleaded guilty to alien smuggling and assault on a federal officer but didn't receive very much jail time in the plea agreement. That bothered Moreno, but he'd seen it before and was somewhat used to it. He hadn't been injured, and the driver claimed that he wasn't trying to hurt Moreno; he was only trying to get away. Moreno was fortunate again and didn't let it affect his work; he just tried to take lessons from the experience and be comforted knowing that he could make that decision to respond with deadly force, if necessary. This is the life of a Border Patrol agent, and this is the nature of the fight north of the border.[1]

The two federal agencies responsible for US domestic security are the Department of Homeland Security (DHS) and the US Department of Justice (USDOJ); the latter oversees the Drug Enforcement Administration (DEA) and the Bureau of Alcohol, Tobacco, Firearms, and Explosives (ATF).

In addition, tens of thousands of police officers, analysts, state employees, contractors, and military personnel are also actively involved in this mission at the state and local levels. This chapter explores how the US government and law enforcement agencies protect the people from the effects of Mexico's drug war, and how they go about their missions.

US HOMELAND SECURITY AND THE STRUGGLE TO KEEP UP

The DHS is like the "hydra" of federal agencies because it has so many different branches, and if one branch is dissolved, it seems that two or three more appear in its place. Currently there are eighteen components and seven agencies that fall under DHS. "Homeland security" covers so many different disciplines and responsibilities that it's hard to encapsulate everything in one organization in any other way. Border security is separated into two divisions: enforcing immigrations and customs laws, run by Immigration and Customs Enforcement (ICE), and conducting inspections at the border, handled by Customs and Border Protection (CBP).

US Customs and Border Protection

Customs and Border Protection is responsible for guarding nearly seven thousand miles of the land border that the United States shares with Canada and Mexico and two thousand miles of coastal waters: those surrounding the Florida peninsula, and off the coast of Southern California. The agency also protects ninety-five thousand miles of maritime border in partnership with the US Coast Guard. CBP officers and agents work at official ports of entry as well as between the ports, preventing illegal entry into America of people and contraband. CBP has the largest law enforcement air force in the world, patrolling the nation's land and sea borders to stop terrorists and smugglers before they enter the country.[2]

Any American who has ever traveled to a foreign country and returned to the United States has had a brief conversation with a CBP inspector, at the airport, a cruise terminal, or a border crossing. These are the folks along the southwest border who check passports, inspect bags, have dogs sniff around vehicles, and sometimes tear apart those same vehicles suspecting that they have well-hidden compartments containing illegal drugs. It's not always a fun job, especially in the summer heat, to be in a black uniform, standing up for several hours at a time, and bearing the responsibility of preventing drugs and terrorists from entering the country. But someone has to do it, and it's the CBP that's doing it at all border crossings.

US Border Patrol

The US Border Patrol is the part of the CBP that protects the borders between the ports of entry. In many respects, the Border Patrol's job is even more unforgiving because of the often-brutal environment in which they're required to operate. The Border Patrol's overall mission is, and has been since 1924, to detect and prevent the illegal entry of aliens into the United States. However, their focus was modified after 9/11 to include the detection, apprehension, and/or deterrence of terrorists and terrorist weapons.

As in the story at the beginning of this chapter, one of the most important activities of a Border Patrol agent is what's called the "line watch": trying to catch bad guys—smugglers, coyotes, terrorists, and others—by hiding, watching, and using teamwork. Agents have several tools at their disposal, but they also have many different responsibilities: following up leads, responding to electronic-sensor television systems, aircraft sightings, and interpreting and following tracks, marks, and other physical evidence. All these activities mean that agents are often in trucks, on all-terrain vehicles, or on foot in the desert, the rugged hills, the mountainous terrain, and other remote places.

The most well-known USDOJ agency is the Federal Bureau of Investigation (FBI), but two other agencies play a much bigger role in Mexico's drug war.

The Drug Enforcement Administration

The Drug Enforcement Administration's mission is twofold: First, they enforce US drug laws and bring to the justice system those involved in the manufacture or distribution of illegal drugs already in or headed toward the United States. Second, the DEA supports programs aimed at reducing the availability of illegal drugs on the domestic and international markets. The DEA currently has seven resident offices in Mexico from which they work with the Mexican government and law enforcement to conduct investigations and provide training and assistance.[7]

While the DEA has had many major successes against Mexican drug cartels, it has also suffered some tragic setbacks. In the early 1980s, DEA agent Enrique "Kiki" Camarena began working against drug trafficking organizations in Mexico after several years of success in the agency. In February 1985, he was working undercover against a major drug supplier when he was kidnapped on his way to meet his wife for lunch. Members of the drug operation he was targeting had identified him as an undercover agent and proceeded to brutally torture Camarena before murdering him. His body was found one month later, and Camarena's death quickly became a symbol for the US struggle against the drug trade. Soon after, people in several US communities started wearing red ribbons to show their commitment to prevent the spread of drug use and demand. That movement has evolved into the national Red Ribbon Campaign.

The DEA has something of a "bad boy" reputation in the law enforcement community. Because of the type of work they do, they play a little rough and often look the part. The DEA also has a heightened frequency of agents "going bad," especially after too much undercover work and regular exposure to a lot of drugs and money.

The Bureau of Alcohol, Tobacco, Firearms, and Explosives

The Bureau of Alcohol, Tobacco, Firearms, and Explosives truly has one of the more prominent roles in US government efforts to combat Mexican drug cartels. The ATF's official mission is to protect communities from violent criminals, criminal organizations, the illegal use and trafficking of firearms, the illegal use and storage of explosives, acts of arson and bombings, acts of terrorism, and the illegal diversion of alcohol and tobacco products. The ATF also works to investigate violators of the federal firearms and explosives laws and to ensure that licensees and permit holders are operating within established laws and regulations.

ATF's largest role in Mexico's drug war is to prevent the illegal southbound flow of firearms from US sources into the hands of Mexican cartels. They do this in two different ways, depending on which side of the border they're working. In America, the ATF works with gun sellers at shops and gun shows to identify straw-purchasing activity by conducting regular inspections of sales records and by talking to sellers to let them know what to look out for. Through their investigative efforts, agents can identify and arrest people suspected of violating federal firearms laws or of planning to smuggle US-origin firearms across the southwest border into the waiting hands of drug traffickers.[8] Just like the DEA, the ATF has several offices in Mexico from which they work with the Mexican government and law enforcement agencies to identify weapons trafficking activity.

STATE AND LOCAL AGENCIES

There are four US states, twenty-three counties, several dozen towns and cities, half a dozen Indian reservations, and twelve million people that share a border with Mexico. This means that hundreds of people working for state agencies, fusion centers (where multiple agencies work under the same roof to improve information-sharing), sheriffs' offices, local police departments, and tribal agencies are all actively involved in the border security mission.

Each southwest border state has its own government agency responsible for border security, among other emergency management functions. The state agencies are actively involved in the management of and participation in their state fusion centers.

There are seventy-two designated fusion centers across the entire country. In the southwest border states, five are in California and one each in Arizona, New Mexico, and Texas. Fusion centers are designed to bring multiple state, local, and federal agency representatives under the same roof to more effectively share domestic threat information. The author personally spent four years working as an analyst at the primary fusion center in California and so is familiar with how hard these analysts work to stay up to speed on the security situation in Mexico. They read through dozens of law enforcement and national-level intelligence reports to make sense of all the shifts and movements going on in the drug war. Their analyses are shared with state, local, and federal agencies that also track developments south of the border.

Law enforcement officers from local police departments and sheriffs' offices along the southwest border form the front line of defense against southwest border violence. They deal with drug-related violence in a wide variety of situations—from vehicle chases in downtown El Paso to tracking footprints in rural Arizona ranch lands. For example, in January 2006, several men in Mexican military–style uniforms crossed the Rio Grande near Neely's Crossing—roughly fifty miles east of El Paso, Texas—on a marijuana smuggling mission. They were confronted by officers from the Hudspeth County Sheriff's Office, but fortunately no shots were fired. The men retreated across the border into Mexico with most of their drug load, but abandoned more than half a ton of marijuana in an SUV that got stuck in the river. They managed to set the SUV on fire before fleeing. A spokesman for the sheriff's office later said that the men were using a Mexican military-issue Humvee and weapons, but the Mexican government denied that any soldiers were involved.[9]

No one knows the lay of the land in these places better than the local cops. They know what gangs operate in their jurisdictions, what types of drugs they're distributing, and often which Mexican cartels have personnel in the area. Many departments even conduct liaison meetings with their Mexican law enforcement partners across the border, particularly in places where sister cities are separated by only the Rio Grande or a fence. Other larger departments have even developed task forces to address specific threats stemming from drug-related violence. For example, in June 2008, the Phoenix Police Department created an anti-kidnapping task force to directly address the increasing number of cross-border kidnapping cases in the city.

MILITARY SUPPORT

Both the Department of Defense (DoD) and the National Guard have active roles in border security. US Northern Command is the unified military command responsible for homeland security. One of its roles is to provide military support to federal law enforcement agencies in the identification and interdiction of threats along the border. Those threats include activities conducted by Mexican cartels, like drug trafficking and human smuggling. Some people worry about the military helping cops with their jobs, but these task forces mainly provide support to the locals so they can do their jobs more effectively. Some examples of the assistance that the Defense Department provides include airborne reconnaissance, radar surveillance, ground sensor operations, vulnerability assessments, intelligence support, engineering support, mobile training, and border tunnel detection.[10]

The National Guard also plays a huge role in southwest border security. For instance, between May 2006 and July 2008, more than twenty-nine thousand National Guard members were deployed to the four southwest border states. Their mission was to provide administrative and civil engineering support to CBP and Border Patrol so they would be freer to engage in their own law enforcement missions. Essentially, the Guard acted as thousands of extra eyes and ears for these agencies whose personnel could actually go out and apprehend people engaging in illegal activity along the border. During that time, they also helped build roads, erect fences, and create vehicle barriers.

The Guard's mission along the border ended in 2008, although many of the southwest border governors wanted them to stay. The federal government denied their requests for continued support, despite the presentation by the states of statistics showing the effectiveness of their deployment. The murder of Arizona rancher Robert Krentz in March 2010 intensified the calls for Guard support by local politicians and congressional representatives alike.

In the spring of 2010, President Obama announced that 1,200 National Guard troops would be deployed to the southwest border to augment Border Patrol and CBP operations.[11] Compared to the number of Guard troops used in the previous border deployment, this was a drop in the bucket and was seen largely as window dressing during a time of highly publicized violent incidents on the Arizona side of the border.

JOINT INITIATIVES

One thing an agency involved in border security can't afford to do is to work in a vacuum. Accordingly, literally dozens of joint initiatives are dedicated to addressing the threat posed by drug trafficking, weapons trafficking, human smuggling, and other criminal activity associated with the drug war.

One is the Border Enforcement Security Task Force (BEST), a series of multi-agency teams developed to identify, disrupt, and dismantle criminal organizations posing significant threats to border security. The teams are designed to increase information sharing and collaboration, and they incorporate personnel from several different key federal, state, local, and foreign law enforcement agencies. There are currently seventeen such teams in place in nine states; eleven of those teams are in the four southwest border states.[12]

In 2003, ICE created the San Diego Tunnel Task Force, which is also made up of several federal, local, and military investigative agencies. It uses an array of high-tech equipment and intelligence information to pinpoint the location of drug tunnels along the border in the region. As of December 2009, federal authorities had discovered more than 120 cross-border tunnels along the southwest border, partly due to the assistance provided by this task force.

In 1974, the Department of Justice submitted a report to the Office of Management and Budget that provided recommendations on how to improve drug and border enforcement operations along the southwest border. One of those recommendations proposed the establishment of a regional intelligence center to collect and disseminate information relating to drug, alien, and weapon smuggling in support of law enforcement agencies throughout the area. In response to that study, the El Paso Intelligence Center (EPIC) was created and was initially staffed by representatives from the DEA, the then–US Customs Service, and the then–Immigration and Naturalization Service. Initially, EPIC focused on the southwest border, with an emphasis on Mexico's heroin traffickers and illegal alien smugglers. After 9/11, EPIC's mission evolved from supporting interdiction efforts and investigations regarding drug trafficking, alien and weapon smuggling, and other criminal activities to include counterterrorism in its efforts. Currently, there are more than a dozen federal, state, and local agencies represented at EPIC.[13]

Despite the number of agencies and personnel working on securing the border, there are still many issues in getting the job done. Unfortunately, the more agencies there are, the more communication- and information-sharing problems occur.

CHALLENGES TO US HOMELAND SECURITY AGENCIES

Mike Allen slapped his neck for what felt like the hundredth time. As usual, the mosquitoes were unrelenting near the Rio Grande, and he and his partner, John Ridge, were supplying the bug buffet for the night. The two Border Patrol agents had been on stakeout since two in the morning, waiting for a possible narcotics drop. Despite the pleasant seventy-degree weather, the circumstances were anything but pleasant. Allen and Ridge had been dropped off a good distance from where they needed to hunker down, so they started the thirty-minute hike through dense brush and trees in almost total darkness.

If they had been wearing hiking gear, they might have been more comfortable, but Allen and Ridge were in their standard dark-green uniforms with bright-gold badges. They had their .40-caliber pistols and M-4 rifles with them, but the only tactical gear they had were some night-vision goggles. Fortunately, those goggles were able to help them get to their observation spot without incident, where they began a long five-hour wait. Allen and Ridge fought to stay awake. It was important that they stay alert for the sounds of approaching drug smugglers and dangerous wildlife. Allen was happy there were no snakes out and about that night; he swears his ever-present sense of paranoia comes from constantly trying to differentiate between the sounds made by a cartel scout and a rattler. He just continued to sit on the ground, shifting around every so often to keep the blood flowing, and tried to stay hydrated.

The two agents, who were lying about seventy-five feet from each other and roughly thirty feet from the river, suddenly perked up when they heard sounds coming from the east. Shortly after sunrise, they noticed several vehicles on the Mexican side of the river. The next noise, they could tell, was a "load vehicle" on the US side coming to pick up the narcotics the smugglers had just brought across the river. Allen and Ridge took off on foot, running as fast as they could to try to apprehend the smugglers, but they weren't able to catch up. The driver of the load vehicle bailed out and got away, but Border Patrol mobile units were able to block in the vehicle itself. And the reward for their long and uncomfortable wait? That was the seizure of 1,400 pounds of Mexican marijuana, which would be either sent for storage in an evidence warehouse or incinerated.

Allen says most people don't realize that parts of the US-Mexico border are like a war zone. Agents patrol, set up an observation post, and try to avoid being ambushed. The bad guys send out scouts to look for them, and they have to remain silent or blow the entire operation. If they're lucky, they seize the marijuana and get an arrest. If they're not lucky, their car gets rammed by a bad guy and they go to the hospital to get checked out. They never know what will happen. Many times, they don't seize anything for all those hours spent waiting, looking, and listening. But on the occasions when agents like Allen and Ridge do make a seizure, the work is worth it: hours and hours of mind-numbing boredom and discomfort for eight to ten minutes of excitement and the adrenaline rush that comes with discovering hundreds of pounds of Mexican dope. These are the situations and decisions that face law enforcement agencies along the southwest border and beyond, every day.[14]

No one ever said that securing the border was an easy job. As if the threats of gun-toting drug traffickers, rock-throwing border crossers, and unforgiving temperatures and terrain weren't enough, border agencies have their own internal troubles to deal with. Anyone who has ever worked for any kind of government agency knows that not everyone always gets along. Interagency rivalries and squabbles have been around as long as the agencies themselves, and while they're usually harmless, those squabbles can sometimes seriously interfere with agencies' abilities to get their missions accomplished.

One example is the "cold war" between ICE and the ATF. Both agencies have an investigative function; however, these responsibilities often overlap. This has resulted in turf battles and an unwillingness to share information across agency lines. The situation got so bad that in June 2009 the two agencies had to sign a memorandum of understanding, or MOU, to clearly establish how ICE and the ATF were to share intelligence and to work together on firearms investigations.[15] It appears that even this major directive didn't help matters much. In September 2010, the USDOJ's Inspector General published a report that said the ATF and ICE "do not work effectively" together and "rarely conduct joint investigations" or even notify each other about cases they are working on. The result was that intelligence about gun trafficking activities that could have potentially led to arrests and smuggling prosecutions at the borders never got passed along[16]—further evidence that an agency's general attitude regarding its willingness to share information and cooperate on investigations can greatly influence the effectiveness of border security efforts.

Another case in point is the integration of state fusion centers into the border security process. The nine fusion centers in the border states are designed to bring federal, state, and local Homeland Security and law enforcement officials under the same roof to more effectively share information. In some cases, the system works well. In others, it barely functions. This happened frequently in the fusion center in Sacramento with the contract analysts. The center was located in the building of a state law enforcement agency, and analysts had security clearances for the highest levels of classified information. However, they were often denied access to materials as simple as police reports by agencies elsewhere in the state that had never heard of them and were less than excited about sharing intelligence with contractors. On countless occasions, analysts would call the ATF for information and spend copious amounts of time explaining who they were and what the fusion center was, passing on their agency's information so they could verify the analysts' clearances. In one case, it took a full month for one agency to confirm one particular analyst's identity and her authorization to view their law enforcement reports. Only after several years, lots of phone calls and conversations with the same people, and meeting agents in person at several conferences was she able to establish her reputation as someone who knew what she was doing and could be trusted.

Another challenge to border agencies is corruption. While many people would prefer to ignore the realities, border agents and inspectors do sometimes accept bribes from Mexican drug smugglers to ignore certain vehicles passing through inspection lanes at ports of entry or let coyotes enter the country with large groups of illegal immigrants. Fortunately, border agencies have become considerably less tolerant of this kind of behavior, and agents are much less willing to cover up for their colleagues' illegal activities. Between 2004 and early 2009, eighty-four officers were arrested and sixty-two convicted on corruption charges.[17]

Since 2007, investigators have arrested at least four border agents who they believe were sent by drug cartels to infiltrate the CBP.[18] In late 2009, US authorities discovered CBP agent Martha Garnica was engaging in criminal activity more likened to a double agent than to an inspector. Press reports said Garnica "devised secret codes, passed stacks of cash through car windows, and sketched out a map for smugglers to safely haul drugs and undocumented workers across the border. For that, she was richly rewarded; she lived in a spacious house with a built-in pool, owned two Hummers, and vacationed in Europe." In late August 2010, a US district judge sentenced her to twenty years in prison after she pleaded guilty to six counts of drug smuggling, human trafficking, and bribery. She was, in the words of prosecutors, a "valued asset" of the crime syndicate "La Linea" based in Ciudad Juárez; she was "directing the movements of at least five men, four of whom are now in prison or dead."[19]

In September 2010, a CBP inspector was charged with conspiring to smuggle cocaine and methamphetamine through his inspection lane at the California-Mexico border crossing in Calexico. The officer, a two-year veteran, allegedly "accepted $52,000 in bribes from informants and federal undercover agents posing as drug traffickers in exchange for allowing what he believed were drug-laden cars to pass through his lane without inspection. The agent allegedly coordinated the smuggling attempts carefully, providing his work schedule to an informant to reveal in which lane he was working. When the informant arrived at his inspection booth on the first attempt in June 2009, the agent allegedly scanned his passport, grinned, and let him through."[20]

That same month, another CBP agent was arrested on corruption conspiracy charges, accused of "accepting bribes in exchange for allowing vehicles filled with illegal immigrants and marijuana to pass through his inspection lanes at the Otay Mesa and San Ysidro border crossings in California." The seventeen-year veteran received up to $20,000 for each vanload of illegal immigrants that passed through his lane without inspection. Witnesses said the agent "would alert smugglers of his lane assignments ahead of time so they knew where to cross." One witness allegedly made eight to ten payments of about $10,000 each to the agent.[21]

DHS says that it has a good explanation for the increase in corruption cases. Homeland Security statistics suggest that the rush to fill thousands of border enforcement jobs in response to increasing border violence has translated into lower hiring standards. Reports said: "Barely 15 percent of CBP applicants undergo polygraph tests; of those, 60 percent were rejected by the agency because they failed the polygraph or were not qualified for the job. The number of CBP corruption investigations opened by the inspector general climbed from 245 in 2006 to more than 770 in 2010. Corruption cases at its sister agency, ICE, rose from 66 to more than 220 over the same period. The vast majority of these cases involve illegal trafficking of drugs, guns, weapons, and cash across the southwest border."[22]

While corruption is definitely a challenge that border agencies need to be concerned about, it shouldn't detract from the successes those agencies are experiencing or the needs they still have. Currently, there are roughly seventeen thousand border agents working along the US-Mexico border, which means that only 4.5 percent of those agents were investigated on corruption charges in 2010. Of course, that number should be much lower, and some would say that any percentage above zero is unacceptable. It's a disturbing side effect of the fortune and glamour associated with the drug trade, and it's inevitable that those things will tempt some who are involved in the border security business. The challenge is to recognize when those temptations become irresistible to border agents and more important, to do something about it.

FUTURE HOPE FOR US-MEXICO COOPERATION

Thankfully, the United States and Mexico are experiencing an unprecedented degree of cooperation as a result of addressing the increased violence along parts of their shared border. It's important to note that intelligence sharing and cross-border law enforcement cooperation are not new for these governments. However, after 9/11, the drug trafficking threat took a backburner to terrorism, and the reorganization of dozens of US law enforcement agencies under DHS threw some traditional mechanisms of cooperation into a tangle. Because border security is a concern shared by both countries these days, they've been able to better organize the mechanisms they use to share intelligence and increase the information flow in the years since 9/11.

One of the biggest challenges to information exchange is the extensive corruption that plagues Mexican institutions all at levels. US agencies are reluctant to share intelligence with their Mexican counterparts because they know there's a decent chance that the intelligence will end up in the hands of cartel members and possibly compromise a delicate operation. The ATF has deployed its eTrace firearms tracing system to several locations throughout Mexico for use by Mexican federal authorities, but they had to reduce the original number of deployment locations over concerns about corrupt agents manipulating the information to assist the cartels.

One thing that is helping matters is the in-country presence of agencies like the ATF and DEA. This allows members of American law enforcement agencies to work more closely with Mexican agents, providing solid training and establishing personal relationships that foster trust and the motivation to stay clean. A decent portion of Mérida Initiative funds will be going toward US-agency training of Mexican law enforcement officials.

This kind of collaboration is also happening right on the border. In September 2009, Border Patrol agents started conducting "parallel patrols" with Mexican federal police along an eighty-mile stretch of the border near Nogales, Arizona. Each morning, US agents would advise the Mexican police of the locations they planned to scout that day, and Mexican officers would patrol across the border in what the officials called "mirrored enforcement." Jeffrey D. Self, acting deputy chief of the Border Patrol, said that the program had led to "all different levels of communication that have never been established before" between the Border Patrol and Mexican Public Security agents. This program does not involve local Mexican police officers from border cities, where drug corruption has reduced some municipal police forces to disarray, but rather federal law enforcement agents. Through training and daily consultations, Border Patrol agents have gradually identified "good, honest police on the Mexican side," Mr. Self said.[23]

This is only one example of programs that Mérida Initiative funds are designed to encourage. It's part of a larger game plan for future counterdrug cooperation between the United States and Mexico, but many are skeptical about its potential for success. They are concerned that it too closely resembles Plan Colombia, which was hatched as a way to reduce the volume of cocaine entering the United States and to dismantle groups like the Revolutionary Armed Forces of Colombia. Most of that money went toward the Colombian military and counterdrug operations.

However, there are important differences. Mexico isn't dealing with the FARC who want to take over the government, although the cartels are just as vicious and probably better armed. And some of the Mérida money is going toward US training of law enforcement personnel, as opposed to US military deployments to Mexican army bases.

The biggest similarity—at least at the outset—is the lack of return on investment thus far. Plan Colombia has been going on for over a decade, and while the FARC have taken hard hits on their leaders and membership, they're still pumping out cocaine. Trafficking routes from Colombia through the Caribbean into the southeast United States are much quieter than they were, but there has not been a dramatic drop in cocaine imports since the plan's implementation.

A Government Accountability Office (GAO) report that was highly critical of the Mérida Initiative had some great suggestions for improving the plan. Some aspects of the drug war are hard to measure, but others aren't. Some goals and benchmarks could include a percentage increase in drug seizures, a percentage decrease in weapons and cash successfully making it across the border into Mexico, and a percentage reduction in murder and kidnapping rates.

Accountability is also important, especially when US tax dollars are involved, and this isn't an area where the government has been strong when it comes to giving money to Latin American countries. It doesn't work to rely on the Mexican authorities to confirm that the equipment that was sent actually made it into (and more important, stayed in) the right hands. This is a cooperative effort, so there's no reason that US agencies can't be more hands-on when it comes to seeing firsthand where money and equipment are going.

More publicity regarding successes derived from the initiative would be beneficial. When a major cartel kingpin is captured, did the authorities use one of the helicopters provided by the initiative? When crime rates go down in a formerly violent border city, is it because initiative funds helped train its police force?

The Mérida Initiative is different from other foreign aid packages because it doesn't involve the potential for serious harm to come to the troops. Even though a lot of taxpayer money could potentially be going down the drain, the lack of a significant American death rate means that it won't make headlines. Part of the challenge of accountability will be reminding Congress that, even though the United States is not losing soldiers to mortars and car bombs, it's important to not lose ground in the drug wars during a time of economic hardship when it is tempted to cut funding.

Finally, there needs to be some sort of limit or cap to the funding of Mérida, even if that means attaching an ultimatum. The United States is not in a financial position to endlessly fund a drug war that isn't going away any time soon. The initiative needs to show concrete and positive results, as well as significant progress toward mutual goals by a certain time.

Mexico is not on the brink of becoming a failed state. It really does have a lot going for it as a country, although that's overshadowed by the drug violence. Currently, one out of every four Mexicans supports US military assistance with the drug war, and that number has risen since this situation started deteriorating. If things continue to get worse, that statistic will likely rise considerably as time passes.

CHAPTER 9

MARIJUANA GROWERS IN THE UNITED STATES

LET'S SAY YOU LIVE in North Carolina—roughly 1,400 miles from the US border with Mexico—with your spouse and two kids. You decide to go on a camping trip for a week, deep in the hills near a national park. You pack up all your gear, the kids, and the dog and head toward that remote, peaceful spot where you can do all the hiking and exploring you want, completely undisturbed, far from tourists or fellow campers.

On your second day of vacation, you're out hiking, and your son spots a deer. He wants to follow it, so you and your family veer off the trail and venture into the North Carolina woods, enjoying the adventure. Ahead of you, the deer scampers into a clearing, and suddenly you're staring at a huge field that extends as far as the eye can see. That field is filled with nothing but marijuana plants. Your dog starts to bark excitedly, capturing the attention of the men armed with powerful assault rifles on the other side of the field, defending it against intruders. Those men work for Mexican drug cartels and will do anything to make sure you don't tell the authorities what you just saw. All of a sudden, the southwest border and the extreme violence beyond don't seem so far away.

MEXICAN CARTELS INFILTRATING US PARKS AND FORESTS

This might sound like a far-fetched scenario, but unfortunately it's becoming more and more common. Marijuana grows controlled by Mexican cartels have been in the United States since at least 2003. In 2006, the top ten outdoor marijuana production states—some containing grows run by Americans and some by Mexicans—were, in order, California, Tennessee, Kentucky, Hawaii, North Carolina, Washington, Alabama, West Virginia, Georgia, and Arkansas.[1] Note that out of those ten states, only one is actually on the southwest border. Other nonborder states that are increasing in popularity for growers include Colorado and Utah, where higher elevations are being used, and even states as far north as Wisconsin and Michigan.

The La Crosse County Sheriff's Department in Wisconsin has said that for years they've had people calling them to say they've found a plot of marijuana. In Wisconsin, authorities have actually started to post signs warning hikers and other park visitors about telltale signs that they might be approaching a grow.[2] In 2010, a total of 1,500 marijuana plants were removed from Michigan national forests. That was when authorities started finding marijuana gardens operated by large Mexican drug trafficking organizations on Michigan's public lands, and they're probably going to start finding many more in the years to come.[3] In July 2010, authorities uncovered a remote site hidden in the Chattahoochee National Forest just two miles from Helen, Georgia. More than twenty-six thousand plants—worth an estimated $52 million—were growing on a patchwork of plots under the thick canopy.[4]

The sheer sizes and street values of some of these grows are alarming. In late April 2009, deputies from the Santa Clara County Sheriff's Office in California discovered a grow of seven thousand plants worth $10 million in the rural hills above Saratoga. The Mexican man tending the garden was armed with a loaded gun. In 2006, federal and state authorities seized over 550,000 marijuana plants worth an estimated $1 billion in Kentucky's remote Appalachian counties.[5] In early June 2010, narcotics officers in Arkansas found ninety-seven marijuana plants worth $100,000 growing in two separate locations in a city park near Fayetteville. Investigators said the patches were close enough to a hiking trail that someone walking in the park could have spotted them.[6] In September 2009, Tennessee narcotics agents cut down 151,000 marijuana plants near Indian Mound State Park, close to the Kentucky state line. In April 2010, 457 marijuana plants were found growing in a remote area of Eglin Air Force Base—a secured military installation—in the Florida panhandle.

Before a grow can be set up, a site has to be chosen. By far, the most popular locations for Mexican drug cartel–controlled marijuana farms are the US tax dollar–funded National Forests and Parks, which conveniently cover 10 percent of the country's landmass. The choice to use public acreage is disturbing on several levels, but it makes sense from the cartels' point of view. Many National Forests and Parks are in very remote locations, have limited road access to most parts, and have few visitors.[7]

The problem of cartel-run marijuana grows on public lands is the most serious in California. Back in 2003, US Forest Service officials said they had identified five separate Mexican drug trafficking organizations operating in the state, one of which had marijuana cultivation operations in seven different forests in nine counties.[8] Networks of backcountry fire and logging roads, rich soil, abundant sun, and reliable water sources provide drug traffickers easy access and ideal growing conditions on the relatively secluded Forest Service lands in the state.[9]

The best places to grow marijuana are between four thousand and six thousand feet above sea level, and all the states that made the top-ten list have lower-range mountainous regions that fit that description. Growers also look for sites with nearby access to water sources and thick stands of bushes like manzanita. They get rid of the smaller shrubbery and plant marijuana, leaving the canopy from the taller trees in place to camouflage the grow from aerial detection.[10]

Once a site is selected, the cartels bring in people and equipment to get things up and running. Drug gangs have imported marijuana experts and unskilled labor to help find the best land or build irrigation systems. Recruiting Mexican nationals to work these grows isn't difficult because the cartels bring them across the border and pay them a decent wage. These laborers often think the work isn't going to be that hard or that big of a crime to just water some plants in a park. Recruiters look for people who still have family in Mexico, so they can use them as leverage to keep the farmers working—and to keep them quiet.[11]

After the labor is hired, cartels haul in tons of equipment, including plastic irrigation piping, fertilizer, drip timers, weapons, booby traps, propane tanks, camping equipment, and food to sustain them through the growing season and harvest. According to Nores and Swan, as the marijuana plants begin to germinate, "streams are dammed and miles of black plastic irrigation pipelines are laid, connecting the crops with pools of water seasoned with fertilizers and pesticides to create a cocktail that makes the plants grow rapidly. Deer and bear that wander into the gardens become meals. The growers are kept supplied with food and water by carefully planned drops, and soon piles of cans and garbage begin to accumulate."[12]

The fertilizers and pesticides are actually one of the biggest dangers posed by these grows. Marijuana growers use chemicals that are many times stronger than those approved for use on US lawns and therefore are illegal. The chemicals start seeping into the soil pretty quickly, and while the pesticides kill bugs and other parasites right off, fertilizer runoff contaminates local waterways and aids in the growth of algae and weeds. The vegetation that results interferes with water flows that are critical to the survival of several animal species.[13]

During Operation Trident, a 2010 large-scale multi-agency marijuana enforcement operation in three California counties, "15.5 tons of trash, 29 miles of irrigation line, and 4,580 pounds of fertilizer were removed from cartel-controlled marijuana grow sites." Approximately 270 acres of land had been either completely altered or destroyed by illegal marijuana cultivation during the months-long duration of those operations.[14]

The marijuana growing season starts in the spring and runs four to five months long, with the harvest in September or October. During that time, cartel-employed crop tenders work from their camps embedded within the grows—making sure that the plants are watered, setting drip timers, making any necessary repairs to irrigation lines, conducting security patrols, and ferrying in supplies from the predetermined drop locations. They also take steps to avoid detection by park rangers and Forest Service officers; fortunately for the workers, that's not too difficult.

To say that the US Forest Service and National Park Service are ill prepared to manage the threat posed by domestic marijuana grows is a gross understatement. As of late 2010, there were roughly 640 law enforcement officers and special agents who policed the country's 191.6 million acres of national forests. Special agents investigate serious crimes, including arson, fire, timber theft, and drug production. Officers actively assist those cases while tackling daily patrol duties that range from campground disturbances to backcountry rescues and forest resource uses. In California, only 130 officers and agents patrol nearly twenty-five million acres of backcountry, spread among eighteen national forests—an area equal to nearly one-fifth of the entire state. Ken Harp, a patrol captain in San Bernardino National Forest, said, "We have eight people in [California] that are dedicated to drug enforcement. This one cartel has 60 or 80." Harp, a thirty-three-year Forest Service veteran, oversees patrol operations for a 700,000-acre forest that receives six million visitors annually with a staff of only five.[15] Calling this an uphill battle doesn't even begin to describe the challenges these officers face.

State and federal governments are trying to do what they can to help, but their efforts are falling very short of what's truly needed. Forest Service law enforcement staff was doubled from fourteen to twenty-eight agents in California between 2007 and 2008. Congress is sending some funds, with a $3-million supplemental appropriation secured by Senator Dianne Feinstein (D-California) that allowed the Park Service to add twenty-five new law enforcement officers to its Pacific Region parks. This is a paltry sum, but any extra hands are better than none, especially when the domestic marijuana business is booming.

Official reports say the number of marijuana plants confiscated by Forest Service officials between 2004 and 2008 "rose by an average of 51 percent in each of those years, reaching a high of 3.3 million plants in 2008. The number of plants seized in California national forests alone rose steadily from 569,000 in 2003 to 2.4 million in 2008." In July 2009, $2.5 million worth of marijuana was seized from a high-tech grow in the mountains near Colorado's Cheesman Reservoir in the Pike National Forest. In early June 2009, hikers in a remote area of southwest Idaho stumbled upon a marijuana crop that netted 12,545 plants with an estimated street value of $6.3 million.[16] That all sounds like a lot, but it's a drop in the bucket. Asked in late 2009 to estimate how much of the overall marijuana crop was being caught, Wayne Hanson, who heads the marijuana unit of the Humboldt County Sheriff's Office in California, said, "I would truthfully say we're lucky if we're getting 1 percent."[17]

In many cases, it has been difficult for law enforcement agencies to positively identify individuals managing the grows and their possible associations with Mexican drug trafficking organizations. One could make the assumption that grows in certain states are ultimately run by cartels in closest proximity, but that might not be the case. Grows in Texas would be operated by associates of the Gulf cartel, Los Zetas, or the Juárez cartel, and grows in California would be run by the AFO under this logic; but at this point, it's hard to say for sure. Intelligence suggests that the major cartels are directly behind much of the marijuana growth that is taking place on public lands. However, it has been difficult for US authorities to prove the connection, partly because the individuals who cultivate the plants have no idea whom they are working for and are able to give little information when arrested.[18]

The most dangerous time for both law enforcement and Mexican growers is the harvest in September and October. The under-the-radar maintenance work of watering and fertilizing is done, and the more labor-intensive work of cutting down the plants and manipulating them to be processed into usable marijuana is more noticeable. The advantage for law enforcement agencies involved in domestic marijuana eradication is that finding these grows is slightly easier during this time. The disadvantage is that Mexican growers are prepared to fight to the death to protect their crops. The NDIC says Mexican growers "reportedly employ armed guards to protect both indoor and outdoor plants. They warn off intruders with flares and use pits filled with punji stakes, fishhooks dangling at eye level, guard dogs, or trip wires linked to shotguns, grenades, or other explosives."[19]

Growers have increasingly armed themselves with high-caliber assault rifles, shotguns, and other firearms. During a June 2003 raid on a Shasta-Trinity National Forest garden, agents seized AK-15 and SKS assault rifles with military-style, double-stacked ammunition clips. Law enforcement officers and agents say hikers, hunters, and other backcountry users have been chased away at gunpoint after stumbling onto marijuana gardens. In early October 2003, two deer hunters pressing into the backcountry of the Los Padres National Forest outside Ojai, California, reported shots fired at them by marijuana farmers. The previous month, things took a fatal turn during one deadly week when law enforcement officers shot and killed four marijuana growers of Mexican citizenship in two separate incidents in Shasta and Butte counties. Reports said the growers had "leveled assault rifles as authorities raided gardens located adjacent to national forest lands." Investigators said the plots were run by Mexican drug trafficking organizations.[20]

By October, Mexican marijuana growers have tended a fine crop and avoided detection by US authorities. They harvest the plants by cutting them down, trimming off the large leaves, and carefully trimming the leaves that surround the marijuana buds. Then the marijuana plants have to be dried out; the time for this stage of the process varies depending on the potency the growers want the buds to reach. They can even be cured for up to two weeks after drying, but some growers might not have the luxury of performing this step. After the buds are sufficiently dried out, the growers will cut the buds off the stems. They can be stored for shipment to the owners of the crop, as well as for further processing into packaged ready-to-sell and ready-to-smoke marijuana.

THE US COMPETITION: A BRIEF HISTORY AND CURRENT LAWS

Life is getting harder for Mexican cartels running US grows. Now they have some problems from a place they might not have expected: competition from American marijuana producers. There's no better place to start looking at the widespread cultivation of marijuana by American growers than the history of medical marijuana in California. It began with a legal measure called Proposition 215, also known as the Compassionate Use Act. Prop 215 was a voter-based initiative, meaning it was written and proposed to the California legislature to be put up for a vote by the public. It passed with approximately 56 percent of voters in favor and 44 opposed, and it was enacted in November 1996. In essence, it allows—under state law only—the legal cultivation and distribution of marijuana by registered dispensaries that fill prescriptions for patients with a doctor's prescription. Those doctors and patients are also supposed to be protected from prosecution under state law.[21] Unfortunately for the patients, doctors, and dispensaries in California—as well as the other twelve states with medical marijuana laws—they're not protected at all under federal law, which always supersedes state law.

The federal Controlled Substances Act of 1970 lists marijuana as a Schedule I drug. This means that marijuana, according to the federal government, has a high potential for abuse, has no accepted use in medical treatment of any ailment, and lacks accepted safety measures for its use under the supervision of a doctor. Schedule I is the most restrictive and condemning list for drugs, and the placement of marijuana in that schedule is highly controversial. First, whether or not the use of marijuana has medical benefits has been debated heatedly for decades between cancer survivors, who swear by it to reduce pain and chemo-induced nausea, and government opponents, who think marijuana is a "gateway drug" to other substances like cocaine and heroin. Some people find it strange that marijuana is considered by anyone to be a gateway drug to stronger and more deadly drugs, because cocaine and heroin are both listed in the less-restrictive Schedule II. (As an aside, Schedule II drugs do have a currently accepted medical use in the United States, according to the act.[22])

Since the implementation of state laws authorizing the use of medical marijuana, the federal government under Presidents Bill Clinton and George W. Bush has made plenty of announcements that federal law still rules in the drug business and that such activity won't be tolerated. Indeed, there have been plenty of raids by the DEA of medical marijuana producers and dispensaries in every state where medical marijuana is legal under state law. In 2008, the USDOJ, under President Obama, instructed US attorneys to allow medical marijuana growers and distributors to operate as long as they're complying with state law. However, the DEA raids have continued in multiple states.

In areas where American growers and dispensaries can operate relatively unimpeded by the feds, it's still not an easy business to navigate. State laws are vague when it comes to the nuts and bolts of actually growing medical marijuana, so those interested in getting into the business are forced underground. Some California cities are trying to streamline the process for granting permits to grow medical marijuana on a larger scale in order to prevent the environmental damage that the grows are known for. However, the permits come with a $211,000 annual fee, and growers would have to implement environmental protections, security, labor standards, transparent finances, and inventory tracking. It seems to be worth the trouble and the learning curve; an economic analysis prepared for a nonprofit seeking one of the Oakland cultivation permits found that a 100,000-square-foot growing facility could generate up to $71 million in annual sales.[23]

Thousands of "mom and pop" grows in the United States are threatening cartel profits, partly because of those recent changes in state laws that allow the legal use of medical marijuana. Currently fifteen states allow doctors to prescribe medical marijuana to people with a wide range of diseases and their associated symptoms or treatment side effects, including cancer, HIV, multiple sclerosis, and glaucoma. In some states like California, the requirements to obtain such a prescription are loose, at best. Critics say the legalization of medical marijuana has sparked an "underground pot culture" in states that sanction its use. Estimates are that about 1,000 illegally operated marijuana shops are located in Los Angeles alone.[24]

There are several reasons why Mexican cartels are growing marijuana on US public lands in the first place. They don't have to worry about smuggling it across the border, they have direct access to markets for American consumers, and they can compete more directly with American growers who are starting to cut into their profits—and the profits to be made can be huge. One marijuana plant can produce between one and two pounds of refined marijuana. Depending on the quality—which can be much higher than marijuana grown and maintained in poor conditions in Mexico—the value of those two pounds can reach up to $9,000 on the street and many times that if grown under tightly controlled conditions.[25]

In a rather ironic development between Mexican dope and American dope, growers in Mexico are starting to adopt marijuana cultivation techniques used in the United States because they make for higher-quality—and higher-priced—dope. The going rate for top-quality US-grown marijuana is around $2,500 per pound, while Mexican types sell for under $500 per pound. Officials say that the new cultivation tactics are a sign that Mexico is being forced to compete with growers north of the border, especially in California where business is booming, spurred on by marijuana sold for medical use. Growers in Mexico have typically cultivated their marijuana in outdoor fields but are now increasingly turning to the use of greenhouses in which they can produce plants with a higher content of THC, the psychoactive ingredient in marijuana. Another advantage is that the new greenhouses are harder for the army to detect with flyovers because they resemble tomato plots common in Sinaloa.[26]

THE FUTURE OF US MARIJUANA GROWS

The landscape of marijuana grows in the United States has shifted considerably in the last two decades, and it's likely to continue doing so, based on a couple of factors. First, the general attitude toward legalizing marijuana is becoming more favorable. While the country as a whole isn't ready for that yet—and even California voters shot down Proposition 19 in 2010, which would have legalized its recreational use under state law—more states might move to legalize medical marijuana under their laws in the next few years. If that happens, additional American growers are going to get into the lucrative pot-growing business.

Second, Mexican drug cartels are getting squeezed by US and Mexican law enforcement, and growing their biggest moneymaking product so close to their ultimate markets is an increasingly attractive solution. They don't have to worry about smuggling bales of dope across the border under dangerous conditions, they have more control over the quality and quantity of the marijuana going to market, and they don't have to worry all that much about detection by US law enforcement. If marijuana seizures along the border increase and it becomes decidedly more difficult to move marijuana into the country through more traditional methods, more Mexican cartels are likely to shift to starting grows within US borders.

These two trends mean one disturbing thing: a lot more pot is probably going to be grown on public lands, and the agencies responsible for stopping it just aren't equipped to deal with the problem. Even if the number of Forest Service and state agents dedicated to finding and eradicating these farms were quadrupled, state officials say it is still difficult to make arrests on pot farms. The growers have to be caught in the act of cultivating to be charged. More often than not, they are able to escape before law enforcement moves in.[27] At that point, all officers can do is pull the plants and remove all the equipment sustaining them. However, as one California National Guard counterdrug veteran once said, that's like mowing the grass in the yard: it looks great as soon as it's done, but a week later, it's ready for cutting all over again.

Unfortunately, it doesn't appear that the Forest Service has a good grasp of the severity of the problem. On the department's website, it says that only a small fraction—forty thousand out of 193 million acres, or 2 percent—of National Forest System lands are affected by illegal marijuana cultivation. Considering how incredibly difficult it is to detect grows, and that only a tiny percentage of them have likely been discovered to date, it seems unlikely that this is an accurate estimate.

The US Forest Service was granted a budget of $6.1 billion overall in 2010, which some might consider generous. But only $135 million were set aside for "law enforcement operations," a mere $3-million increase from 2008's budget. It's less than the amount budgeted for "forest products" ($329 million) and "inventory and monitoring" ($168 million). What's mind boggling is that the Forest Service spent only a small fraction of that already small budget in 2008—$15.1 million out of $131.9 million—to combat marijuana growers.

This leads one to believe that there is no overarching strategy for tackling the problem of marijuana growing on public lands. To start, they need a small army of helicopters and personnel to find the grows scattered among the millions of acres of national park foliage. And when one is found, they need another small army on the ground to go in and pull everything out. That's a nice stopgap measure, but the odds of catching the cartel employees running the grows are still very small. That means they'll just wait out the authorities and start another grow soon after. What's more, it's a dangerous business to go in after those growers, so that "small army" would need even more funding for weapons, armor, and other protective measures. Getting Congress to appropriate enough money for that array of helicopters, agents and rangers, and guns and armor is a pipe dream.

One solution, a double-edged sword, is increasing the public-awareness campaigns about the existence of these grows. On the one hand, visitors to parks and forests can be great assets because they multiply the pairs of eyes that can locate illegal grows. In fact, several states have posted signs and flyers at park entrances informing visitors about the signs that would alert them that they've stumbled upon a grow: strong chemical smells, propane tanks, camping equipment where there should be none, piles of garbage, and more. With one phone call from a hiker, park service rangers can respond to a specific area, with law enforcement backup, without having to search for endless hours.

On the other hand, announcing the likely existence of Mexican cartel–controlled grows inside a park or National Forest might be a big turnoff for some potential visitors. Or curiosity might embolden some visitors or put them in danger if they encounter growers. The Forest Service website tries to be reassuring, saying it is using all available means to combat the problem, and it constantly seeks to establish a safe environment for visitors. But it also warns, "If you encounter a drug operation, back out immediately! Never engage the growers as these are extremely dangerous people." And you thought running into a hungry bear would be your biggest problem during your next camping trip.

It appears that the future health and safety of public lands will be in increasing jeopardy due to the rising acceptance of medical marijuana use and cultivation and to the financial benefits to Mexican cartels of growing marijuana within US borders. The only ways to mitigate the problem are to dramatically reduce demand for the drug (unlikely), legalize marijuana nationwide and designate cultivation areas outside public lands where the environment will be minimally affected (almost as unlikely), or throw significantly more money, equipment, and people at the problem from an enforcement perspective. The third option is the most practical, but every government agency is clamoring for money in a very tight economy. It's unlikely that federal, state, and local agencies working in the domestic marijuana eradication business will acquire enough additional resources over the next few years to make a significant dent in the problem. Until something changes, it will be just as important for someone to be able to identify a marijuana leaf as to recognize poison ivy on his or her next backpacking adventure.

CHAPTER 10

RESTORING FAITH AND TAKING MEXICO BACK FROM THE NARCOS

ONE OF THE MAIN OBSTACLES to both the Mexican and US governments in effectively dealing with Mexican cartels is being stuck on traditional notions of how to label the threat. Enemies these days generally fall into one of three categories: terrorists, insurgents, or criminals. Governments and militaries have strategies and tactics for how to deal with each type of enemy in a variety of circumstances. But what happens when the enemy displays characteristics of all three groups, yet only one (often inaccurate) label is used? Usually, the strategy ends up failing.

Violent acts committed by cartels and their enforcer groups on both sides of the border are regarded as criminal. Yet, many of these acts are similar in nature to those committed by terrorist organizations like al-Qa'ida, the FARC, and the IRA, and with similar intentions. Beheadings and dismemberments typical for some of these organizations have become the norm for cartel enforcers when they want to send a strong message to rivals or to the government.

In 2008, US counterterrorism sources reported that the Gulf cartel—in its weakened state at the time—was incapable of engaging the Mexican army, head to head. Because of this, the Gulf leadership had decided that using insurgent tactics against the military would give it an advantage, and they were right. Other Mexican cartels had been using insurgent-style tactics for quite some time against the military and Mexican law enforcement—including ambushes and hit-and-run tactics against convoys, highway checkpoints, and police and military installations. In 2008, the Mexican army and federal police forces used anti-insurgency tactics against cartels, in many cases preferring those to standard law enforcement procedures.[1]

The "traditional organized crime" label no longer fits Mexican cartels. There are two more or less generally accepted models of how organized crime groups operate: the American model and the Colombian model. In the United States, the Italian Mafia and other groups, like the Russian Mafia, operate under a certain "civilized" code of conduct. As this code has evolved over the years, it's become more conservative and likes to fly under the radar. Organized crime still flourishes in certain areas of the country, and the Mob is active in racketeering, prostitution, gambling, and extortion. They also still eliminate rivals and traitors in violent fashions, but they do so quietly. More important, they make it a point not to touch family members of targeted victims.

Unfortunately, it looks more and more like Mexican cartels have gone down the path of Colombian organized crime—a model that combines traditional criminal activity with insurgency against the government, military, and law enforcement. Cartels don't follow the "civilized" rules of the Italian Mafia; they have no problem kidnapping, torturing, or killing family members of rivals or people who have somehow done them wrong. They are also extremely overt about sending messages when they kill police officers, government officials, or soldiers, often leaving signed notes attached to bodies. Narco banners are routinely hung in busy thoroughfares across the country, with messages claiming or ducking responsibility for certain killings or warning the public that their government can't protect them from the cartels. The Mafias in the United States have never done business that way.

So if Mexican organized crime groups clearly engage in activities that can be likened to terrorism, insurgency, and nontraditional organized crime, why do governments on both sides of the border insist on labeling them and treating them as traditional organized crime? This substantially limits any strategy. US enforcers would never send thousands of soldiers into New York City to deal with the Mob, just as they would never send a few dozen cops from the Los Angeles Police Department into Pakistan to deal with al-Qa'ida. The situation in Mexico has evolved beyond one caused simply by organized crime. Cartels are now hybrid organizations that have to be regarded as such if the Mexican government wants to truly make a dent in their operations. The US government needs to make this distinction as well, if federal, state, and local law enforcement agencies are ever to be provided with adequate resources to deal with violent situations stemming from cartel activities.

A dramatic shift in thinking is necessary, as Mexican authorities have already been engaging in counterinsurgency tactics against the cartels for some time. The most appropriate term in recent years to describe the Mexican cartels is "criminal insurgency." It still retains the criminal nature of the conflict, but adds an extra—and much needed—dimension necessary for the government to get behind the allocation of extra resources and an added sense of urgency to address the problem.

The Mexican government has started to realize the benefit of treating narcos more like terrorists than like criminal thugs. In December 2010, Mexico's Chamber of Deputies (equivalent to the US House of Representatives) approved a legal amendment under which drug cartels qualify as terrorist organizations. This allows judges to impose sentences ranging from ten to fifty years in prison for those who "intimidate society through the spread of activities that create fear." Some examples where the new law would apply include the September 2008 grenade attack in Morelia and the use of car bombs in Ciudad Juárez. The deputies wouldn't say how effective they think this new law will actually be, in that only 2 percent of drug-related crimes are ever successfully investigated through prosecution to sentencing.[2] However, it's a step in the right direction.

Here are a few ways to start shifting how the US government (and ostensibly the Mexican government as well) views cartels as organizations:

DHS can host conferences or roundtable sessions with leading academics and analysts who follow the drug war to discuss the full meaning and impact of a change in label.

The US government can communicate clearly to all federal, state, and local agencies involved in border security (e.g., Border Patrol, CBP, El Paso Sheriff's Office) what the new label means and what the change means for the way they do their jobs.

DHS can explore new sources of funding that will become available to its agencies, as well as to state and local agencies, after cartels are reclassified as a new type of hybrid organization.

New and more powerful strategies can be developed by governments on both sides of the border to combat cartels as a type of insurgency, rather than simply as criminal groups.

Right now, it's necessary to think and work outside the box. When a strategy is obviously failing to make any significant gains, it's time to explore other, less orthodox options.

ROOTING OUT CARTEL DOMINANCE FROM WITHIN

This book's discussion of the history of corruption in Latin America in general, and in Mexico specifically, provides a good understanding of why the effective reduction (notice that doesn't say "elimination," which is a pipe dream) of corruption in Mexico is so difficult. But that's not to say that President Calderón isn't trying and even making a little bit of headway. In June 2007, Calderón replaced the federal police chiefs from each of the country's thirty-one states and the Federal District, pending polygraph and drug tests to determine whether or not they were on the right side of the law. In January 2008, federal agents arrested eleven city and state police on drug charges, and army troops have confiscated weapons from about 300 Mexican police who were under investigation for corruption along the Texas border. In October 2008, five top officials at the federal organized crime task force were arrested for accepting bribes after being identified by an informant who worked for both the US embassy in Mexico City and the Sinaloa Federation. In late May 2009, federal forces swooped into corruption-plagued Michoacán state and hauled off ten mayors and seventeen other government officials on narco-corruption charges. The week before, three police officers in Morelos state were arrested on similar charges, and a police chief and the former state security chief were detained for questioning.

These stories are just a drop in the bucket compared to the entire catalog of government and law enforcement purges that Calderón has initiated. Yet, the process—however noble—seems to be futile, considering the fact that little has changed in day-to-day operations against the cartels. Local police are still notoriously unreliable, and even the army is coming under fire for human rights abuses. Some of the more recent takedowns of high-profile cartel leaders have been conducted by revamped federal agencies and navy commandos. Calderón might be having some success in cleaning up his federal agencies, but he's running out of options for using his military. Despite the extreme uphill battle to root out corruption in Mexico, Calderón can't afford to quit now. He needs to stay the course and continue to send the message that corruption in the ranks won't be tolerated.

But cleaning house of corrupt police and politicians isn't enough. The justice system needs to be fixed and made transparent so that police and politicians arrested for colluding with criminals are actually successfully tried, convicted, and sent to jail for a definitive stay. Imprisoning a high-ranking member of government or a cartel does no good when the criminal and the public know he won't be spending much time there, and if he does, that he'll be living like a king.

In spite of recent reform attempts, Mexico's legal system is still unsatisfactory and requires the implementation of major changes to a significant number of federal laws—for example, how trials are conducted, and rules of evidence—to produce real progress. It's not that making those changes to laws and the court system would be impossible but that they would take a lot of time and political willpower. Just think of the impact such changes would have on the people of Mexico once they were able to access trial details of a suspected drug trafficker or a corrupt prison guard, mayor, or police officer. Prison systems could be redesigned to compartmentalize access to certain areas. That way, no one guard could access everything, and prison "escapes" could be reduced. Mexican prisons also need to become places where narcos live miserably.

However, even the reforms that are being enacted already are not going well. During a national security dialogue in August 2010 between President Calderón and business leaders, nongovernmental organizations (NGOs), the clergy, leaders of the political parties, the judicial branch, and the governors, he asked why the state of Chihuahua suffers from the highest levels of violence when it is the entity that to date has implemented the judicial reforms most completely. The president also asked why there are so few criminals sentenced in comparison to the great number of those detained.

In response, Supreme Court Chief Ortiz stated that the police "have still not been fully trained in the procedures necessary for real investigative work in legal proceedings where proper rules of evidence apply." He added that prosecutors still have very little experience in the new justice system. The Attorney General of the Republic in 2010, Arturo Chávez, said that the new criminal justice system is "flawed in states where implementation has begun and that public support has turned against the reforms seen as failing to stem the growing violence and lawlessness." The Attorney General also acknowledged that the Forfeiture Act, a cornerstone of the criminal law reform designed to seize the assets of convicted drug traffickers, has run into problems and will need to be redrafted. The Supreme Court President conceded that the Forfeiture Act is very rarely used.[3]

Reform will definitely be a stop-and-start process because of the system-wide breakdown of efficiency and transparency. Nevertheless, as long as Mexico has a president and a decent number of top officials who want to make changes and, more important, to see those changes take root and start working, there might actually be some hope for justice reform.

GOING AFTER THE MONEY

President Calderón made it very clear when he entered office in December 2006 that his top priorities included going after the cartels and reducing the levels of violence across the country. He has employed new strategies, like sending in the military to narco hot spots, and has purged government offices and police departments of dirty politicians and cops. But there is one aspect of pursuing organized criminal groups that the Mexican government has yet to fully explore or even make modest efforts to improve its track record: going after the drug money.

One facet of the Prohibition era is relevant here, and that's the manner in which Al Capone and his organization were eventually brought down. Because Capone made most of his money from bootlegging, prostitution, and gambling, many believe that he was eventually arrested for one of these crimes. In fact, Al Capone was arrested, tried, convicted, and jailed for tax evasion. It took a lot of work, and more than a few lucky breaks, by the Internal Revenue Service (IRS) investigator on his case to run a successful inquiry. In the end, one of the biggest gangsters in US history wasn't brought down because of booze, hookers, or horses; he was brought down because the US government went after the money. Along somewhat similar lines, when the US government goes after foreign terrorist organizations like al-Qa'ida or Hezbollah, they don't only go after the operatives or their weapons; they go after the money used to fund their operations.

So why isn't the Mexican government going after the profits of drug trafficking organizations? Part of the reason is that Mexico's laws regarding money laundering are weak. Although comprehensive, they don't meet international standards, so they need to be strengthened for better implementation. Even more concerning, money laundering offenses aren't adequately investigated. Mexican authorities have obtained only twenty-five convictions for money laundering since it was criminalized in 1989. From 2004 to 2007, prosecutors secured 149 indictments, but only two were related to investigations by the Mexican financial intelligence unit, the governmental agency charged with rooting out this particular form of corruption.[4] Mexico has made some progress in developing its system for combating money laundering, but it still has a long way to go.

Another part of the problem is the fact that Mexico's economy relies heavily on drug money that is poured back into the system while being laundered, as well as on the pesos spent by high-rolling kingpins and entourage members. The Mexican economy receives between $35 billion and $40 billion each year in drug-related income. This does not represent all of the cartels' profits, however, as they hold some back to invest elsewhere, and drug profits need to remain liquid and undetectable to be usable. While some drug money clearly flows out of Mexico, the smugglers are able to influence the behavior of the Mexican government by investing some of it at home. For these reasons, negative ramifications on the Mexican government or economy would result from completely shutting down the drug trade.[5]

This isn't to say that the Mexican government isn't trying to stop money laundering, at least enough to decrease the levels of violence. The consistent message is that government agencies don't have sufficient personnel or financial resources to adequately investigate money laundering and associated crimes. And changing existing laws or implementing new ones—even for something as important as this—isn't an easy task. It takes a lot of time and a lot of negotiation to get legislation passed through the Mexican congress. Ultimately, the conflict of interest when it comes to strengthening anti–money laundering laws will be the main obstacle to any legislative changes.[6]

President Calderón has started taking some baby steps to reduce money laundering. In June 2010, he announced some of the toughest restrictions in Mexico's history on cash transactions of US dollars. Tourists and Mexicans without bank accounts are now limited to exchanging a maximum of US$1,500 per month. According to the Associated Press, "The measure is meant to help stem the flood of about $10 billion per year in suspicious cash flows that are thought to be linked to drug trafficking."[7]

The onus of strengthening these efforts falls on the Mexican government, but that doesn't mean that the United States can't help. The US government has been using the Foreign Narcotics Kingpin Designation Act (more succinctly known as the Kingpin Act) to cut off the money supply to dozens of cartel members and cartel-owned businesses. The Mexican government could model new legislation after the Kingpin Act. It could also work more closely with the US Office of Foreign Assets Control—the agency that manages entities on the Kingpin Act list—to develop a stronger anti–money laundering program of its own.

It appears that US banks need to get on the ball when it comes to detecting suspicious financial transactions with a possible drug trafficking nexus. In April 2006, soldiers searched a DC-9 jet at Ciudad del Carmen airport, 500 miles east of Mexico City, and found 5.7 tons of cocaine. They discovered that the plane was bought with drug money laundered through Wachovia Bank and Bank of America. Wachovia had made a habit of helping to move money for Mexican drug smugglers, and Wells Fargo Bank, which bought Wachovia in 2008, admitted in court that its unit "failed to monitor and report suspected money laundering by narcotics traffickers, including the cash used to buy four planes that shipped a total of twenty-two tons of cocaine." Wachovia admitted that it didn't do enough to spot illicit funds in handling $378.4 billion for Mexican currency exchange houses from 2004 to 2007.[8]

Wachovia hasn't been alone in its ignorance or complicity. Miami-based American Express Bank International paid fines in 1994 and 2007 after admitting that it had failed to identify and report drug dealers laundering money through its accounts. Drug traffickers used accounts at Bank of America in Oklahoma City to buy three planes that carried ten tons of cocaine, according to Mexican court filings. Federal agents caught people who work for Mexican cartels depositing illicit funds in Bank of America accounts in Atlanta, Chicago, and Brownsville, Texas, from 2002 to 2009. Wachovia was eventually charged with violating the Bank Secrecy Act by failing to run an effective anti–money laundering program. Wells Fargo promised in a Miami federal courtroom to take a hard look at its program and revamp its system for identifying suspicious transactions. Wachovia's new owner paid $160 million in fines and penalties, and if Wells Fargo keeps its pledge, the US government, according to an agreement, was supposed to drop all charges against the bank in March 2011.[9]

Current US laws that regulate the banking system are partly to blame for these egregious oversights. The 1970 Bank Secrecy Act requires banks to report all cash transactions above $10,000 to regulators and to tell the government about other suspected money laundering activity. However, no big American bank has ever been indicted for violating the Bank Secrecy Act or any other federal law. Instead, the Justice Department settles criminal charges by using deferred-prosecution agreements, in which a bank pays a fine and promises not to break the law again. These "get out of jail free" cards need to be revoked, and cash transactions with possible ties to drug trafficking scrutinized much more closely, with harsher punishments to follow.

SAVING THE YOUTH OF TOMORROW

Creating a world of opportunity for youth within Mexico might be the greatest challenge yet for President Calderón and his pledge to defeat the narcos. It's hard enough to make changes to government structures and organizations that already exist. But Calderón has to figure out a way to make something out of nothing: job and educational opportunities for young people in Mexico's cities and countless poor, rural areas where currently there are none.

But first and foremost, the Mexican people have to fight for their kids. They can't resign their children to a violent fate that seems inescapable. Right now in places like Tijuana and Ciudad Juárez, small children are inventing kidnapping games and forming playground gangs at elementary schools. Instead of looking up to policemen and firefighters, they're idolizing drug lords and dreaming of how rich they could be if they could grow up to become narcos. Social workers in Mexico report that much of the blame belongs on parents who are absent from the home while working long hours in fields or in factories. The kids have little access to good schools, and they see from their parents' examples that long hours of hard work bring little reward compared to the narco lifestyle of little work and big riches.[10]

Part of what needs to be overcome is the cultural aspect of the narcos' influence. Parents need to ingrain in their children that the narco lifestyle is unacceptable, much as one would endeavor to teach children that being a gangster is not a good career choice. Just as it's extremely difficult for a child raised in a broken home surrounded by drug dealers in a US city to escape that life and become a valuable member of society, the same uphill battle must be fought for Mexican children. It can be done—but not without a major societal restructuring that the Mexican people might not yet be prepared to do.

The Mexican government, for its part, has to help provide educational opportunities for children as well as social programs that extend beyond the school day. They can reach out to NGOs within Mexico as well as in the United States, Canada, and elsewhere in the hemisphere for help to set up small schools in rural areas where children of poppy farmers can start receiving more positive messages about their future. Children also need a place to go and constructive things to do after their school day ends; this is another area where NGOs and charitable groups can help. Effective after-school programs in the United States have done a world of good for many American children at high risk of joining gangs and using drugs. The Mexican ninis need to find positive outlets for their energy and time, whether it's through sports, music and the arts, or volunteerism. Their parents also need to be right behind them with strong words of encouragement.

Once their formal education ends, Mexico's youth need employment options other than drug trafficking. It's obvious that the Mexican government and the private sector have problems providing sufficient gainful employment for citizens; if that weren't the case, millions of Mexicans wouldn't try every year to enter the United States illegally, looking for better-paying jobs. Many of Mexico's youth will never attend college, so there needs to be a focus on job-training and the creation of jobs for less-skilled workers. The

Mexican and American media love to publicize how US car manufacturers and other big industry giants are opening up new factories and plants in Mexico as a sign of defiance to cartel violence and a sagging economy. But an auto plant that employs 700 Mexican workers who are trained to build cars does nothing to help a sixteen-year-old Mexican teenager who has no hope of receiving either further education or skills training for worthwhile employment.

Part of the problem might be that no one wants to talk about the lack of prospects for Mexico's youth. In October 2010, Juan Martin Perez, head of a Mexican NGO, Network for the Rights of Children, told Reuters, "The worst thing is that there is no official response to try to prevent children dying, to stop them being used in organized crime. Practically nobody is talking about this." The silence is probably because the Mexican government doesn't want to acknowledge that it can't compete with the cartels. Unskilled youngsters in Ciudad Juárez can earn $700 a month working as junior drug hit men, three times what they would earn in an assembly plant producing microwaves or car parts for the US market.[11]

Like its attempts to fix the justice system, Mexican government attempts to improve the education system aren't really taking hold. Calderón's predecessor, Vicente Fox, did start an internationally acclaimed program of handing cash to families in return for kids' school attendance. The program, called "Oportunidades," reaches 5.8 million families across Mexico and has been ramped up in Ciudad Juárez to help 26,000 families, up from 12,000 at the end of 2009. Mexico spends 5.5 percent of its gross domestic product on education, only a little below Britain and France, according to the most recent CIA (Central Intelligence Agency) data. Although Mexicans are not known as big readers, the country has an 86-percent literacy rate. On average, Mexicans complete thirteen years in school—well within United Nations guidelines for the progress of developing countries. According to Catherine Bremer, Calderón "visited Ciudad Juárez twice this year and pledged to increase spending on schools, social services, nurseries and soccer pitches for the city, which has hardly any green spaces or parks. But he gave no details on funding. The government says that since February [2010] it has awarded thousands of educational grants for Ciudad Juárez, renovated some 50 schools and opened rehab centers. . . . [But] nonprofit workers who spend afternoons playing soccer and skipping rope games with poor kids in dusty yards [say] they have seen no evidence of any money being spent."[12]

One tiny ray of light that was widely reported in early December 2010 was the creation of a youth orchestra in Ciudad Juárez, by a former heroin addict. After recovering from drug addiction at the age of thirty-five, Alma Rosa Gonzalez was inspired by Venezuela's famous network of orchestras known as "El Sistema" (The System), which aims to rescue poor young people through music. She realized that she had a lot of musical resources in the city, primarily in the form of musicians who came to Juárez from across Mexico and even from as far away as Eastern Europe. To date, the program "has helped more than 400 children in the city, despite threats, robberies, and students dropping out when parents have been kidnapped. But the parents of children in the program are undaunted, knowing that this might be the only opportunity their children have to escape the drug violence literally lurking around the corner." Some of the kids have actually gone on to study music in Mexico City. While Gonzalez acknowledges that "not all of the children in the program will become virtuosos," she feels it's one of the better options available to them under the city's current circumstances. Although for years she relied solely on charity, Gonzalez now receives federal government help to fund her orchestra program, which operates at a series of schools and community centers.[13]

Mexico is in crisis, not only because its present is plagued with drug-fueled violence, but also because its future is already slipping away. There are dozens of potential solutions to help reduce drug-related violence in Mexico, but those solutions are only words on paper if no one with authority does anything to put them into action. Calderón and his administration—as well as anyone intending to make a run for the office of president in 2012—need to take a hard look at making some difficult changes. The Mexican people also need to find the last ounces of fight left inside them. This is not only so the government and the people can take back their Mexico from the narcos, but so they can keep the narcos from taking their most prized resource—their children.

CHAPTER 11

IMPROVING SECURITY ALONG THE BORDER AND BEYOND

BY NOW IT IS CLEAR that the drug war and all of its associated ills aren't confined to only the southwest border. It is also apparent that this multifaceted problem involves not only illegal drugs, but also guns, money, and an invasion of US public lands. Any strategy designed to prevent Mexico's drug war from completely exploding into America has to address all of these issues in a comprehensive fashion. But before DHS, or the USDOJ, or the White House can address issues of security along the border and beyond, the problems themselves have to be understood. This is where the trouble begins.

THE DEBATE OVER BORDER VIOLENCE SPILLOVER

Despite all the evidence presented in these pages to the contrary, plenty of people in US governments and law enforcement agencies believe that the drug war isn't a big problem for the United States. They cite low crime statistics in American border cities and the lack of shootouts in broad daylight, à la Ciudad Juárez. DHS has published several assessments with a bottom line that there is no evidence to suggest that border violence spillover is happening. On the flip side are politicians like Arizona governor Jan Brewer and Texas governor Rick Perry, sheriffs like Paul Babeu in Pinal County, Arizona, and hundreds of ranchers in rural areas who say that US borders are being invaded by violent criminals who can't be stopped.

One of the biggest reasons for the discrepancy is the lack of an agreed-upon definition of "spillover violence." It was defined as follows in a report to Congress by a DEA Special Agent in 2009: "Spillover violence entails deliberate, planned attacks by the cartels on U.S. assets, including civilian, military, or law enforcement officials, innocent U.S. citizens, or physical institutions such as government buildings, consulates, or businesses. This definition does not include trafficker on trafficker violence, whether perpetrated in Mexico or the U.S."[1]

The problem is that this definition hasn't been officially adopted by anyone. So when peer agencies or individuals start talking about spillover violence, either in official reports or in stories in the media, it's like comparing apples to oranges.

Looking strictly at crime statistics, spillover doesn't appear to be a problem at all. Crime levels in San Diego have remained steady or dropped over the last six years, which is roughly when the dramatic crime spike began in Tijuana. San Diego's overall crime rate plunged 18 percent in 2009, with a decrease of 25.5 percent in homicides and 15.4 percent in rapes.[2] In November 2010, CQ Press—a major publisher of books and web products on American politics and current affairs—ranked El Paso as the safest city in the United States, based on 2009's crime statistics. FBI Uniform Crime Reports and statistics provided by police agencies show that crime rates in Nogales, Douglas, Yuma, and other Arizona border towns have remained essentially flat for the past decade.[3] Even local citizens say the talk about spillover is hype. "I have to say, a lot of this is way overblown," said Gary Brasher of Tuboc, Arizona, president of the Coalition for a Safe and Secure Border.[4]

On the other hand are dozens—if not hundreds—of confirmed reports of violent activity being perpetrated on US soil or against US citizens. These include the murder of rancher Robert Krentz, the grenade tossed into the Texas strip club, and attacks on US law enforcement by cartel-affiliated marijuana growers. Despite the different opinions on spillover, there is no disputing that Mexican drug cartels are present in America, and it's not just the southwest border that's feeling the effects of their activities. Just ask the sheriff in Shelby County, Alabama, who found those tortured bodies of Mexicans who owed money to the Gulf cartel, or the parents of Cole Puffinburger, who was kidnapped from his home in Las Vegas allegedly because his grandfather owed money to a cartel.

To be clear, cartel-sanctioned hit men are not wandering through US city streets in broad daylight and walking up to cars at stop signs so they can put two bullets into someone's head. Decapitated corpses with snarky notes from a cartel attached are not being piled up in front of a local elementary school. While these things are happening on the Mexican side of the border and not on the US side, that doesn't mean that American federal, state, and law enforcement agencies have what they need to combat existing drug-related crime in the United States.

Mexico's drug war is not just a border security problem, or a drug smuggling problem, or a southbound weapons smuggling problem. It is a national security problem that is quiet and insidious. Gang members who work for Mexican cartels threaten US children by making offers of cheap drugs and by recruiting them using glamorized visions of the gang lifestyle. Cartel members use US highways and cities to move and hide drugs and people. They pose as law-abiding citizens and buy guns, allowed by US laws, so they can send them to brutal assassins across the border. The drug war has been here for some time, and it will remain here unless governments on both sides of the border can come up with some brave and creative solutions to attack this drug-fueled plague.

SENDING MORE RESOURCES TO THE RIGHT PLACES

It is well known that money is tight everywhere right now, and there aren't enough police officers and federal agents to go around. But effective resource allocation is key when a war is on the doorstep. Too many reports and personal stories from local cops and federal agents along the border reveal aging or scanty equipment, and guns and protective gear that don't stack up to the firepower of their adversaries.

The National Guard and Department of Defense have provided a lot of assistance by way of loaned gear—drones, night-vision goggles, scopes, and the like—to the agencies that work along the border. When they leave, however, often their gear goes with them. Sometimes, USBP sectors have to borrow gear from neighboring sectors or other agencies because their budgets don't allow them to buy their own. Many roads along the southwest border are made impassable at certain times of the year due to inhospitable weather conditions. Sometimes, the USBP doesn't have the funding to make those roads usable or to obtain all-terrain vehicles that would allow them access to certain parts of their own sector. Of course, that means it's also hard for drug and human smugglers to access those same areas. But if they know the USBP can't get there quickly enough to catch them, they're certainly going to try them out.

State-of-the-art technology has been even more of a disaster for the border security mission than the problems of day-to-day funding. The "virtual fence" idea with so many remotely accessed cameras and sensors has been a waste of one billion taxpayer dollars; and that was just for the pilot program in Arizona, which covered only fifty-three miles of the border. Fortunately, the program was eliminated in January 2011 because it "does not meet current standards for viability and cost effectiveness," per Secretary Napolitano. Seismic sensors designed to detect border tunnels work on occasion, but running over the entrance to one with a truck is still one of the best detection methods. Coming across a group of migrants or smugglers while on routine patrol is a great find, but advance notice from informants or Mexican agency counterparts would minimize that patrol time. The new Predator drones being deployed to the border can do and see some amazing things as high-tech eyes in the sky for Border Patrol and CBP. But without experienced agents to respond to situations that the drones catch on camera, their flight time is wasted. Good technological products are definitely needed and have their place in the border security mission. Nevertheless, technology shouldn't be expected to take the place of good human enforcement, or source operations, or liaison relationships between agencies.

One of the biggest problems is that there simply are not enough people to go around to all the different sectors, stations, and offices staffed by multiple agencies and departments along the border. Back in March 2009, Secretary Napolitano responded to southwest border security concerns by announcing that DHS was going to beef up its staffing in the region. The plan called for the deployment of 360 officers and agents at the border and in Mexico. That included doubling the staffing of BEST teams, tripling the number of assigned analysts, deploying one hundred more USBP agents, and sending border agencies more equipment, like x-ray scanners and canine units. In some cases, this has been a big help. But in other cases, it's been merely window dressing. For example, a good number of the additional USBP agents sent to the border are fresh out of training. That means that each has to spend a mandatory period as a probationary agent, learning the ropes and doing everything with a partner. Sometimes it takes up to two years before a new Border Patrol agent can get in a truck and go out on patrol alone. That's not exactly a force multiplier.

Similarly, the ATF doesn't have enough people to effectively address the southbound weapons trafficking problem. Following is a sample of the challenges that the ATF is dealing with.

The National Tracing Center is the only place in the nation authorized to trace gun sales. Here, ATF researchers make phone calls and pore over handwritten records from across the country to track down gun owners. In contrast with such state-of-the-art, twenty-first-century crime-fighting techniques as DNA matching and digital fingerprint analysis, gun tracing is an antiquated, laborious process done mostly by hand.[5] When gun dealers go out of business for whatever reason, they have to send their paper records to this center, where the records are scanned by machine onto microfiche sheets. Remember: microfiches are clear plastic sheets that have document pages printed on them in miniature, and a huge metal apparatus is needed to magnify the printing for reading. The government has been prohibited from putting gun ownership records into an easily accessible format, such as a searchable computer database; for decades, the NRA has lobbied successfully to block all attempts at such computerization, arguing against any national registry of firearm ownership.[6]

The NRA's efforts to limit the ATF's capabilities have tremendously politicized the southbound weapons trafficking issue. The NRA actually wanted to completely abolish the ATF through the 1980s and 1990s; then it backpedaled, thinking "it preferred the devil it knew to some other regulatory agency that might make life more difficult for the lobbying group. In 2008, gun dealers got a huge boost in business when the NRA ran TV ads saying that President Obama planned to ban handguns and to close 90 percent of gun shops, despite the fact that he never said such things." Obama did say he was interested in reinstating the assault weapons ban and closing the gun show loophole and that he planned to repeal the ATF-restricting Tiahrt Amendment. As of late 2010, however, the Obama Administration has changed virtually nothing with regard to gun legislation and regulations.[7]

Currently, the ATF doesn't even have enough personnel to fully inspect the firearms and explosives dealers already under its charge. The bureau has about 600 inspectors to cover more than 115,000 firearms dealers—about 55,000 collectors and about 60,000 retail sellers. By law, the ATF can inspect dealers for compliance only once a year. But officials acknowledge that, on average, dealers are inspected only about once a decade. When inspectors document persistent or severe violations, they can issue warning letters or hold warning conferences with licensees. When problems are critical, they can move to take away the license. Dealers, however, "can drag out the process for years and sell guns the entire time."[8]

One of the ATF's chief concerns is missing guns. Nationwide, dealers lose track of an enormous number of guns. Since 2005, ATF visits to conduct 3,847 inspections have documented 113,642 guns that cannot be found, and it is unknown how many of those guns have made their way into Mexico. The process is complicated because dealers, by law, do not have to take inventory. As a result, ATF inspectors sometimes have to spend days or weeks poring through a dealer's paperwork and physically matching it to the guns on hand.[9] These are significantly less-than-ideal circumstances under which any US agency should be working—especially one charged with the huge responsibility of stopping southbound weapons trafficking.

I know from personal experience that one of the hardest things to do as an agent out in the field is to firmly tell superiors—often located in a comfortable office far away from the realities of the field—that the job can't get done the way it needs to be because there aren't enough people or there isn't enough gear. Even tougher is when agents actually manage to communicate that and their superiors give them the dreaded response of "Too bad; you'll have to do more with less." Given the climate along the southwest border these days, that kind of attitude is completely unacceptable. Some measures that DHS specifically, and the US government in general, can take include:

- Conduct a thorough assessment to determine (through anonymous reports from field agents, if necessary) the actual shortfalls and limitations occurring at patrol stations and field offices along the border.

- Don't saddle the ATF alone with the prevention of southbound weapons trafficking; USDOJ needs to work more closely with state agencies responsible for firearms law enforcement. Often this is a funding problem for the states, but they need to realize the necessity of contributing their own state agents to the fight.
- Develop a thorough, strict, and standardized accounting procedure for keeping track of federal grant monies that go to state and local law enforcement agencies for border-security missions. Sometimes funds are used wisely and appropriately, but very often they're not, and that's taxpayer money that might be better spent elsewhere if certain agencies are demonstrating that they can't spend it right.
- Take a good, hard look at federal government priorities. If border security isn't toward the top of the list, it needs to be moved there. And funding priorities need to follow; examine where resources can be pulled from other uses and move them to those priority areas.
- Revisit the repeal of the Tiahrt Amendment and other regulations that prevent the ATF from accomplishing its mission and making a dent in the southbound weapons flow.

Yes, these things are more easily said than done; many have seen first-hand how slowly the cogs of the federal government can move. But that doesn't mean that something can't be done or that it shouldn't be done. Notice how quickly policies and priorities can change, and how quickly money can flow, when there's a national emergency. The situation on the border with Mexico isn't a national emergency for the United States right now, but where's the wisdom in waiting for an emergency to start making decisions that could have prevented that kind of escalation?

Illegal immigration and immigration reform are two hot-button issues that affect border security. How to properly enforce immigration laws is being debated on Capitol Hill, by talking heads on the news, and in the nation's highest courts. As it turns out, the agencies that are charged with protecting the borders from drug traffickers, criminals, and terrorists are also charged with keeping out illegal immigrants. Out of those four groups of people, the last group comprises the largest number of people and demands the allocation of a large volume of US-agency resources. Yet, some might argue that the first three groups, although smaller in number, pose a much greater threat to national security, and therefore the limited law enforcement resources should be focused on them. Immigration laws should not be ignored—far from it—but when the immigration reform process finally begins, it should include a method for law enforcement agencies to more efficiently separate terror suspects, drug traffickers, and other criminals from immigrant groups so that agency resources can focus on the more prominent threats.

CHANGING US DRUG AND GUN LAWS

First and foremost in considering changes to drug laws is to clarify the difference between legalization and decriminalization. This is a very important distinction, partly because one of them has already been implemented in Mexico and partly because the repercussions of each are very different. In essence, with decriminalization, people do not go to jail for possessing certain small amounts of designated drugs. It's still illegal to manufacture and sell those drugs, but a person is no longer looked upon as a criminal for possessing small amounts of drugs or for getting caught using them. Under decriminalization, the authorities are going after the suppliers as the real criminals, not the users, because the suppliers are the ones profiting from the sale of illegal goods.

In June 2009, the Mexican legislature quietly voted to decriminalize the possession of small amounts of marijuana, cocaine, methamphetamine, and other drugs. Oddly enough, it was President Calderón's idea. He felt it made sense to distinguish between small-time users and big-time dealers, while retargeting major crime-fighting resources away from the consumers and toward the dealers and their drug lord bosses. Under Mexico's decriminalization initiative, users caught with small amounts—up to 5 grams of marijuana, 500 milligrams of cocaine, 40 milligrams of methamphetamine, or 50 milligrams of heroin—clearly intended for "personal and immediate use" will not be criminally prosecuted. They will be told of available clinics and encouraged to enter a rehabilitation program.[10]

A year later, it's apparent that the controversial measure hasn't made a significant difference in the levels of violence across Mexico or in the volume of illegal drugs flowing throughout the country. In May 2010, *National Journal* interviewed Arturo Sarukhan, Mexico's ambassador to the United States, and the interviewer specifically asked him about the results so far of his country's decriminalization policy. In his two-paragraph response, he explained the law's intention, but not once did he even allude to any results—positive or negative. His unsatisfactory answer suggests that the controversial measure isn't working out the way the Calderón administration had expected or hoped and that Mexico's law enforcement agencies and justice system are just as overburdened as ever.

Drug legalization is a different matter because it essentially authorizes the production, sale, distribution, and use of one or several illegal substances. It's true that a change could legalize only one drug and not all; the current debate in the United States over legalization has centered on marijuana alone. The movement has been picking up steam in recent years, partly because Americans are acknowledging in greater numbers that "traditional" drug policy has done very little to reduce the demand for marijuana in America and also because violent cartels in Mexico smuggle in more marijuana than any other illegal drug.

Consider that the repeal of Prohibition worked to a certain extent in alleviating the effects of organized crime, but it didn't eliminate them. Likewise, the domestic legalization of marijuana is a worthwhile debate to have because it will likely alleviate some of the negative effects of the drug war, but it's not the perfect answer that many people think it is.

Basic economic theory of supply and demand says that if a lot of people want something that they can't easily purchase, it's going to cost more to obtain that something. This adds an even higher premium to the overall price of illegal drugs, and subsequently means even bigger profits for the cartels that manufacture and distribute them. Cartels work in a very similar fashion to major corporations: their primary motive for doing what they do is profit generation. That's the be-all and end-all of their very existence. If something could take the big profits away from cartels, they wouldn't be left with a reason to operate.

The current debate over legalization covers only marijuana. Legalization, regulation, and taxation of marijuana's sale, production, and use in the United States would dramatically drive down its price and have a major negative impact on Mexican cartels' profit margins. That's just the way the free market works, and it has nothing to do with the moral aspects of legalization. However, this doesn't mean that Mexican cartels would go out of business. Organized crime groups in Chicago and New York didn't disappear in the early 1930s when Prohibition was repealed. That's because they adapted and got into the legal alcohol trade. They also still had other illegal activities they could bank on, such as gambling and prostitution. It would likely work the same way for Mexican cartels. They could still rely on the illegal trafficking of cocaine, methamphetamine, and heroin while entering into the legal market for marijuana. They could also remain engaged in kidnapping, extortion, and human smuggling activities to keep their income sources diversified.

That might sound discouraging, but it doesn't mean that the US government should keep the option of legalization completely off the table. International studies conducted by the World Bank show that in several countries around the globe, tobacco use decreases when cigarette taxation increases; it's possible that would apply to marijuana use as well. These same studies also examine the effectiveness of a combined approach between high tobacco taxes and education and awareness campaigns.[11] In light of these studies, there are several concrete steps that the US government can take regarding marijuana legalization to determine its feasibility and potential effectiveness against Mexican cartel activity:

- Commission a new, independent, and completely transparent study of how the economics of marijuana supply, demand, and taxation, along with public awareness campaigns, might compare to that of tobacco and alcohol.
- Explore regulatory options for the production, sale, and distribution of marijuana in the United States, similar to those used in the tobacco industry.
- Explore legal and enforcement options for marijuana use, similar to those of tobacco and alcohol (e.g., minimum age requirement, field tests to determine recent marijuana use by drivers, expanded DUI laws).
- Develop potential public awareness campaigns for both underage and adult marijuana users, similar to antitobacco campaigns.

These are just a handful of suggestions, and there are so many more steps that would be involved in such a major US policy change. But it wouldn't have to happen overnight, and it could happen in a measured fashion to allow the public health sector—and more importantly, the public mindset—to keep up. The benefits in the long run would be numerous: significantly reduced profits for the brutally violent Mexican cartels, increased profits for US growers and related businesses entering into a large new market, a much-needed new source of tax income for federal and state governments, and, ideally, reduced demand for marijuana.

Changing US drug laws to allow the recreational use of marijuana might be next to impossible, but the real battle will be over changing the gun laws. The heated debate over the right way to stop US-origin guns from going to Mexico seesaws between adding more gun laws and eliminating existing ones. Some believe the reinstatement of the assault weapons ban is a solution to the southbound weapons trafficking problem. However, most of the weapons on the original 1994 ban list are not the ones going to Mexico. Others claim that the "90 percent" figure (the percentage of weapons seized in Mexico that are traced back to US sources) is an attempt by the antigun lobby to clamp down on US gun sales.[12]

The ATF has analyzed firearms recovered in Mexico from 2005 to 2008 and has identified the weapons most commonly used by the drug cartels: 9mm pistols, .38-caliber revolvers, 5.7mm pistols, .223-caliber rifles, 7.62mm rifles, and .50-caliber rifles. Specifically, certain drug trafficking organizations are fond of the Fabrique Nationale (FN) FiveSeven pistol and the FN-P90, as well as the Barrett .50-caliber sniper rifle. The AK-47 and the AR-15 are very popular with the cartels and are on the ban list, but many "copycat" assault rifles would easily—and legally—be available should the ban ever be reinstated.[13]

In addition to assault weapons legislation, some politicians have attempted to close the "gun show loophole" with new laws. Currently, a private individual selling guns—meaning he or she does not sell guns for a living—can sell personally owned firearms at a gun show without having to run a background check on buyers. In 2009, Senator Frank Lautenberg (D-New Jersey) filed a bill to close the gun show loophole by requiring an unlicensed person who wanted to sell a gun to use a Federal Firearms License (FFL) at a gun show to complete the transaction.

However, one cannot apply for an FFL for the sole purpose of selling guns at a gun show, as the FFL requires a permanent business location for selling the guns. If a law like Lautenberg's were to pass, even though most private sellers would be inconvenienced by not being able to sell their guns at gun shows, it would still be legal, in some states, to sell their weapons to people at their homes, in parking lots, or at any other location as long as it was not a gun show.

The fact remains that the majority of guns purchased in the United States by straw buyers are bought legally (from the seller's perspective, anyway), from both licensed and unlicensed gun sellers. The straw buyers have clean backgrounds, fill out all the requisite forms, claim (falsely) that the guns are for personal use, and leave and pass the guns on to whoever is going to transport them south into Mexico. Passing legislation to close the "gun show loophole" and to remove unlicensed sellers from gun shows probably wouldn't make a dent in the weapons trafficking problem because cartel-bound guns can still be bought through other existing venues.

Stopping the flow of weapons from the United States into Mexico is complicated and difficult for many reasons. Fingers are being pointed at both governments for having weak laws or weak enforcement efforts, but there are so many facets to the problem that it's impossible to address them all at the same time. The drug syndicates have virtually unlimited financial resources and don't have to follow laws to accomplish their goals. The Mexican authorities are dealing with widespread corruption, which allows seized guns to reenter circulation. The United States doesn't have enough enforcement agents or resources but does have constitutionally protected laws being used to the cartels' advantage.

It might be impossible to tackle all of these challenges at once, but there are efforts being made to address them, one at a time. Mexican authorities are making record numbers of gun seizures. The ATF is working closely with Mexican authorities to trace significantly more of the seized guns. The US government is making more personnel and financial resources available to the ATF and other agencies involved in stemming the southbound weapons flow.

An important question is whether US homeland security agencies should take part in southbound inspections in an attempt to stem the flow of weapons into Mexico. There are two schools of thought on this. Some believe that the US government shouldn't be conducting random searches on southbound vehicles because it should be Mexico's responsibility to screen vehicles and people entering their country. However, they rarely do that. US Secretary of State Hillary Clinton and Secretary Napolitano have already assumed some responsibility for this issue, so leaving it entirely up to the Mexican government isn't really an option.

That leaves the second school of thought, which is for the United States to shoulder some of the responsibility (or blame, depending on who is asked) for inspections, since many of the guns in question likely originate in America. Unfortunately, this would lead to citizens' complaining that their own government is causing long backups at border crossings and negatively affecting US businesses whose trucks cross into Mexico. One ATF official cautioned, "The second they start doing southbound inspections and the trucks start backing up 1,500 miles to the Canadian border, there's going to be hell to pay. You've got to be selective."[14] Even so, when CBP and local authorities decide they want to perform southbound vehicle inspections, the cartels would set up spotters just south of the border to observe the inspections; based on what the spotters tell them, they would radio their people on the US side in cars with Mexico-destined guns and tell them not to cross.

Someone is always going to be unhappy with efforts to clamp down on cross-border trafficking and border violence. Nonetheless, it's essential that something be done about the southbound flow of guns. Since it looks like a lot of that is going to fall on the US government, it needs to figure out the best ways to go about it. Changing US gun laws isn't going to be the perfect answer that solves the weapons trafficking problem, just like changing US drug laws to allow the use of marijuana won't end drug trafficking or its associated violence.

When an ATF supervisor was asked why he thought the American people should care about guns sold in the United States going to Mexican cartel members, he vehemently responded, "Mexican drug cartels are thugs. They're violent criminals. If people think they don't have influence in this country, they're wrong. The firearms that they're eagerly acquiring and illegally trafficking are empowering them, making them stronger, more vicious, and more violent. If we can somehow remove that tool, then we can give the Mexicans an opportunity to get ahead of the game."[15]

Former Arizona attorney general Terry Goddard is worried that a lack of concern will eventually come around to bite. "It's only a matter of time until those guns that are sold to cartels end up coming back into the United States and being used against law enforcement here," he said. "The numbers are so large I consider it almost inevitable."[16]

Goddard believes that the cartels' cycle of criminal activity and the components of that cycle—the center of which is the drug trade—are all interrelated. "Like any integrated business operation, if you're going to stop it, you're going to have to eliminate the component parts," he said. "We haven't been very successful at eliminating the drug component, which drives everything." Goddard suggested that governments and law enforcement agencies might have more success by stepping up efforts against the other components, like weapons trafficking, money laundering, and human smuggling. He acknowledged that classic cartel behavior—like beheadings, grenade attacks, and mass killings—is not being seen in the United States right now, but the potential is there. Goddard advised, "Robust, vigorous defensive maneuvering to do whatever we can to support Mexico in the fight against the cartels [along with] decisive actions by US law enforcement are absolutely necessary. We certainly don't want to see that [kind of violent] program succeed in Mexico, or anywhere else."[17]

It won't be easy to solve the many problems on either side of the border. As they say, extreme situations call for extreme measures. It's unfortunate that something drastic has to happen before leaders will take the necessary actions that might have prevented those situations in the first place. Because of the severe political and financial repercussions associated with making big changes in either the United States or Mexico, it is unrealistic to expect some of them to even make it to the table for discussion unless things get much worse along the border—always a possibility—or unless US federal, state, and local governments start agreeing that spillover is happening and that the drug war has officially arrived. Hopefully, the Mexican government will realize it also can't afford for the drug war to get worse, and US officials will realize the situation has made it past the threshold of the doorstep and has settled itself comfortably in America's living room.

CHAPTER 12

CONCLUSIONS

MANAGING A WAR THAT CAN'T BE WON

CAN THE MEXICAN DRUG WAR be won? Historically, determining whether a conflict has been won or lost has been extraordinarily difficult in some cases. One can easily say who won the American Civil War or World War II, but did the United States "win" in Iraq? Technically, Iraq does have some semblance of a democratic government, but the political infighting and insurgent violence continue, albeit on a smaller scale. Is America winning in Afghanistan? If the Taliban retake control after a few years, does that erase the W and chalk up an L? What benchmark would be used to measure success in Mexico and to eventually declare victory? In a situation where everyone knows that all drug trafficking can't be eradicated and that all violence can't be definitively ended, what level of each is low enough or acceptable enough to say that either the Mexican or US government has won?

The Mexican drug war cannot be won. It must be viewed as a conflict that can only be managed. Drug trafficking and associated violence need to be controlled so that the Mexican people can experience a degree of security sufficient to allow them to prosper. It's no different from living with common crime in the United States; criminal activity is present from big cities to small towns, and it's something that everyone has to deal with at some point. But concerns about becoming victims of crime don't keep US citizens from taking their kids to school, or from voting on Election Day, or from going to a certain restaurant or nightclub on date night. Most Americans don't care for politicians very much, and some don't care for the police very much either; but overall, they have enough faith in the governments and the justice system that they can lead normal, peaceful lives.

Obviously, this is not the case in many parts of Mexico. What's even more saddening than the fact that many Mexicans have had their basic freedoms curtailed by drug-related violence is that many have also resigned themselves to their fates. Dirty politicians and dirtier cops are accepted as the norm. Few ordinary citizens have the means or the willpower to fight the plague that has consumed their country; those who do meet all too often with a grisly end.

In late November 2010, several members of a cartel approached seventy-seven-year-old Alejo Garza Tamez on his ranch in Ciudad Victoria. They gave him an ultimatum: abandon his ranch within twenty-four hours, or die. Tamez told his ranch hands to go home, then strategically placed weapons by the windows and doors of his home. When the narcos came back, he opened fire, killing four and injuring two more before he was killed in a volley of gunfire and grenades. They never did get the ranch, and Tamez became a hero as his story spread across Mexico.[1]

Some Mexicans say they're inspired by the story of Tamez's last stand, but most still prefer to just stay out of the way of the narcos. There's not much else they can do; most citizens can't buy guns to arm and protect themselves. They can't trust the police to come to their rescue if they're kidnapped or threatened in any way. Electing different officials probably won't change things much because if they're not corrupted by the cartels going in, chances are they will be before they come out.

Protesting in public over the lack of effort by elected officials can be as dangerous as standing up to the narcos. Marisela Escobedo's daughter Rubi was killed in Ciudad Juárez in 2008, and the mother demanded answers—and action. Contrary to what many people might assume, neither Marisela nor Rubi was involved in any way in the drug trade. A state tribunal cleared the man who was arrested for Rubi's murder—her boyfriend, actually—and Marisela began providing important information about the case to prosecutors and federal police as a way to seek justice for her daughter. In December 2010, while on the steps of the state capitol collecting signatures for a petition, Marisela was seen exchanging words with a man who approached her. The man pulled out a gun and shot her in the head while she attempted to run to safety. This occurred despite the fact that state security officials had been assigned to protect her. The shooter flicked his cigarette onto the ground, got into a white car, and drove away. Officials say they're investigating Marisela's murder, but it's likely that her killer will never be brought to justice—just like her daughter's killer.[2]

Despite the elevated number of arrests by Mexican authorities of so-called major cartel kingpins and high-ranking lieutenants in the last two years, it's hard to be optimistic when not much has really changed as a result. The Mexican government and media love to boast that they've captured this cartel leader or that kingpin. But nine times out of ten, the "leader" or "kingpin" was a mid-level guy, or at most, was in charge of a local *plaza*. This goes for government actions on both sides of the border. In December 2010, Operation Xcellerator produced the largest-ever US federal crackdown on the Federation (Mexico's Sinaloa drug cartel), with 761 people arrested and twenty-three tons of narcotics seized. US Attorney General Eric Holder and DEA chief Michele Leonhart characterized the operation as "a crushing blow" to the cartel. Unfortunately, most of those arrested were mid- to low-level cartel members, and it didn't make much of a dent in Federation operations.[3]

Statistically speaking, the Sinaloa Federation has suffered considerably fewer losses—meaning arrests or deaths due to government action—than any of the other major cartels. This has led many observers to question whether Calderón is in bed with El Chapo and company. Like anything else in Mexico these days, it's always possible, but there might be a plausible explanation. Roughly ten to fifteen years ago, there was a reasonable degree of peace in Mexico. Fewer big cartels existed then, and handshake deals and truces still meant something. Calderón might be trying to return Mexico to a similar situation. Remember, the violence in Mexico is caused by cartels fighting against the military and police as well as fighting each other for territory and drug smuggling routes. The fewer cartels there are, the fewer enemies the government has to worry about, and the fewer narcos who are fighting for control.

Between 2008 and 2010, the vast majority of major cartel kingpins who were captured or killed by Mexican police or the military belonged to the smaller cartels or ones that had been significantly weakened in recent years. If the Mexican government continues to hammer smaller and weaker cartels, this opens up the door for the bigger and stronger cartels, like the Sinaloa Federation and Los Zetas, to eat up more territory. At the end of the day, only two or three "megacartels" would be running the show, instead of six or seven.

Of course, there are benefits and drawbacks to this possible strategy. The main benefit is that fewer cartels usually means less fighting, which translates to less overall violence. Bigger cartels might be more willing to negotiate because they know that all the players have more resources to bring to a fight. The obvious drawback is that the Mexican government would have bigger and more powerful enemies, even if they were fewer in number. At the extreme end of this strategy is the complete takeover of the Mexican drug business by one cartel. If that were ever to happen, there would be a drastic reduction in violence all across the country, because the only fighting would be between the cartel and the government forces. Even that kind of conflict might be limited because such a megacartel could be powerful enough to work as a sort of parallel government in its own right. In exchange for peace, the legitimate Mexican government would likely have to concede some accommodations to the drug trade.

How bad this arrangement would actually be depends on who is asked, and on which side of the border the question is raised. An arrangement between drug traffickers and a democratically elected government harkens back to the days of PRI domination and a culture of looking the other way—dynamics that facilitated the rise of these cartels in the first place. Others might liken it to Mexico's selling its soul to the devil in exchange for a peace that might end up being short-lived. In reality, they'd be taking care of the symptoms but not curing the disease.

Despite all the depressing news, the seemingly insurmountable challenges, and the no-way-out situation that Mexico seems to be in, there are still people who are trying to shine a ray of light into the darkness. Motivated by an October 2010 shooting by federal police of a nineteen-year-old classmate during a peaceful street protest, some twenty students at the Autonomous University of Juárez formed the Asociación Estudiantil Juarense (the Student Association of Juárez). Their primary goal is to seek justice for their classmate, who survived the shooting, but also to help end the corruption of the police and military in the city. They have organized several marches to protest drug-related violence and government corruption, and their message has spread to other parts of Mexico.[4] Even though they're putting themselves in an extremely vulnerable position by speaking out so publicly, these students feel it's more important to let their countrymen know that they've had enough.

For the last seven years, Fernando Gallegos has been coaching Juárez teenagers on how to play American football at a science-focused magnet school in the city. Gallegos says the point isn't to play good football. "We're trying not to lose these children. The idea is to keep this field full of kids, to distract them," he said. "We can't do much about the situation this city is in. Our only weapon is to keep them active." The team lost two players in a massacre in January 2010, and many team members stopped coming to practices shortly thereafter. But Gallegos and other team supporters kept at it, and the team is now stronger than ever.[5]

Right now, it's hard to imagine what Mexico would look like under "normal" and ideal circumstances. If all of the country's problems—those that are its own and those shared with the United States—had been solved yesterday, Alejo Garza Tamez would still be working his ranch. The killers of Marisela Escobedo and her daughter Rubi would be rotting away in a Mexican prison with no chance of escape. Gallegos would be coaching football for football's sake and not because he had to keep a group of Juárez teenagers from becoming the newest hit men for the Sinaloa Federation.

If all the country's problems were to be solved tomorrow, small businesses across the country would spring up and thrive without fear of being extorted, restaurants would fill their tables in the evenings, and nightclubs would attract patrons after dark. During elections, a majority of Mexicans would show up at the polls without fear and with confidence that their vote would actually mean something. The politicians they'd elect would be beholden to their constituents and not to the cartels who currently line their pockets and threaten their families.

North of the border, US residents would stop losing their sons and daughters, sisters and brothers, parents, friends, and coworkers to drug addiction. The biggest concern CBP inspectors would have would be college kids who lost their passports on Spring Break and were trying to reenter the United States without them. Border Patrol agents would face bigger threats from mountain lions and snakes than from drug smugglers trying to pick them off with automatic rifles. The ATF would be able to dedicate more time to tracking down guns used to commit crimes in America than those bought legally for transport to Mexico.

Our relationship with Mexico could flourish like never before. There would be no more cross-border finger-pointing for the causes of drug trafficking, weapons trafficking, human smuggling, and border violence. The tourism sector in Mexico would explode, and Americans would travel to Mexico for business and pleasure in numbers never seen before. Border towns on both sides would be reenergized with an unimpeded back-and-forth flow of visitors. Corruption, no longer being an issue in this ideal world, would cease to obstruct the sharing of intelligence between American and Mexican government and law enforcement agencies. Drug traffickers, human smugglers, terrorists, and criminals of all types would not view the southwest border as an option for surreptitiously entering the United States.

It's really amazing to think of the possibilities for both countries in a world without the Mexican drug wars. The situation becomes that much harder to swallow as a result of knowing that many of these things could possibly become reality if certain people could only make the right decisions. Mexico has such an incredibly long way to go. But Americans also need to take a hard look at domestic laws and policies at home that facilitate the effects of the drug war.

Current US drug policy regarding marijuana needs close scrutiny and possibly baby steps toward legalization to reduce cartel profits and illegal cultivation on public lands. Gun lobby–endorsed legislation needs to be repealed so that law enforcement agencies like the ATF can adequately identify and investigate straw buyers. Agencies like the Border Patrol and Forest Service need more trained officers and enough equipment to accomplish their respective counterdrug missions.

More important, US governments and law enforcement agencies at all levels need to more fully grasp the reality of the situation in Mexico and how it's impacting national security far beyond the southwest border. The debate over border-violence spillover is a thing of the past; not only does spillover exist, but it's affecting every corner of the country. If only for that reason, agencies charged with border security need to improve communication with each other, and federal border agencies need to speak up to their headquarters inside the Beltway. Otherwise, the policy makers in Washington will have a very narrow—and likely skewed—vision of what's going on along the US side of the border.

Just as we opened our eyes to the dark and disturbing world of international terrorism after 9/11, we need to start appreciating the threat posed to our national security by Mexican cartels operating right under our noses. Today cartels are the current major threat to our national security—tens of thousands of violent Mexican cartel members who are living and operating in our cities, communities, and public lands. We've spent over $365 billion on the war in Afghanistan since 2001, and almost 1,400 military members have lost their lives in the process. We've committed only $1.6 billion to the drug war in Mexico—only a few hundred million of which has actually been spent since 2007—and our military isn't allowed to step one foot in-country unless it's for training purposes.

We need to take a good look at our priorities when it comes to national security. Thousands of Americans die every year as a result of using drugs being peddled by Mexican cartels operating in our country. We also need to take into account the cost of interdicting even a small percentage of those drugs at the border, as well as the environmental toll that domestic marijuana cultivation is taking on our nation's landscape.

It's important that all Americans fully understand how the drug war in Mexico affects them, their communities, and the rest of their country. Maybe one day soon, your son or daughter will watch or read a news story about the brutal violence in Ciudad Juárez and make a comment to you about it, or vice versa. That's a prime opportunity to teach them about some of the real-life consequences of drug use. Or maybe you'll have a chance to talk to a policy maker in Washington about the impact of the drug war on our national forests, or the resource shortfall at some Border Patrol stations.

Until drug use ends in the United States and elsewhere in the world, Mexican drug cartels and the havoc they wreak will be a part of our national reality for some time to come. The Mexican government might never be able to bring the violence back down to manageable levels, and if the violence starts heading more fervently in our direction, we need to be fully prepared to deal with the consequences.

NOTES

INTRODUCTION

1. The name of the Border Patrol agent in this story was changed to protect his identity. All details are factual, based on an interview with an active US Border Patrol agent.

CHAPTER 1   THE WAR INSIDE MEXICO

1. Malcolm Beith, *The Last Narco: Inside the Hunt for El Chapo, the World's Most Wanted Drug Lord* (New York: Grove Press, 2010), Kindle edition.
2. Ibid.
3. Ibid.
4. "#701 Joaquin Guzmán Loera," *Forbes* (online), March 11, 2009, accessed October 5, 2010, http://rate.forbes.com/comments/CommentServlet?op=CPage&pageNumber=2&StoryURI=lists/2009/10/billionaires-2009-richest-people_Joaquin-Guzman-Loera_FS0Y.html&sourcename=story.
5. "#41 Joaquin Guzmán," *Forbes* (online), November 11, 2009, accessed October 5, 2010, http://www.forbes.com/lists/2009/20/power-09_Joaquin-Guzman_NQB6.html.
6. Beith, *Narco*.
7. David Luhnow and Jose de Cordoba, "The Drug Lord Who Got Away," *Wall Street Journal,* June 13, 2009, accessed October 3, 2010, http://online.wsj.com/article/SB124484177023110993.html.
8. Jen Phillips, "Mexico's New Super-Cartel Ups Violence in Power Play," *Mother Jones,* April 13, 2010, accessed October 3, 2010, http://motherjones.com/mojo/2010/04/evolution-mexicos-cartel-war.
9. Sylvia Longmire and John P. Longmire IV, "Redefining Terrorism: Why Mexican Drug Trafficking Is More Than Just Organized Crime," *Journal of Strategic Security* 1, no. 1 (November 2008).
10. Ibid.
11. At the time this manuscript went into production, kidnapping statistics for the City of Phoenix were being disputed. Police officials were being accused of inflating the numbers in order to receive additional grant money. Subsequently, they acknowledged there was a problem with the classification of abductions in their computer system that tracks them. Thus, the real number of drug-related abductions was more likely in the two hundreds, rather than 340.
12. Longmire and Longmire, *Journal of Strategic Security.*
13. Ibid.
14. Ibid.
15. Ibid.
16. Ibid.

17. Nick Miroff and William Booth, "Mexican Drug Cartels' Newest Weapon: Cold War–Era Grenades Made in U.S.," *Washington Post,* July 17 2010, accessed March 2, 2011, http://www.washington post.com/wp-dyn/content/article/2010/07/16/AR2010071606252.html.

18. Hannah Strange, "Mexican Drug Gang Killers Cut Out Victims' Hearts," *Times* (London), June 8, 2010, accessed September 6, 2010, http://www.timesonline.co.uk/tol/news/world/us_and _americas/article7145669.ece.

19. George W. Grayson, "La Familia: Another Deadly Mexican Syndicate," *E-Notes,* Foreign Policy Research Institute, February 2009, http://www.fpri.org/enotes/200901.grayson.lafamilia.html.

20. "Juarez Death Toll Is 3,000 So Far in 2010," UPI.com, December 15, 2010, accessed March 2, 2011, http://www.upi.com/Top_News/World-News/2010/12/15/Juarez-death-toll-is-3000-so-far-in-2010/UPI-42941292417150/.

21. Ibid.

22. Tracy Wilkinson, "Mexico Cartel Kills Four in Car Bombing," *Los Angeles Times,* July 17, 2010, accessed August 24, 2010, http://articles.latimes.com/2010/jul/17/world/la-fg-mexico-car-bomb-20100717.

23. "Chaotic Shootout in Mexican Tourist Paradise Leaves 6 Dead," eTurboNews.com, April 15, 2010, accessed September 5, 2010, http://www.eturbonews.com/15547/chaotic-shootout-mexican-tourist-paradise-leaves-6-dead?utm_source=feedburner&utm_medium=feed&utm _campaign=Feed%3A+eturbonews+%28eTurboNews%29&utm_content=Twitter.

24. "19 Patients Killed at Mexican Drug Rehab Facility," CNN (online), June 11, 2010, accessed September 5, 2010, http://edition.cnn.com/2010/WORLD/americas/06/11/mexico.patient.killings/index.html.

25. Oscar Villalba, "Officials Say Gunmen Killed 17 at Party in Mexico," AOL News (Associated Press), July 19, 2010, accessed September 6, 2010, http://www.aolnews.com/world/article/officials-say-gunmen-kill-17-at-party-in-mexico/19558786?icid=main%7Chtmlws-main-n%7Cdl1%7Clink4%7Chttp%3A%2F%2Fwww.aolnews.com%2Fworld%2Farticle%2Fofficials-say-gunmen-kill-17-at-party-in-mexico%2F19558786.

26. Francisco Roséndiz, "Nayarit: cancelan clases por miedo [Nayarit: Classes Canceled due to Fear]," *El Universal,* June 16, 2010, accessed September 6, 2010, http://www.eluniversal.com.mx/primera/35095.html.

27. Chris Hawley, "Mexico's Drug Violence Leads Schools to Teach Students to Dodge Bullets," *Arizona Republic,* July 8, 2010, accessed September 9, 2010, http://www.azcentral.com/arizonarepublic/news/articles/2010/07/08/20100708mexico-drug-violence-affecting-schools-and-students.html.

28. Tim Johnson, "Mexico's Drug Gangs Aim at New Target—Teachers," *Miami Herald,* December 11, 2010, accessed December 13, 2010, http://www.miamiherald.com/2010/12/11/1969153/mexicos-drug-gangs-aim-at-new.html#ixzz17wzyBnKG.

29. Dane Schiller, "Mexican Cartels Infiltrate Houston," *Houston Chronicle,* March 7, 2009, accessed July 12, 2010, http://www.chron.com/disp/story.mpl/metropolitan/6299436.html.

30. Amanda Lee Myers, "Chandler Beheading Raises Fears of Drug Violence," *Arizona Daily Star* (Associated Press), October 30, 2010, accessed December 15, 2010, http://azstarnet.com/news/local/crime/article_c593bd79-e887-59e5-868a-a8179cfe830b.html.

31. Pauline Arrillaga, "Grisly Slayings Bring Mexican Drug War to U.S.," Associated Press, April 19, 2009, accessed June 4, 2010, http://www.foxnews.com/story/0,2933,517078,00.html.

32. Michelle Wayland, "DA: Brutal Kidnapping, Murder Crew Dismantled," NBC San Diego (online), August 14, 2009, accessed May 6, 2010, http://www.nbcsandiego.com/news/local-beat/DA-Brutal-Kidnapping-Murder-Crew-Dismantled----53146782.html.

33. Mary Papenfuss, "Mexican Cartel Crew Indicted in San Diego Kidnap-Murders," Newser.com, August 14, 2009, accessed April 28, 2010, http://www.newser.com/story/66901/mexican-cartel-crew-indicted-in-san-diego-kidnap-murders.html.

34. Angela Kocherga, "Evidence Links U.S., Mexico Grenade Attacks," Texas Cable News, February 17, 2009, accessed October 5, 2010, http://www.txcn.com/sharedcontent/dws/txcn/houston/stories/khou090212_mh_mexico_grenade_attacks.c16c1da.html.

35. Brady McCombs, "Focus in Krentz Killing on Suspect in US," *Arizona Daily Star,* May 3, 2010, accessed May 14, 2010, http://azstarnet.com/news/local/border/article_35ef6e3a-5632-5e58-abe7-e7697ee2f0d5.html.

36. Edwin Mora, "U.S. Alleges Mexican Drug Cartel Rented Apartments in U.S. to Recruit Young Americans," CNSNews.com, January 11, 2011, accessed January 19, 2011, http://www.cnsnews .com/news/article/federal-court-hear-case-mexican-drug-car.

37. Kristina Davis, "San Diego's Crime Rate Fell Again in '09, Stats Show," *San Diego Union-Tribune,* January 28, 2010, accessed April 14, 2010, http://www.signonsandiego.com/news/2010/jan/28/ citys-crime-rate-fell-again-in-09-stats-show/.

38. Dennis Wagner. "Violence Is Not Up on Arizona Border Despite Mexican Drug War," *Arizona Republic,* May 2, 2010, accessed May 14, 2010, http://www.azcentral.com/news/articles/2010/ 05/02/20100502arizona-border-violence-mexico.html.

CHAPTER 2   DRUG TRAFFICKING IN THE TWENTY-FIRST CENTURY

1. *National Drug Threat Assessment 2010,* National Drug Intelligence Center, US Department of Justice, February 2010, accessed April 18, 2010, http://www.justice.gov/ndic/pubs38/38661/ index.htm.

2. "Phoenix Bars Provide Recruiting Ground for Cartels, Authorities Say," FOX News (online), August 27, 2010, accessed October 5, 2010, http://www.foxnews.com/us/2010/08/27/phoenix-bars-provide-recruiting-ground-cartels-authorities-say/.

3. *Border Crossing/Entry Data,* US Bureau of Transportation Statistics public website, accessed March 29, 2010, http://www.TranStats.bts.gov/BorderCrossing.aspx.

4. *CBP Border Wait Times,* US Customs and Border Protection public website, accessed March 29, 2010, http://apps.cbp.gov/bwt/.

5. Brian Fraga, "Sophisticated Hidden Vehicle Compartment Reveals Tricks of Drug Trade," *Standard-Times,* February 20, 2009, accessed April 2, 2010, http://www.southcoasttoday.com/apps/ pbcs.dll/article?AID=/20090220/NEWS/902200346.

6. Sean Holstege, "More Drug Tunnels Being Found on Border," *Arizona Republic,* November 25, 2008, accessed April 22, 2010, http://www.azcentral.com/news/articles/2008/11/25/20081125 tunnels1125.html.

7. "U.S., Mexican Authorities Investigating Cross-Border Tunnel near San Diego," US Immigration and Customs Enforcement public website, December 2, 2009, accessed May 18, 2010, http:// www.ice.gov/pi/nr/0912/091202sandiego.htm.

8. "DEA Intel Aids in Seizure of Fully-Operational Narco Submarine in Ecuador," DEA Press Release, Office of Public Affairs, July 3, 2010, accessed October 5, 2010, http://www.justice.gov/ dea/pubs/pressrel/pr070310.html.

9. Robin Emmott, "Mexico Finds Cocaine Haul Hidden in Frozen Sharks," Reuters, June 17, 2009, accessed March 2, 2011, http://www.reuters.com/article/2009/06/17/us-mexico-drugs-idUSN1631193420090617.

10. "Border Patrol Arrests Surfers Towing Marijuana-Loaded Surfboard," CBP News Release, June 19, 2009, accessed March 2, 2011, http://www.cbp.gov/xp/cgov/newsroom/news_releases/ archives/2009_news_releases/june_2009/06192009_5.xml.

11. George W. Grayson, "Death of Arturo Beltrán Leyva: What Does It Mean for Mexico's Drug War?," *E-Notes,* Foreign Policy Research Institute, February 2010, accessed October 5, 2010, http://www.fpri.org/enotes/201002.grayson.beltranleyva.html.

12. Tim Johnson, "Mexican Marijuana Smugglers Turn to Ultralight Aircraft," McClatchy Newspapers, June 4, 2010, accessed June 16, 2010, http://www.mcclatchydc.com/2010/06/04/95370/ mexican-marijuana-smugglers-turn.html.

13. "Southwest Border Region—Drug Transportation and Homeland Security Issues," *National Drug Threat Assessment 2008,* National Drug Intelligence Center, US Department of Justice, accessed October 5, 2010, http://www.justice.gov/ndic/pubs25/25921/border.htm.

14. "35 Accused of Shipping Drugs from Juarez to Denver," FOX News, November 8, 2010, accessed December 15, 2010, http://www.foxnews.com/us/2010/11/08/accused-shipping-drugs-juarez-denver/. As of the date this book went to press, this case has not been resolved.

15. *National Drug Threat Assessment 2010,* National Drug Intelligence Center.

16. Ben Conery, "Mexican Drug Cartels 'Hide in Plain Sight' in U.S.," *Washington Times,* June 7, 2009, accessed June 6, 2010, http://www.washingtontimes.com/news/2009/jun/07/mexican-drug-cartels-hide-in-plain-sight-in-us/.

17. Ibid.

18. National Clandestine Laboratory Register, US Drug Enforcement Administration, accessed January 19, 2011, http://www.justice.gov/dea/seizures/index.html.

19. "Potent Mexican Crystal Meth on the Rise as States Curb Domestic Meth Production," Partnership for a Drug-Free America, January 25, 2006, http://www.drugfree.org/Portal/DrugIssue/ News/Potent_Mexican_Crystal_Meth_on_the_Rise.

20. Larry Hartstein, "Agents Raid Huge Lawrenceville Meth Lab as Part of Strike on Cartel," *Atlanta Journal-Constitution,* October 22, 2009, accessed May 15, 2010, http://www.ajc.com/news/ gwinnett/agents-raid-huge-lawrenceville-169790.html.

CHAPTER 3   FROM MEXICO TO MAIN STREET: AN ILLEGAL DRUG'S JOURNEY INTO AMERICA

1. Jesus Bucardo et al., "Historical Trends in the Production and Consumption of Illicit Drugs in Mexico: Implications for the Prevention of Blood Borne Infections," National Institutes of Health, April 1, 2005, accessed November 2, 2010, http://www.ncbi.nlm.nih.gov/pmc/articles/ PMC2196212/.

2. "From Flowers to Heroin," Central Intelligence Agency, accessed November 3, 2010, http:// www.erowid.org/plants/poppy/poppy_article2.shtml.

3. "Afghanistan Identifies Cutting Agents for Heroin," World Drug Report 2009 Series, United Nations Office on Drugs and Crime, accessed November 5, 2010, http://www.unodc.org/unodc/ en/frontpage/2009/June/afghanistan-identifies-cutting-agents-for-heroin.html.

4. Personal interview with Phil Jordan, former Drug Enforcement Agency Special Agent in Charge (El Paso) and former Director of the El Paso Intelligence Center, conducted October 28, 2010.

5. *West Texas High Intensity Drug Trafficking Area Drug Market Analysis 2009,* National Drug Intelligence Center, March 2009, accessed November 5, 2010, http://www.justice.gov/ndic/ pubs32/32792/production.htm#Transportation.

6. *National Drug Threat Assessment 2010,* National Drug Intelligence Center, US Department of Justice, February 2010, accessed November 12, 2010, http://www.justice.gov/ndic/pubs38/38661/ index.htm.

7. "Killings, Kin and Luck Helped Drug Lord," *Albuquerque Journal* (undated), accessed November 12, 2010, http://www.abqjournal.com/news/drugs/6drug3-3.htm.

8. *DEA History, 1975–1980,* US Department of Justice Publications, accessed November 12, 2010, http://www.justice.gov/dea/pubs/history/1975-1980.html.

9. *Chicago HIDTA Drug Market Analysis 2010,* National Drug Intelligence Center, April 2010, accessed November 6, 2010, http://www.justice.gov/ndic/pubs40/40385/product.htm #Transportation.

10. "The Almighty Latin Kings Nation," Know Gangs website, accessed November 6, 2010, http:// www.knowgangs.com/gang_resources/profiles/kings/.

11. *Chicago HIDTA,* National Drug Intelligence Center.

CHAPTER 4   THE BIGGEST ARMED FORCE SOUTH OF THE BORDER

1. NRA/ILA Firearms Laws for Arizona, NRA Institute for Legislative Action (AZ Rev. Statutes §§12-714, 13-2904, 13-3101, 13-3102, 13-3105, 13-31-07, 13-3109, 31-3112, 17-301, 17-301.1, 17-305, 17-312), February 2006.

2. "Background Checks and Waiting Periods for Firearms Purchases: State-by-State Breakdown," Brady Campaign to Prevent Gun Violence, accessed April 12, 2010, http://www.bradycampaign .org/facts/issues/?page=waitxstate.

3. NRA/ILA Firearms Laws for New Mexico, NRA Institute for Legislative Action (NM Stat. Ann. §§ 17-2-12; 17-2-33 through 35; 29-19-1 through 12; 30-3-8; 30-7-1 through 16; 32A-2-33), July 2006.

4. NRA/ILA Firearms Laws for Texas, NRA Institute for Legislative Action (TX Penal Code § 46.01 et seq. and TX Govt. Code § 411.171 et seq.), January 2008.

5. NRA/ILA Firearms Laws for Texas, NRA.

6. State of California Penal Code §§ 12001.5, 12020(a)(1).

7. State of California Penal Code § 12220.

8. State of California Penal Code § 12280.

9. State of California Penal Code §§ 12320, 12321.

10. State of California Penal Code § 12072(a).

11. Definitions of weapons and specific gun restrictions are detailed in the California Department of Justice's brochure *California Firearms Laws 2007,* http://ag.ca.gov/firearms/forms/pdf/Cfl2007 .pdf.

12. "Background Checks and Waiting Periods," Brady Campaign.

13. Weapons trace data provided by the ATF indicated that, of the roughly 7,500 weapons provided to them by the Mexican government for tracing in fiscal year 2008, 90 percent of the guns were traced to a person who bought that firearm in the United States—what's known as a "successful trace." The figure dropped by 10 percent in May 2010 when President Calderón said that of the seventy-five thousand firearms Mexico seized in the past three years, an estimated 80 percent came from America.

14. The media don't report that an *unsuccessful* firearms trace can still reveal *where* the firearm was physically purchased. To many, this statistic is more significant than the facts surrounding the actual gun buyers. However, publicly available statistics only tally *successful* traces. That means there is no data about how many additional weapons seized in Mexico that were submitted for tracing led ATF agents to a US point of sale without identifying an actual buyer.

15. Sylvia Longmire, "Making Sense of the Southbound Weapons Flow to Mexico," MexiData.info, August 17, 2009, accessed April 6, 2010, http://mexidata.info/id2366.html.

16. Brian Ross et al., "ATF: Phoenix Gun Dealer Supplied Mexican Cartels," ABC News, May 6, 2008, accessed April 12, 2010, http://abcnews.go.com/Blotter/story?id=4796380&page=1.

17. Joel Millman, "U.S. Gun Trial Echoes in Drug-Torn Mexico," *Wall Street Journal,* March 2, 2009, accessed October 6, 2010, http://online.wsj.com/article/SB123595012797004865 .html.

18. Joel Millman, "Case Against Gun-Store Owner Dismissed," *Wall Street Journal,* March 20, 2009, accessed April 15, 2010, http://online.wsj.com/article/SB123750753535390327.html. As of the date this book went to press, information about whether the civil suit had been resolved was unavailable.

19. Ray Stern, "George Iknadosian, Accused of Supplying Mexican Cartels with Guns, Sues Arizona, City of Phoenix and Terry Goddard," *Phoenix New Times,* March 24, 2010, accessed October 6, 2010, http://blogs.phoenixnewtimes.com/valleyfever/2010/03/george_iknadosian_accused_of _s.php.

20. "Brothers Plead Guilty to Unlawful Gun Trafficking," Press Release, US Department of Justice, November 25, 2009, accessed April 5, 2010, http://www.atf.gov/press/releases/2009/11/112509- sf-brothers-plead-guilty.html.

21. Ibid.

22. Drew Griffin and John Murgatroyd, "Smugglers' Deadly Cargo, Cop-Killing Guns," CNN.com, March 26, 2008, http://www.cnn.com/2008/WORLD/americas/03/26/gun.smuggling/index .html.

23. Zeta Online, "CAF asesina a military," http://www.zetatijuana.com/html/Edicion1803/Principal .html.

24. United States of America v. Uvaldo Salazar-Lopez, Criminal Complaint, US District Court of Nevada, Case 2:09-mj-00002-LRL-LRL, May 1, 2009, accessed through PACER online.

25. "U.S. Guns Pour into Mexico," *Arizona Republic,* January 16, 2007, accessed March 4, 2011, http://www.azcentral.com/arizonarepublic/news/articles/0116americanguns0116.html.

26. "Review of ATF's Project Gunrunner," US Department of Justice, Office of the Inspector General, Evaluations and Inspections Division, November 2010, accessed March 4, 2011, http:// www.justice.gov/oig/reports/ATF/e1101.pdf.

27. Sari Horwitz and James Grimaldi, "Firearms Watchdog on Short Leash," *Washington Post,* October 26, 2010, accessed November 26, 2010, http://www.washingtonpost.com/wp-dyn/content/ article/2010/10/25/AR2010102505588.html?sid=ST2010102600379.

CHAPTER 5   THE SECOND-BIGGEST MONEYMAKER FOR CARTELS: KIDNAPPING

1. Lawrence Mower, "Police Search for Boy Taken from Home," *Las Vegas Review-Journal,* October 16, 2008, accessed May 2, 2010, http://www.lvrj.com/news/31095764.html.

2. Nicholas Riccardi, "Kidnapped Boy Is Safe," *Los Angeles Times,* October 20, 2008, accessed May 6, 2010, http://articles.latimes.com/2008/oct/20/nation/na-kidnap20.

3. Mower, *Las Vegas Review-Journal.*

4. "Police Lift Amber Alert for Abducted Las Vegas Boy," CNN Online, October 18, 2008, accessed October 6, 2010, http://www.cnn.com/2008/CRIME/10/18/nevada.boy.kidnapped/index.html.

5. Sandra Dibble, "Three Arrested in Rosarito Beach Kidnapping, Killing," *San Diego Union-Tribune,* April 15, 2010, accessed October 7, 2010, http://www.signon-san-diegos.com/news/2010/apr/15/three-arrested-rosarito-beach-kidnapping-killing/.

6. Names have been changed and identifying details have been omitted in this true story to protect individuals' identities.

7. Gustavo Ruiz, "20 Kidnapped in Acapulco Had No Criminal Records," Associated Press, October 5, 2010, accessed October 6, 2010, http://www.google.com/hostednews/ap/article/ALeqM5gMi5B2USfJStXxfqgWWr2xjRYpOgD9ILSLM01?docId=D9ILSLM01.

8. Lauren Villagran, "Probes by Authorities Sputter as Violence in Mexico Mounts," *Dallas Morning News,* October 7, 2010, accessed October 7, 2010, http://www.dallasnews.com/shared content/dws/news/world/stories/DN-mexcrime_07int.ART.State.Edition1.488b5bf.html.

9. Eve Conant and Arian Campos-Flores, "The Enemy Within: Cartel-Related Violence Has Moved Well Beyond Border Towns," *Newsweek,* March 14, 2009, accessed April 22, 2010, http://www.newsweek.com/id/189246/page/1.

10. "McCain Says Phoenix Is the Second Kidnapping Capital in the World," Politifact.com, accessed January 20, 2011, http://politifact.com/texas/statements/2010/jun/28/john-mccain/mccain-says-phoenix-second-kidnapping-capital-worl/.

11. In early March 2011, Phoenix Police Department officials conceded that the city's kidnapping statistics had been inflated in order to obtain more federal grant money. There was also significant confusion over how kidnapping cases were classified by officers taking reports. The real number was estimated to be in the 200s, rather than the 368 originally reported for 2008. At the time of this book's publication, the department's process for accounting for kidnapping cases was being reviewed.

12. "Trial: Kidnapping Victim 'Cooked' in Mexico," KGBT News, January 20, 2010, accessed October 7, 2010, http://www.valleycentral.com/news/story.aspx?id=404432.

13. "Mexican Police Rescue Man Kidnapped in Texas," *Latin American Herald Tribune,* May 31, 2010, accessed June 12, 2010, http://laht.com/article.asp?CategoryId=14091&ArticleId=348190.

CHAPTER 6 THE MEXICAN PEOPLE

1. Dudley Althaus, "Mexico Confronting a Drug Addiction Epidemic," *Houston Chronicle,* October 5, 2009, accessed October 7, 2010, http://www.chron.com/disp/story.mpl/metropolitan/6652182.html.

2. Chris Hawley, "Drug Addiction Soars in Mexico," *USA Today,* July 22, 2008, accessed October 7, 2010, http://www.usatoday.com/news/world/2008-07-22-mexaddicts_N.htm.

3. Ibid.

4. Ken Ellingwood, "Mexico Grapples with Drug Addiction," *Los Angeles Times,* October 15, 2008, accessed October 8, 2010, http://www.latimes.com/news/nationworld/world/la-fg-mex addict15-2008oct15,0,4364637.story.

5. Rocío Gallegos, "Se han ido 230 mil de Juárez por la violencia [230,000 Have Left Juárez Because of Violence]," *Vanguardia Informativa,* August 26, 2010, accessed September 19, 2010, http://www.vanguardiainformativa.com/index.php/notas-rotativas/2454-se-han-ido-230-mil-de-juarez-por-la-violencia.

6. Adriana Gómez Licón, "Juárez Cancels Sept. 16 Celebration," *El Paso Times,* August 30, 2010, accessed September 13, 2010, http://www.elpasotimes.com/ci_15935968?source=most_viewed.

7. "Mexicans Continue Support for Drug War," Pew Global Attitudes Project, Pew Research Center, August 12, 2010, accessed September 12, 2010, http://pewglobal.org/2010/08/12/mexicans-continue-support-for-drug-war/.

8. Nicholas Casey, "Mexico Under Siege," *Wall Street Journal,* August 19, 2010, accessed March 4, 2011, http://online.wsj.com/article/SB10001424052748704557704575437762646209270.html.

9. Ibid.

10. Lourdes Cardenas, "Chihuahua and Its Disenchantment with Elections," *El Paso Times* (blog), June 15, 2010, accessed September 18, 2010, http://elpasotimes.typepad.com/mexico/2010/06/chihuahua-and-its-disenchantment-with-elections.html.

11. Mica Rosenberg, "Mexico Drug Cartels Use Gory Videos to Spread Fear," Reuters, August 4, 2010, accessed September 6, 2010, http://www.reuters.com/article/idUSTRE6734E720100804.

12. José Gil Olmos, "The Mexican *Ninis*," *Proceso* (Mexico), February 3, 2010, accessed November 10, 2010, http://bit.ly/g9A0Ca.

13. Ioan Grillo, "Mexico's Lost Youth: Generation Narco," *Time* (online), November 7, 2010, accessed November 10, 2010, http://www.time.com/time/world/article/0,8599,2028912,00.html.

14. Matt Sanchez, "In Mexico, Journalists Are Becoming an Endangered Species," FOX News (online), August 18, 2010, accessed September 6, 2010, http://www.foxnews.com/world/2010/08/18/mexico-journalists-increasingly-endangered-species/.

15. Ibid.

16. Ibid.

17. Personal interview with "Jose" (name changed), conducted via e-mail on September 28, 2010.

18. Ibid.

19. Personal interview with "Sonia" (name changed), conducted via e-mail on September 30, 2010.

20. "Migrantes Pierden 150 mdd por Extorsiones: PRI," *El Universal,* December 12, 2010, accessed December 16, 2010, http://www.eluniversal.com.mx/notas/729900.html.

21. Karl Penhall, "Brave Few Break Mexico Drug War's Code of Silence," CNN Online, June 21, 2010, accessed September 16, 2010, http://edition.cnn.com/2010/WORLD/americas/06/21/mexico.drug.war/index.html.

22. "Ejecutan a Tres Los 'Mata Zetas,'" *El Universal,* June 19, 2009, accessed March 4, 2011, http://www.eluniversal.com.mx/nacion/169098.html.

23. "Video en Internet Confirma Existencia de Grupo 'Mata Zetas,'" *Terra,* July 2, 2009, accessed March 4, 2011, http://www.terra.com.mx/articulo.aspx?articuloId=842793&ref=1.

24. Sylvia Longmire, "The More Deadly Side of Growing Vigilantism in Mexico," MexiData.info, November 2, 2009, accessed September 16, 2010, http://www.mexidata.info/id2451.html.

25. "Is the Fuse Lit? Uprising/Lynching in Chihuahua," *Chihuahua News,* September 22, 2010.

26. Ibid.

CHAPTER 7   FELIPE CALDERÓN'S PLAN TO SAVE MEXICO

1. "Profile: Felipe Calderón," BBC News, September 5, 2006, accessed November 16, 2010, http://news.bbc.co.uk/2/hi/americas/5318434.stm.

2. Ibid.

3. "Mexican Military Losing Drug War Support," MSNBC.com (Associated Press), July 26, 2010, accessed September 20, 2010, http://www.msnbc.msn.com/id/25851906/.

4. Ibid.

5. Steve Fainaru and William Booth, "Mexican Army Using Torture to Battle Drug Traffickers, Rights Groups Say," *Washington Post,* July 9, 2009, accessed December 16, 2010, http://www.washingtonpost.com/wp-dyn/content/article/2009/07/08/AR2009070804197.html.

6. "Militarization of Mexico by 'Common Citizen,'" *Borderland Beat* (blog), April 13, 2010, accessed September 16, 2010, http://www.borderlandbeat.com/2010/04/militarization-of-mexico-by-common.html#comments.

7. Tracy Wilkinson, "Mexico Army Handling of Civilian Death Inquiries Questioned," *Los Angeles Times,* May 5, 2010, accessed September 2, 2010, http://articles.latimes.com/2010/may/05/world/la-fg-mexico-dead-civilians-20100505.

8. "PRI impulsa ley contra excesos militares [PRI Pushes Law Against Military Abuses]," *El Universal,* September 8, 2010, accessed September 18, 2010, http://www.eluniversal.com.mx/notas/707353.html.

9. "Mexico Sacks 10% of Police Force in Corruption Probe," BBC News (UK online), August 30, 2010, accessed September 15, 2010, http://www.bbc.co.uk/news/world-latin-america-11132589.

10. Chris Hawley, "Drug Cartels Outmatch, Outgun Mexican Forces," *Republic* Mexico City Bureau, *Borderland Beat* (blog), June 16, 2010, accessed September 12, 2010, http://www.borderlandbeat.com/2010/06/drug-cartels-outmatch-outgun-mexican.html.

11. "Data: Limited Progress in Vetting Police Forces," *Reforma* (online), September 19, 2010, accessed September 20, 2010.

12. Rodrigo Vera, "La Policía Federál pide auxilio [The Federal Police Asks for Help]," *Proceso* (online), August 2, 2010, accessed September 18, 2010, http://www.proceso.com.mx/rv/mod Home/detalleExclusiva/81985.

13. Jorge Ramos et al., "Acuerdan una sola policía por entidad [Agreement on One Unified Police Force]," *El Universal,* June 4, 2010, accessed September 22, 2010, http://www.eluniversal.com .mx/notas/685409.html.

14. "Alcaldes de la ZMG rechazan el mando único en la policía [ZMG Mayors Reject Plan for Unified Police Force]," *Milenio* (online), June 24, 2010, accessed September 19, 2010, http://www .milenio.com/node/471947.

15. Chris Hawley and Sergio Colache, "Mexico Cracks Down on Police Corruption," *USA Today,* February 6, 2008, accessed March 4, 2011, http://www.policeone.com/international/ articles/1658569-Mexico-cracks-down-on-police-corruption/.

16. "Mexico's Criminal Justice System: A Guide for U.S. Citizens Arrested in Mexico," US Consulate in Tijuana, accessed on November 16, 2010, http://tijuana.usconsulate.gov/root/pdfs/telegal criminalguide.pdf.

17. Brady McCombs, "U.S. to Aid Mexico's Judicial Reforms," *Arizona Daily Star,* September 27, 2010, accessed on November 16, 2010, http://azstarnet.com/news/local/border/ article_7025a974-11b4-5544-b646-6a1f9e7215f7.html.

18. David Luhnow, "Presumption of Guilt," *Wall Street Journal,* October 17, 2009, accessed March 4, 2011, http://online.wsj.com/article/SB10001424052748704322004574475492261338318 .html.

19. Ken Ellingwood and Tracy Wilkinson, "Corruption Sweep in Mexico's Michoacan Unravels in the Courts," *Los Angeles Times,* December 12, 2010, accessed December 15, 2010, http://www .latimes.com/news/nationworld/world/la-fg-mexico-michoacan-20101212,0,6080015.story.

20. Ibid.

21. "Resignation in Mexican Missing Girl Paulette Case," BBC News, May 26, 2010, accessed November 16, 2010, http://www.bbc.co.uk/news/10168243. The result of this case was not known at the time this book went to press.

22. Ibid.

23. Tracy Wilkinson, "Mexico Sees Inside Job in Prison Break," *Los Angeles Times,* May 18, 2009, accessed November 16, 2010, http://articles.latimes.com/2009/may/18/world/fg-mexico-prison18.

24. McCombs, *Arizona Daily Star.*

25. Miguel Sarré, "Mexico's Judicial Reform and Long-Term Challenges," presented at the Policy Forum: U.S.-Mexico Security Cooperation and the Merida Initiative, convened by the Mexico Institute of the Woodrow Wilson Center for International Scholars, Capitol Building, Washington, DC, May 9, 2008.

26. Tracy Wilkinson, "Mexico Moves Quietly to Decriminalize Minor Drug Use," *Los Angeles Times,* June 21, 2009, accessed September 14, 2010, http://articles.latimes.com/2009/jun/21/world/ fg-mexico-decriminalize21.

27. Jim DeMint, "Finish the Border Fence Now," *Human Events,* May 17, 2010, accessed September 27, 2010, http://www.humanevents.com/article.php?id=37025.

28. "Mexico Still Indignant Over Wall," *Taipei Times* (Associated Press), December 22, 2005, accessed March 4, 2011, http://www.taipeitimes.com/News/world/archives/2005/12/22/2003285521.

29. "A Fence for the Southern Border of . . . Mexico," *The Blaze,* September 22, 2010, accessed on November 16, 2010, http://www.theblaze.com/stories/a-fence-for-the-southern-border-of-mexico/.

30. "How Mexico Treats Its Illegal Aliens," Creators.com, accessed on November 16, 2010, http:// www.creators.com/conservative/michelle-malkin/how-mexico-treats-its-illegal-aliens.html.

31. Chris Hawley, "Activists Blast Mexico's Immigration Law," *USA Today,* May 25, 2010, accessed November 16, 2010, http://www.usatoday.com/news/world/2010-05-25-mexico-migrants_N .htm.

32. "U.S. Foreign Economic and Military Aid Programs: 1980 to 2007," US Census Bureau website, accessed September 14, 2010, http://www.census.gov/compendia/statab/2010/tables/10s1262.pdf.

33. "Mérida Initiative: The United States Has Provided Counternarcotics and Anticrime Support but Needs Better Performance Measures," US Government Accountability Office (GAO-10-837), July 21, 2010, accessed September 20, 2010, http://www.gao.gov/products/GAO-10-837.

CHAPTER 8   THE FIGHT TO STOP CARTELS NORTH OF THE BORDER

1. The name of the Border Patrol agent in this story was changed to protect his identity. All details are factual, based on an interview with an active US Border Patrol agent.

2. "This Is CBP," US Customs and Border Protection public website, accessed May 12, 2010, http://www.cbp.gov/xp/cgov/about/mission/cbp_is.xml.

3. "Who We Are and What We Do," US Border Patrol public website, accessed May 12, 2010, http://www.cbp.gov/xp/cgov/border_security/border_patrol/who_we_are.xml.

4. "Hereford Ranch Hand Accused of Smuggling," KSWT13 News (online), December 18, 2010, accessed December 19, 2010, http://www.kswt.com/Global/story.asp?S=13708128. The result of this case was not known at the time this book went to press.

5. "ICE Operation in Florida Nets 95 Arrests," USA Today, December 13, 2010, accessed December 19, 2010, http://www.miamiherald.com/2010/12/13/1971290/ice-operation-in-florida-nets.html.

6. "Francisco Javier Arellano-Felix Sentenced to Life in Prison," Imperial Valley News, November 6, 2007, accessed December 19, 2010, http://imperialvalleynews.com/index.php?option=com_content&task=view&id=277&Itemid=2.

7. "DEA Mission Statement," Drug Enforcement Administration public website, accessed May 12, 2010, http://www.justice.gov/dea/agency/mission.htm.

8. "Strategic Plan—Fiscal Years 2010–2016," Bureau of Alcohol, Tobacco, Firearms, and Explosives public website, accessed May 13, 2010, http://www.atf.gov/publications/general/strategic-plan/.

9. Alicia Caldwell, "Mexico Army Likely Part of Border Incident (Says Hudspeth County Sheriff)," Free Republic (Associated Press), January 27, 2006, accessed December 21, 2010, http://www.freerepublic.com/focus/f-news/1566642/posts.

10. "Homeland Security Support," Joint Task Force North public website, accessed May 18, 2010, http://www.jtfn.northcom.mil/subpages/homeland_s.html.

11. Maria Recio, "Obama May Send Guard to Help Stem Border Violence," Houston Chronicle, March 12, 2009, accessed May 20, 2010, http://www.chron.com/disp/story.mpl/nation/6306226.html.

12. "Border Enforcement Security Task Forces," US Immigration and Customs Enforcement public website, November 3, 2009, accessed May 18, 2010, http://www.ice.gov/pi/news/factsheets/080226best_fact_sheet.htm.

13. "El Paso Intelligence Center," US Drug Enforcement Agency public website, accessed May 18, 2010, http://www.justice.gov/dea/programs/epic.htm.

14. The names of the two Border Patrol agents in this story were changed to protect their identities. All details are factual, based on an interview with an active US Border Patrol agent.

15. "ATF, ICE Update Partnership Agreement to Maximize Investigative Efforts," Press Release, US Immigration and Customs Enforcement, June 30, 2010, accessed November 19, 2010, http://www.ice.gov/news/releases/0906/090630albuquerque.htm.

16. Michael Isikoff, "U.S. Bid to Stem Flow of Weapons to Mexico Cartels Misfires," MSNBC.com, September 21, 2010, accessed January 21, 2011, http://www.msnbc.msn.com/id/39282887/ns/us_news-crime_and_courts/.

17. Rick Jervis, "Arrests of Border Agents on the Rise," USA Today, April 24, 2009, accessed November 19, 2010, http://www.usatoday.com/news/nation/2009-04-23-borderagent_N.htm.

18. Ibid.

19. Ceci Connolly, "Woman's Links to Mexican Drug Cartel a Saga of Corruption on U.S. Side of Border," Washington Post, September 25, 2010, accessed November 19, 2010, http://www.washingtonpost.com/wp-dyn/content/article/2010/09/11/AR2010091105687.html?tid=nn_twitter.

20. Richard Marosi, "U.S. Border Inspector Charged with Drug Conspiracy," *Los Angeles Times,* September 25, 2010, accessed November 19, 2010, http://www.latimes.com/news/local/la-me-corruption-20100925,0,6470787.story.

21. Richard Marosi, "U.S. Border Officer Accused of Accepting Bribes to Allow Illegal Immigrants to Cross Border," *Los Angeles Times,* September 30, 2010, accessed November 19, 2010, http://latimesblogs.latimes.com/lanow/2010/09/us-border-officer-accused-of-accepting-bribes-to-allow-illegal-immigrants-to-cross-border.html.

22. Connolly, *Washington Post.*

23. Julia Preston, "Officers on Border Team Up to Quell Violence," *New York Times,* March 25, 2010, accessed November 19, 2010, http://www.nytimes.com/2010/03/26/world/americas/26border .html?_r=1&src=tptw.

CHAPTER 9   MARIJUANA GROWERS IN THE UNITED STATES

1. John Gettman, "Marijuana Production in the United States (2006)," *The Bulletin of Cannabis Reform,* December 2006, accessed May14, 2010, http://www.drugscience.org/Archive/bcr2/ MJCropReport_2006.pdf.

2. Cynthia Schweigert, "Growing Marijuana on Public Land," WKBT.com, May 13, 2010, accessed November 22, 2010, http://www.wkbt.com/global/story.asp?s=12473429.

3. "National Forests Urge Awareness of Drug Operations," *The Daily Reporter,* November 22, 2010, accessed November 24, 2010, http://www.thedailyreporter.com/newsnow/x96441365/ National-forests-urge-awareness-of-drug-operations.

4. "Sheriff: Mexican Cartels Growing Pot in Georgia Parks," WSBTV.com, November 9, 2010, accessed November 24, 2010, http://www.wsbtv.com/news/25675125/detail.html.

5. "State of Kentucky Profile of Drug Indicators," Office of National Drug Control Policy, Drug Policy Information Clearinghouse, February 2008, accessed March 5, 2011, http://www.white housedrugpolicy.gov/statelocal/ky/ky.pdf.

6. Russell Jones, "Marijuana Found Growing at Fort Smith Park," KFSM5 News Online, June 2, 2010, accessed June 16, 2010, http://www.kfsm.com/news/kfsm-news-marijuana-found-at-city-park,0,2583938.story.

7. Sean Markey, "Marijuana War Smolders on U.S. Public Lands," *National Geographic News,* November 4, 2003, accessed November 20, 2010, http://news.nationalgeographic.com/ news/2003/11/1103_031104_marijuana.html.

8. Katherine Peters, "Losing Ground," *Government Executive,* December 1, 2010, accessed November 20, 2010, http://www.govexec.com/story_page.cfm?filepath=/features/1203/1203s2.htm.

9. Markey, *National Geographic News.*

10. Lt. John Nores Jr. and James A. Swan, *War in the Woods: Combating Drug Cartels on Our Public Lands,* excerpted in *Crime Magazine,* November 14, 2010, accessed November 20, 2010, http:// www.crimemagazine.com/war-woods-combating-marijuana-cartels-our-public-lands.

11. Alicia Caldwell and Manuel Valdes, "Public Lands Sprouting Marijuana Farms," *San Francisco Chronicle,* March 14, 2010, accessed November 20, 2010, http://articles.sfgate.com/2010-03-14/news/18831119_1_drug-gangs-marijuana-farms-mexican-growers/2.

12. Nores and Swan, *War in the Woods.*

13. Phil Taylor, "Cartels Turn U.S. Forests into Marijuana Plantations, Creating Toxic Mess," E&E Publishing, July 30, 2009, accessed November 21, 2010, http://www.eenews.net/public/Land letter/2009/07/30/1.

14. "Operation Trident Results in Seizure of Thousands of Marijuana Plants Worth More Than $1.7 Billion," Press Release, US Drug Enforcement Administration, August 11, 2010, accessed November 21, 2010, http://www.justice.gov/dea/pubs/states/newsrel/2010/sanfran081110.html.

15. Markey, *National Geographic News.*

16. Taylor, E&E Publishing.

17. Steve Fainaru and William Booth, "Cartels Face an Economic Battle," *Washington Post,* October 7, 2009, accessed November 22, 2010, http://www.washingtonpost.com/wp-dyn/content/ article/2009/10/06/AR2009100603847.html?sid=ST2009100603892.

18. Ibid.

19. Sylvia Longmire, "Mexican Cartels Are Taking Over U.S. Marijuana Production," MexiData .info, October 19, 2009, accessed May 10, 2010, http://www.mexidata.info/id2437.html.

20. Taylor, E&E Publishing.

21. Scott Imler, "Medical Marijuana in California: A History," *Los Angeles Times,* March 6, 2009, accessed November 22, 2010, http://www.latimes.com/features/health/la-oew-gutwillig-imler6-2009mar06,0,2951626.story.

22. 21 U.S.C. Chapter 13, *Drug Abuse Prevention and Control,* February 1, 2010, accessed November 22, 2010, http://uscode.house.gov/download/pls/21C13.txt.

23. "NorCal Cities Bring Pot Growing into the Light," FOX News (Associated Press), November 20, 2010, accessed November 23, 2010, http://www.foxnews.com/us/2010/11/20/norcal-cities-bring-pot-growing-light/.

24. Patrick Stack and Clare Suddath, "A Brief History of Medical Marijuana," *Time,* October 21, 2009, accessed November 22, 2010, http://www.time.com/time/health/article/0,8599,1931247,00.html.

25. Ibid.

26. Mica Rosenberg, "Mexico Marijuana Growers Learn New Tricks from U.S.," Reuters, December 14, 2010, accessed December 16, 2010, http://af.reuters.com/article/worldNews/idAFTRE6BD3LA20101214?sp=true.

27. "Sheriff: Mexican Cartels Growing Pot in Georgia Parks," WSBTV.com, November 9, 2010, accessed March 5, 2011, http://www.wsbtv.com/news/25675125/detail.html.

CHAPTER 10   RESTORING FAITH AND TAKING MEXICO BACK FROM THE NARCOS

1. Sylvia Longmire and John P. Longmire IV, "Redefining Terrorism: Why Mexican Drug Trafficking Is More Than Just Organized Crime," *Journal of Strategic Security* 1, no. 1 (November 2008).

2. "Diputados cambian ley para que narcos sean considerados terroristas," SDPNoticias.com, December 15, 2010, accessed December 29, 2010, http://sdpnoticias.com/sdp/contenido/nacional/2010/12/15/1003/1179591.

3. Gerardo Carrillo, "Felipe Calderón and the National Security Dialog," *Borderland Beat* (blog), August 13, 2010, accessed November 26, 2010, http://www.borderlandbeat.com/2010/08/felipe-calderon-and-national-security.html.

4. "Mexico: Detailed Assessment Report on Anti–Money Laundering and Combating the Finance of Terrorism," International Monetary Fund, September 11, 2008, accessed May 2, 2010, http://www.imf.org/external/pubs/ft/scr/2009/cr0907.pdf.

5. George Friedman, "Mexico and the Failed State Revisited," STRATFOR Geopolitical Intelligence Report, April 6, 2010, accessed November 26, 2010, http://www.stratfor.com/weekly/20100405_mexico_and_failed_state_revisited?utm_source=facebook&utm_medium=official&utm_campaign=link.

6. Sylvia Longmire, "Mexico: Why Calderón Isn't Going After Drug Money," Examiner.com, July 14, 2009, accessed May 2, 2010, http://www.examiner.com/x-17196-South-America-Policy-Examiner-y2009m7d14-Mexico-Why-isnt-Calderon-going-after-drug-money.

7. "In Mexico, Transactions with Dollars Face Scrutiny," *The New York Times* (Associated Press), June 15, 2010, accessed November 26, 2010, http://www.nytimes.com/2010/06/16/world/americas/16mexico.html.

8. Michael Smith, "Banks Financing Mexico Gangs Admitted in Wells Fargo Deal," Bloomberg.com, June 28, 2010, accessed November 26, 2010, http://www.bloomberg.com/news/2010-06-29/banks-financing-mexico-s-drug-cartels-admitted-in-wells-fargo-s-u-s-deal.html.

9. Ibid.

10. Julian Cardona, "'Cops and Narcos' Playground Games for Mexico Kids," Reuters, May 17, 2010, accessed November 26, 2010, http://www.reuters.com/article/idUSTRE64G5FJ20100517.

11. Catherine Bremer, "Special Narcos' Playground Games for Mexico Kids," Reuters, October 6, 2010, accessed November 26, 2010, http://af.reuters.com/article/worldNews/idAFTRE69530J20101006?sp=true.

12. Ibid.

13. Julian Cardona, "Youth Orchestra a Ray of Hope in Mexico Drug War," Reuters, December 6, 2010, accessed December 15, 2010, http://uk.reuters.com/article/idUKTRE6B541D20101206.

CHAPTER 11   IMPROVING SECURITY ALONG THE BORDER AND BEYOND

1. *Southwest Border Violence: Issues in Identifying and Measuring Spillover Violence,* CRS Report to Congress, Congressional Research Service, February 16, 2010, accessed March 5, 2011, http://trac.syr.edu/immigration/library/P4351.pdf.

2. Kristina Davis, "San Diego's Crime Rate Fell Again in '09, Stats Show," *San Diego Union-Tribune,* January 28, 2010, accessed April 14, 2010, http://www.signonsandiego.com/news/2010/jan/28/citys-crime-rate-fell-again-in-09-stats-show/.
3. Dennis Wagner, "Violence Is Not Up on Arizona Border Despite Mexican Drug War," *Arizona Republic,* May 2, 2010, accessed May 14, 2010, http://www.azcentral.com/news/articles/2010/05/02/20100502arizona-border-violence-mexico.html.
4. "AP Impact: Despite Calls for More Troops, Data Shows US-Mexico Border Is Actually Pretty Safe," FOXNews.com (Associated Press), June 3, 2010, accessed June 16, 2010, http://www.foxnews.com/world/2010/06/03/ap-impact-despite-calls-troops-data-shows-mexico-border-actually-pretty-safe/.
5. Sari Horwitz and James Grimaldi, "Firearms Watchdog on Short Leash," *Washington Post,* October 26, 2010, accessed November 26, 2010, http://www.washingtonpost.com/wp-dyn/content/article/2010/10/25/AR2010102505588.html?sid=ST2010102600379.
6. Ibid.
7. Sari Horwitz and James Grimaldi, "NRA-Led Gun Lobby Wields Powerful Influence Over ATF, U.S. Politics," *Washington Post,* December 15, 2010, accessed December 29, 2010, http://www.washingtonpost.com/wp-dyn/content/article/2010/12/14/AR2010121406045.html?hpid=topnews&sid=ST2010121406431.
8. Horwitz and Grimaldi, *Washington Post,* October 26, 2010.
9. Ibid.
10. Tracy Wilkinson, "Mexico Moves Quietly to Decriminalize Minor Drug Use," *Los Angeles Times,* June 21, 2009, accessed January 23, 2011, http://articles.latimes.com/2009/jun/21/world/fg-mexico-decriminalize21.
11. *Tobacco Control in Developing Countries,* published by the OUP for the World Bank and World Health Organization, 2000, accessed April 14, 2010, http://www1.worldbank.org/tobacco/tcdc.asp.
12. Sylvia Longmire, "Making Sense of the Southbound Weapons Flow," MexiData.info, August 17, 2009, accessed March 5, 2011, http://mexidata.info/id2366.html.
13. Ibid.
14. Telephone interview with senior ATF official who wished to remain anonymous.
15. Ibid.
16. Telephone interview with Arizona Attorney General Terry Goddard, December 22, 2010.
17. Ibid.

CHAPTER 12 CONCLUSIONS: MANAGING A WAR THAT CAN'T BE WON

1. Will Ripley, "Rancher's Last Stand," KRGV.com, November 25, 2010, accessed November 25, 2010, http://www.krgv.com:80/news/local/story/Ranchers-Last-Stand/pBhPy5JwMUmR52HL7IB1Hg.cspx?rss=1652.
2. Daniel Borunda, "Woman Activist Slain in Chihuahua: Quest to Find Daughter's Killer Drove Self-Made Investigator," *El Paso Times,* December 18, 2010, accessed December 29, 2010, http://www.elpasotimes.com/news/ci_16889727.
3. Martha Mendoza and Elliot Spagat, "AP IMPACT: Big Crackdowns on Mexican Drug Cartels Had Little, If Any, Effect on Drug Trade," *Star Tribune* (Associated Press), December 1, 2010, accessed December 15, 2010, http://www.startribune.com/nation/111106914.html.
4. Alex Peña, "No Mas: Mexico Students Unite to Stop Drug War," ABC News (online), December 23, 2010, accessed December 29, 2010, http://abcnews.go.com/International/mas-mexico-students-unite-stop-drug-war/story?id=12462284.
5. Dudley Althaus, "Inside Juarez: Hope Amid the Despair," *Houston Chronicle,* December 19, 2010, accessed December 29, 2010, http://www.chron.com/disp/story.mpl/world/7346645.html.

BIBLIOGRAPHY

"#41 Joaquin Guzmán." *Forbes* (online), November 11, 2009. Accessed October 5, 2010. http://www
.forbes.com/lists/2009/20/power-09_Joaquin-Guzman_NQB6.html.

"#701 Joaquin Guzmán Loera." *Forbes* (online), March 11, 2009. Accessed October 5, 2010. http://
rate.forbes.com/comments/CommentServlet?op=CPage&pageNumber=2&StoryURI=lists/
2009/10/billionaires-2009-richest-people_Joaquin-Guzman-Loera_FS0Y.html&sourcename
=story.

"19 Patients Killed at Mexican Drug Rehab Facility." CNN (online), June 11, 2010. Accessed September
5, 2010. http://edition.cnn.com/2010/WORLD/americas/06/11/mexico.patient.killings/index
.html.

21 U.S.C. Chapter 13, *Drug Abuse Prevention and Control,* February 1, 2010. Accessed November 22,
2010. http://uscode.house.gov/download/pls/21C13.txt.

"35 Accused of Shipping Drugs from Juarez to Denver." FOX News, November 8, 2010. Accessed December 15, 2010. http://www.foxnews.com/us/2010/11/08/accused-shipping-drugs-juarez-denver/.

"55 Persons Charged in Federal Court in Connection with Multi-Agency Marijuana Eradication Effort."
Press Release, US Department of Justice, July 29, 2010. Accessed November 21, 2010. http://
www.justice.gov/usao/cae/press_releases/docs/2010/07-29-10TridentPR.pdf.

"A Fence for the Southern Border of . . . Mexico." *The Blaze,* September 22, 2010. Accessed November
16, 2010. http://www.theblaze.com/stories/a-fence-for-the-southern-border-of-mexico/.

"Afghanistan Identifies Cutting Agents for Heroin." World Drug Report 2009 Series, United Nations
Office on Drugs and Crime. Accessed November 5, 2010. http://www.unodc.org/unodc/en/front
page/2009/June/afghanistan-identifies-cutting-agents-for-heroin.html.

Aguilar, Julian. "Law Enforcement Indicate Jailbreak Was to Swell Cartel Ranks." *Texas Tribune,* December 18, 2010. Accessed December 30, 2010. http://www.texastribune.org/texas-mexico-
border-news/texas-mexico-border/law-enforcement-indicate-jailbreak-was-swell-carte/.

"Alcaldes de la ZMG rechazan el mando único en la policía [ZMG Mayors Reject Plan for Unified Police Force]." *Milenio* (online), June 24, 2010. Accessed September 19, 2010. http://www.milenio
.com/node/471947.

"The Almighty Latin Kings Nation." Know Gangs website. Accessed November 6, 2010. http://www
.knowgangs.com/gang_resources/profiles/kings/.

Althaus, Dudley. "Inside Juarez: Hope Amid the Despair." *Houston Chronicle,* December 19, 2010. Accessed December 29, 2010. http://www.chron.com/disp/story.mpl/world/7346645.html.

———. "Mexico Confronting a Drug Addiction Epidemic." *Houston Chronicle,* October 5, 2009.
Accessed October 7, 2010. http://www.chron.com/disp/story.mpl/metropolitan/6652182.html.

"AP Impact: Despite Calls for More Troops, Data Shows US-Mexico Border Is Actually Pretty Safe."
FOXNews.com (Associated Press), June 3, 2010. Accessed June 16, 2010. http://www.foxnews

.com/world/2010/06/03/ap-impact-despite-calls-troops-data-shows-mexico-border-actually-pretty-safe/.

Arrillaga, Pauline. "Grisly Slayings Bring Mexican Drug War to U.S." Associated Press, April 19, 2009. Accessed June 4, 2010. http://www.foxnews.com/story/0,2933,517078,00.html.

"ATF, ICE Update Partnership Agreement to Maximize Investigative Efforts." Press Release, US Immigration and Customs Enforcement, June 30, 2010. Accessed November 19, 2010. http://www.ice.gov/news/releases/0906/090630albuquerque.htm.

"ATF Says E. Washington Source of Mexico Guns." *The Spokesman-Review* (Associated Press), November 13, 2009. http://www.spokesman.com/stories/2009/nov/13/atf-says-e-washington-source-mexico-guns/.

"Authorities: Arrests 'Major' Blow to Trans-National Gangs." KETV7 News, June 3, 2009. http://www.ketv.com/news/19647462/detail.html.

"Background Checks and Waiting Periods for Firearms Purchases: State-by-State Breakdown." Brady Campaign to Prevent Gun Violence. Accessed April 12, 2010. http://www.bradycampaign.org/facts/issues/?page=waitxstate.

Beith, Malcolm. *The Last Narco: Inside the Hunt for El Chapo, the World's Most Wanted Drug Lord.* New York: Grove Press, 2010. Kindle edition.

Border Crossing/Entry Data. US Bureau of Transportation Statistics public website. Accessed March 29, 2010. http://www.TranStats.bts.gov/BorderCrossing.aspx.

"Border Enforcement Security Task Forces." US Immigration and Customs Enforcement public website, November 3, 2009. Accessed May 18, 2010. http://www.ice.gov/pi/news/factsheets/080226best_fact_sheet.htm.

Borja, Elizabeth. *Brief Documentary History of the Department of Homeland Security, 2001–2008.* History Office, US Department of Homeland Security, 2008. http://www.dhs.gov/xlibrary/assets/brief_documentary_history_of_dhs_ 2001_2008.pdf.

Borunda, Daniel. "Activist Slain in Chihuahua: Quest to Find Daughter's Killer Drove Self-Made Investigator." *El Paso Times,* December 18, 2010. Accessed December 29, 2010. http://www.elpasotimes.com/news/ci_16889727.

Bremer, Catherine. "Special Narcos' Playground Games for Mexico Kids." Reuters, October 6, 2010. Accessed November 26, 2010. http://af.reuters.com/article/worldNews/idAFTRE69530J20101006?sp=true.

"Brothers Plead Guilty to Unlawful Gun Trafficking." Press Release, US Department of Justice, November 25, 2009. Accessed April 5, 2010. http://www.atf.gov/press/releases/2009/11/112509-sf-brothers-plead-guilty.html.

Bucardo, Jesus, Kimberly C. Brouwer, Carlos Magis-Rodríguez, Rebeca Ramos, Miguel Fraga, Saida G. Perez, Thomas L. Patterson, and Steffanie A. Strathdee. "Historical Trends in the Production and Consumption of Illicit Drugs in Mexico: Implications for the Prevention of Blood Borne Infections." National Institutes of Health, April 1, 2005. Accessed November 2, 2010. http://www.ncbi.nlm.nih.gov/pmc/articles/PMC2196212/.

Burton, Fred, and Ben West. "The Barrio Azteca Trial and the Prison Gang-Cartel Interface." STRATFOR, *Global Security and Intelligence Report,* November 19, 2008. http://www.stratfor.com/weekly/20081119_barrio_azteca_trial_and_prison_gang_cartel_interface.

Burton, Fred, and Scott Stewart. "Mexico: The Third War." STRATFOR, February 19, 2009. Accessed March 5, 2011. http://www.stratfor.com/weekly/20090218_mexico_third_war.

———. "Worrying Signs from Border Raids." STRATFOR, *Global Security and Intelligence Report,* November 12, 2008. http://www.stratfor.com/weekly/20081112_worrying_signs_border_raids/?utm_source=Tweekly-utm.

Caldwell, Alicia. "Mexico Army Likely Part of Border Incident (Says Hudspeth County Sheriff)." Free Republic (Associated Press), January 27, 2006. Accessed December 21, 2010. http://www.freerepublic.com/focus/f-news/1566642/posts.

Caldwell, Alicia, and Manuel Valdes. "Public Lands Sprouting Marijuana Farms." *San Francisco Chronicle,* March 14, 2010. Accessed November 20, 2010. http://articles.sfgate.com/2010-03-14/news/18831119_1_drug-gangs-marijuana-farms-mexican-growers/2.

California Firearms Laws 2007. California Department of Justice. http://ag.ca.gov/firearms/forms/pdf/Cfl2007.pdf.

Cardenas, Lourdes. "Chihuahua and Its Disenchantment with Elections." *El Paso Times* (blog), June 15, 2010. Accessed September 18, 2010. http://elpasotimes.typepad.com/mexico/2010/06/chihuahua-and-its-disenchantment-with-elections.html.

———. "Renewing the Mexican Police . . . Is It possible?" *El Paso Times* (blog), June 4, 2010. http://elpasotimes.typepad.com/mexico/2010/06/renewing-the-mexican-policeis-it-possible.html.

———. "Vulnerable Citizens in the Middle of the Drug War." *El Paso Times* (blog), July 19, 2010. http://elpasotimes.typepad.com/mexico/2010/07/vulnerable-citizens-in-the-middle-of-the-drug-war-.html.

Cardona, Julian. "'Cops and Narcos' Playground Games for Mexico Kids." Reuters, May 17, 2010. Accessed November 26, 2010. http://www.reuters.com/article/idUSTRE64G5FJ20100517.

———. "Youth Orchestra a Ray of Hope in Mexico Drug War." Reuters, December 6, 2010. Accessed December 15, 2010. http://uk.reuters.com/article/idUKTRE6B541D20101206.

Carrillo, Gerardo. "Felipe Calderón and the National Security Dialog." *Borderland Beat* (blog), August 13, 2010. Accessed November 26, 2010. http://www.borderlandbeat.com/2010/08/felipe-calderon-and-national-security.html.

Casey, Nicholas. "Mexico Under Siege." *Wall Street Journal,* August 19, 2010. http://online.wsj.com/article/SB10001424052748704557704575437762646209270.html.

Castañeda, Jorge. "Mexico's Failed Drug War." CATO Institute Economic Development Bulletin, No. 13, May 6, 2010. http://www.cato.org/pub_display.php?pub_id=11746.

CBP Border Wait Times. US Customs and Border Protection public website. Accessed March 29, 2010. http://apps.cbp.gov/bwt/.

"Chaotic Shootout in Mexican Tourist Paradise Leaves 6 Dead." eTurboNews.com, April 15, 2010. Accessed September 5, 2010. http://www.eturbonews.com/15547/chaotic-shootout-mexican-tourist-paradise-leaves-6-dead?utm_source=feedburner&utm_medium=feed&utm_campaign=Feed%3A+eturbonews+%28eTurboNews%29&utm_content=Twitter.

Chicago HIDTA Drug Market Analysis 2010. National Drug Intelligence Center, April 2010. Accessed November 6, 2010. http://www.justice.gov/ndic/pubs40/40385/product.htm#Transportation.

Clark, Jonathan. "Elite Team Was Trained to Flush Out Border Bandits." *Nogales International,* December 17, 2010. Accessed December 19, 2010. http://www.nogalesinternational.com/articles/2010/12/17/news/doc4d0b842a54a0f734379356.txt.

Conant, Eve, and Arian Campos-Flores. "The Enemy Within: Cartel-Related Violence Has Moved Well Beyond Border Towns." *Newsweek,* March 14, 2009. Accessed April 22, 2010. http://www.newsweek.com/id/189246/page/1.

Conery, Ben. "Drug Cartels 'Hide in Plain Sight' in U.S." *Washington Times,* June 7, 2009. Accessed June 6, 2010. http://www.washingtontimes.com/news/2009/jun/07/mexican-drug-cartels-hide-in-plain-sight-in-us/.

Connolly, Ceci. "Woman's Links to Mexican Drug Cartel a Saga of Corruption on U.S. Side of Border." *Washington Post,* September 12, 2010. Accessed November 19, 2010. http://www.washingtonpost.com/wp-dyn/content/article/2010/09/11/AR2010091105687.html?tid=nn_twitter.

Cook, Colleen. "Mexico's Drug Cartels." Congressional Research Service, February 5, 2008. http://www.fas.org/sgp/crs/row/RL34215.pdf.

"Data: Limited Progress in Vetting Police Forces." *Reforma* (online), September 19, 2010. Accessed September 20, 2010.

Davis, Kristina. "San Diego's Crime Rate Fell Again in '09, Stats Show." *San Diego Union-Tribune,* January 28, 2010. Accessed April 14, 2010. http://www.signonsandiego.com/news/2010/jan/28/citys-crime-rate-fell-again-in-09-stats-show/.

DEA History, 1975–1980. US Department of Justice Publications. Accessed November 12, 2010. http://www.justice.gov/dea/pubs/history/1975-1980.html.

"DEA Intel Aids in Seizure of Fully-Operational Narco Submarine in Ecuador." DEA Press Release, Office of Public Affairs, July 3, 2010. Accessed October 5, 2010. http://www.justice.gov/dea/pubs/pressrel/pr070310.html.

"DEA Mission Statement." Drug Enforcement Administration public website. Accessed May 12, 2010. http://www.justice.gov/dea/agency/mission.htm.

DeMint, Jim. "Finish the Border Fence Now." *Human Events,* May 17, 2010. Accessed September 27, 2010. http://www.humanevents.com/article.php?id=37025.

Dibble, Sandra. "Three Arrested in Rosarito Beach Kidnapping, Killing." *San Diego Union-Tribune,* April 15, 2010. Accessed October 7, 2010. http://www.signon-san-diegos.com/news/2010/apr/15/three-arrested-rosarito-beach-kidnapping-killing/.

"Diputados cambian ley para que narcos sean considerados terroristas." SDPNoticias.com, December 15, 2010. Accessed December 29, 2010. http://sdpnoticias.com/sdp/contenido/nacional/2010/12/15/1003/1179591.

"Drug Interdiction." US Coast Guard public website. Accessed May 12, 2010. http://www.uscg.mil/hq/cg5/cg531/drug_interdiction.asp.

Ellingwood, Ken. "Mexico Grapples with Drug Addiction." *Los Angeles Times,* October 15, 2008. Accessed October 8, 2010. http://www.latimes.com/news/nationworld/world/la-fg-mexaddict15-2008oct15,0,4364637.story.

Ellingwood, Ken, and Tracy Wilkinson. "Corruption Sweep in Mexico's Michoacan Unravels in the Courts." *Los Angeles Times,* December 12, 2010. Accessed December 15, 2010. http://www.latimes.com/news/nationworld/world/la-fg-mexico-michoacan-20101212,0,6080015.story.

"El Paso Intelligence Center." US Drug Enforcement Agency public website. Accessed May 18, 2010. http://www.justice.gov/dea/programs/epic.htm.

Emmott, Robin, and Julian Cardona. "85 Prisoners Escape Jail on Mexico-U.S. Border." Reuters, September 10, 2010. Accessed November 16, 2010. http://www.reuters.com/article/idUSTRE68944P20100910.

Fainaru, Steve, and William Booth. "Cartels Face an Economic Battle." *Washington Post,* October 7, 2009. Accessed November 22, 2010. http://www.washingtonpost.com/wp-dyn/content/article/2009/10/06/AR2009100603847.html?sid=ST2009100603892.

———. "Mexican Army Using Torture to Battle Drug Traffickers, Rights Groups Say." *Washington Post,* July 9, 2009. Accessed December 16, 2010. http://www.washingtonpost.com/wp-dyn/content/article/2009/07/08/AR2009070804197.html.

Fraga, Brian. "Sophisticated Hidden Vehicle Compartment Reveals Tricks of Drug Trade." *Standard-Times,* February 20, 2009. Accessed April 2, 2010. http://www.southcoasttoday.com/apps/pbcs.dll/article?AID=/20090220/NEWS/902200346.

"Francisco Javier Arellano-Felix Sentenced to Life in Prison." *Imperial Valley News,* November 6, 2007. Accessed December 19, 2010. http://imperialvalleynews.com/index.php?option=com_content&task=view&id=277&Itemid=2.

Friedman, George. "Mexico and the Failed State Revisited." STRATFOR Geopolitical Intelligence Report, April 6, 2010. Accessed November 26, 2010. http://www.stratfor.com/weekly/20100405_mexico_and_failed_state_revisited?utm_source=facebook&utm_medium=official&utm_campaign=link.

"From Flowers to Heroin." Central Intelligence Agency. Accessed November 3, 2010. http://www.erowid.org/plants/poppy/poppy_article2.shtml.

"Fiscal Year 2011: The Interior Budget in Brief." US Department of the Interior, Feburary 2010. Accessed November 24, 2010. http://www.doi.gov/budget/2011/11Hilites/2011_Highlights_Book.pdf.

"FY 2011 Budget in Brief." US Department of Homeland Security. Accessed November 24, 2010. http://www.dhs.gov/xlibrary/assets/budget_bib_fy2011.pdf.

Gallegos, Rocío. "Se han ido 230 mil de Juárez por la violencia [230,000 Have Left Juárez Because of Violence]." *Vanguardia Informativa,* August 26, 2010. Accessed September 19, 2010. http://www.vanguardiainformativa.com/index.php/ notas-rotativas/2454-se-han-ido-230-mil-de-juarez-por-la-violencia.

Gettman, John. "Marijuana Production in the United States (2006)." *The Bulletin of Cannabis Reform,* December 2006. Accessed May 14, 2010. http://www.drugscience.org/Archive/bcr2/MJCropReport_2006.pdf.

Gómez Licón, Adriana. "Juárez Cancels Sept. 16 Celebration." *El Paso Times,* Aug. 30, 2010. Accessed September 13, 2010. http://www.elpasotimes.com/ci_15935968?source=most_viewed.

Gonzalez, Daniel, and Dan Nowicki. "Napolitano Confirms Gang Killed Border Agent in Battle." *USA Today,* December 18, 2010. Accessed December 19, 2010. http://www.usatoday.com/news/nation/2010-12-18-border-agent-killed_N.htm.

Grayson, George. *Mexico: Narco-Violence and a Failed State?* (Piscataway, NJ: Transaction, 2009).

Grayson, George W. "Death of Arturo Beltrán Leyva: What Does It Mean for Mexico's Drug War?" *E-Notes,* Foreign Policy Research Institute, February 2010. Accessed October 5, 2010. http://www.fpri.org/enotes/201002.grayson.beltranleyva.html.

———. "La Familia: Another Deadly Mexican Syndicate." *E-Notes,* Foreign Policy Research Institute, February 2009. http://www.fpri.org/enotes/200901.grayson.lafamilia.html.

Griffin, Drew, and John Murgatroyd, "Smugglers' Deadly Cargo, Cop-Killing Guns," CNN.com, March 26, 2008, http://www.cnn.com/2008/WORLD/americas/03/26/gun.smuggling/index.html.

Grillo, Ioan. "Mexico's Lost Youth: Generation Narco." *Time* (online), November 7, 2010. Accessed November 10, 2010. http://www.time.com/time/world/article/0,8599,2028912,00.html.

Hartstein, Larry. "Agents Raid Huge Lawrenceville Meth Lab as Part of Strike on Cartel." *Atlanta Journal-Constitution,* October 22, 2009. Accessed May 15, 2010. http://www.ajc.com/news/gwinnett/agents-raid-huge-lawrenceville-169790.html.

Hawley, Chris. "Activists Blast Mexico's Immigration Law." *USA Today,* May 25, 2010. Accessed November 16, 2010. http://www.usatoday.com/news/world/2010-05-25-mexico-migrants_N.htm.

———. "Drug Addiction Soars in Mexico." *USA Today,* July 22, 2008. Accessed October 7, 2010. http://www.usatoday.com/news/world/2008-07-22-mexaddicts_N.htm.

———. "Drug Cartels Outmatch, Outgun Mexican Forces." *Republic* Mexico City Bureau, *Borderland Beat* (blog), June 16, 2010. Accessed September 12, 2010. http://www.borderlandbeat.com/2010/06/drug-cartels-outmatch-outgun-mexican.html.

———. "Drug Violence Leads Schools to Teach Students to Dodge Bullets." *Arizona Republic,* July 8, 2010. Accessed September 9, 2010. http://www.azcentral.com/arizonarepublic/news/articles/2010/07/08/20100708mexico-drug-violence-affecting-schools-and-students.html.

———. "Mexico Focuses on Police Corruption." *USA Today,* February 5, 2008. http://www.usatoday.com/news/world/2008-02-05-mexico-police_N.htm.

Hawley, Chris, and Sergio Colache. "Mexico Cracks Down on Police Corruption." *USA Today,* February 6, 2008. Accessed March 4, 2011. http://www.policeone.com/international/articles/1658569-Mexico-cracks-down-on-police-corruption/.

"Hereford Ranch Hand Accused of Smuggling." KSWT13 News (online), December 18, 2010. Accessed December 19, 2010. http://www.kswt.com/Global/story.asp?S=13708128.

Holstege, Sean. "More Drug Tunnels Being Found on Border." *Arizona Republic,* November 25, 2008. Accessed April 22, 2010. http://www.azcentral.com/news/articles/2008/11/25/20081125tunnels1125.html.

"Homeland Security Support." Joint Task Force North public website. Accessed May 18, 2010. http://www.jtfn.northcom.mil/subpages/homeland_s.html.

Hoover, William, ATF Deputy Director for Field Operations. Statement Before the Senate Committee on the Judiciary, Subcommittee on Crime and Drugs, March 17, 2009.

Horwitz, Sari, and James Grimaldi. "Firearms Watchdog on Short Leash." *Washington Post,* October 26, 2010. Accessed November 26, 2010. http://www.washingtonpost.com/wp-dyn/content/article/2010/10/25/AR2010102505588.html?sid=ST2010102600379.

———. "NRA-Led Gun Lobby Wields Powerful Influence Over ATF, U.S. Politics." *Washington Post,* December 15, 2010. Accessed December 29, 2010. http://www.washingtonpost.com/wp-dyn/content/article/2010/12/14/AR2010121406045.html?hpid=topnews&sid=ST2010121406431.

"How Mexico Treats Its Illegal Aliens." Creators.com. Accessed November 16, 2010. http://www.creators.com/conservative/michelle-malkin/how-mexico-treats-its-illegal-aliens.html.

H. Res. 1540 for the 111th Congress, December 8, 2010. Accessed December 15, 2010. http://thomas.loc.gov/cgi-bin/query/D?c111:2:./temp/~c111aFRZHb::.

"ICE Operation in Florida Nets 95 Arrests." *USA Today,* December 13, 2010. Accessed December 19, 2010. http://www.miamiherald.com/2010/12/13/1971290/ice-operation-in-florida-nets.html.

Imler, Scott. "Medical Marijuana in California: A History." *Los Angeles Times,* March 6, 2009. Accessed November 22, 2010. http://www.latimes.com/features/health/la-oew-gutwillig-imler6-2009mar06,0,2951626.story.

"In Mexico, Transactions with Dollars Face Scrutiny." *The New York Times* (Associated Press), June 15, 2010. Accessed November 26, 2010. http://www.nytimes.com/2010/06/16/world/americas/16mexico.html.

Isackson, Amy. "Mexican Southbound Screening Snarling San Ysidro Traffic." KPBS.org, October 28, 2009. http://www.kpbs.org/news/2009/oct/28/mexican-southbound-screening-snarling-san-ysidro-t/.

Isikoff, Michael. "U.S. Bid to Stem Flow of Weapons to Mexico Cartels Misfires." MSNBC.com, September 21, 2010. Accessed January 21, 2011. http://www.msnbc.msn.com/id/39282887/ns/us_news-crime_and_courts/.

"Is the Fuse Lit? Uprising/Lynching in Chihuahua." *Chihuahua News,* September 22, 2010.

Jervis, Rick. "Arrests of Border Agents on the Rise." *USA Today,* April 24, 2009. Accessed November 19, 2010. http://www.usatoday.com/news/nation/2009-04-23-borderagent_N.htm.

Johnson, Tim. "Mexican Corruption: Getting Worse?" *Mexico Unmasked* (McClatchy blogs), December 10, 2010. Accessed December 15, 2010. http://blogs.mcclatchydc.com/mexico/2010/12/mexican-corruption-getting-worse.html.

———. "Mexican Marijuana Smugglers Turn to Ultralight Aircraft." McClatchy Newspapers, June 4, 2010. Accessed June 16, 2010. http://www.mcclatchydc.com/2010/06/04/95370/mexican-marijuana-smugglers-turn.html.

———. "Mexico's Drug Gangs Aim at New Target—Teachers." *Miami Herald,* December 11, 2010. Accessed December 13, 2010. http://www.miamiherald.com/2010/12/11/1969153/mexicos-drug-gangs-aim-at-new.html#ixzz17wzyBnKG.

Jones, Russell. "Marijuana Found Growing at Fort Smith Park." KFSM5 News Online, June 2, 2010. Accessed June 16, 2010. http://www.kfsm.com/news/kfsm-news-marijuana-found-at-city-park,0,2583938.story.

"Juarez Death Toll Is 3,000 So Far in 2010." UPI.com, December 15, 2010. Accessed March 2, 2011. http://www.upi.com/Top_News/World-News/2010/12/15/Juarez-death-toll-is-3000-so-far-in-2010/UPI-42941292417150/.

"Killings, Kin and Luck Helped Drug Lord." *Albuquerque Journal* (undated). Accessed November 12, 2010. http://www.abqjournal.com/news/drugs/6drug3-3.htm.

Knight, Meribah. "Families Fear Phone Call from Mexico's Cartels." *The New York Times,* July 31, 2010. http://www.nytimes.com/2010/08/01/us/01cnccartel.html?_r=1.

Kocherga, Angela. "Evidence Links U.S., Mexico Grenade Attacks." Texas Cable News, February 17, 2009. Accessed October 5, 2010. http://www.txcn.com/sharedcontent/dws/txcn/houston/stories/khou090212_mh_mexico_grenade_attacks.c16c1da.html.

Lomnitz, Claudio. "Understanding History of Corruption in Mexico." *University of Chicago Chronicle* 15, no. 6 (November 27, 1995). http://chronicle.uchicago.edu/ 951127/lomnitz.shtml.

Longmire, Sylvia. "Are Mexican Cartels Expanding for Profit or Survival?" MexiData.info, September 21, 2009. http://www.mexidata.info/id2411.html.

———. "Making Sense of the Southbound Weapons Flow to Mexico." MexiData.info, August 17, 2009. Accessed April 6, 2010. http://mexidata.info/id2366.html.

———. "Mexican Cartels Are Taking Over U.S. Marijuana Production." MexiData.info, October 19, 2009. Accessed May 10, 2010. http://www.mexidata.info/id2437.html.

———. "Mexico: Why Calderón Isn't Going After Drug Money." Examiner.com, July 14, 2009. Accessed May 2, 2010. http://www.examiner.com/x-17196-South-America-Policy-Examiner~y2009m7d14-Mexico-Why-isnt-Calderon-going-after-drug-money.

———. "Mexico's Rising Drug Use and Addiction—Who Is to Blame?" MexiData.info, October 12, 2009. http://mexidata.info/id2430.html.

———. "The More Deadly Side of Growing Vigilantism in Mexico." MexiData.info, November 2, 2009. Accessed September 16, 2010. http://www.mexidata.info/id2451.html.

Longmire, Sylvia, and John P. Longmire IV. "Redefining Terrorism: Why Mexican Drug Trafficking Is More Than Just Organized Crime." *Journal of Strategic Security* 1, no. 1 (November 2008).

Luhnow, David. "Presumption of Guilt." *Wall Street Journal,* October 17, 2009. Accessed March 4, 2011, http://online.wsj.com/article/SB10001424052748704322004574475492261338318.html.

Luhnow, David, and Jose de Cordoba. "The Drug Lord Who Got Away." *Wall Street Journal,* June 13, 2009. Accessed October 3, 2010. http://online.wsj.com/article/SB124484177023110993.html.

Markey, Sean. "Marijuana War Smolders on U.S. Public Lands." *National Geographic News,* November 4, 2003. Accessed November 20, 2010. http://news.nationalgeographic.com/news/2003/11/1103_031104_marijuana.html.

Marosi, Richard. "U.S. Border Inspector Charged with Drug Conspiracy." *Los Angeles Times,* September 25, 2010. Accessed November 19, 2010. http://www.latimes.com/news/local/la-me-corruption-20100925,0,6470787.story.

———. "U.S. Border Officer Accused of Accepting Bribes to Allow Illegal Immigrants to Cross Border." *Los Angeles Times,* September 30, 2010. Accessed November 19, 2010. http://latimesblogs.latimes.com/lanow/2010/09/us-border-officer-accused-of-accepting-bribes-to-allow-illegal-immigrants-to-cross-border.html.

"McCain Says Phoenix Is the Second Kidnapping Capital in the World." Politifact.com. Accessed January 20, 2011. http://politifact.com/texas/statements/2010/jun/28/john-mccain/mccain-says-phoenix-second-kidnapping-capital-worl/.

McCombs, Brady. "Focus in Krentz Killing on Suspect in US." *Arizona Daily Star,* May 3, 2010. Accessed May 14, 2010. http://azstarnet.com/news/local/border/article_35ef6e3a-5632-5e58-abe7-e7697ee2f0d5.html.

———. "U.S. to Aid Mexico's Judicial Reforms." *Arizona Daily Star,* September 27, 2010. Accessed November 16, 2010. http://azstarnet.com/news/local/border/article_7025a974-11b4-5544-b646-6a1f9e7215f7.html.

Mendoza, Martha, and Elliot Spagat. "AP IMPACT: Big Crackdowns on Mexican Drug Cartels Had Little, If Any, Effect on Drug Trade." *Star Tribune* (Associated Press), December 1, 2010. Accessed December 15, 2010. http://www.startribune.com/nation/111106914.html.

"Merida Initiative: The United States Has Provided Counternarcotics and Anticrime Support but Needs Better Performance Measures." US Government Accountability Office (GAO-10-837), July 21, 2010. Accessed September 20, 2010. http://www.gao.gov/ products/GAO-10-837.

"Mexican Drug Cartels: Two Wars and a Look Southward." STRATFOR, December 16, 2009.

"Mexican Military Losing Drug War Support." MSNBC.com (Associated Press), July 26, 2010. Accessed September 20, 2010. http://www.msnbc.msn.com/id/25851906/.

"Mexican Police Rescue Man Kidnapped in Texas." *Latin American Herald Tribune,* May 31, 2010. Accessed June 12, 2010. http://laht.com/article.asp?CategoryId=14091&ArticleId=348190.

"Mexicans Continue Support for Drug War." Pew Global Attitudes Project, Pew Research Center, August 12, 2010. Accessed September 12, 2010. http://pewglobal.org/2010/08/12/mexicans-continue-support-for-drug-war/.

Mexico: Detailed Assessment Report on Anti–Money Laundering and Combating the Finance of Terrorism. International Monetary Fund, September 11, 2008. Accessed May 2, 2010. http://www.imf.org/external/pubs/ft/scr/2009/cr0907.pdf.

"Mexico Sacks 10% of Police Force in Corruption Probe." BBC News (UK online), August 30, 2010. Accessed September 15, 2010. http://www.bbc.co.uk/news/world-latin-america-11132589.

"Mexico's Ambassador on Controlling the Border." *Nation Journal,* May 18, 2010. http://insiderinterviews.nationaljournal.com/2010/05/mexico.php.

"Mexico's Criminal Justice System: A Guide for U.S. Citizens Arrested in Mexico." US Consulate in Tijuana. Accessed November 16, 2010. http://tijuana.usconsulate.gov/root/pdfs/telegalcriminalguide.pdf.

"Migrantes pierden 150 mdd por extorsiones: PRI." *El Universal,* December 12, 2010. Accessed December 16, 2010. http://www.eluniversal.com.mx/notas/729900.html.

"Militarization Increased Drug Violence in Mexico, According to Experts." EFE News, August 26, 2010. http://mywordismyweapon.blogspot.com/2010/08/militarization-increased-drug-violence.html.

"Militarization of Mexico by 'Common Citizen.'" *Borderland Beat* (blog), April 13, 2010. Accessed September 16, 2010. http://www.borderlandbeat.com/2010/04/militarization-of-mexico-by-common.html#comments.

Millman, Joel. "Case Against Gun-Store Owner Dismissed." *Wall Street Journal,* March 20, 2009. Accessed April 15, 2010. http://online.wsj.com/article/SB123750753535390327.html.

———. "U.S. Gun Trial Echoes in Drug-Torn Mexico." *Wall Street Journal,* March 2, 2009. Accessed October 6, 2010. http://online.wsj.com/article/SB123595012797004865.html.

Miroff, Nick, and William Booth. "Mexican Drug Cartels' Newest Weapon: Cold War–Era Grenades Made in U.S." *Washington Post,* July 17, 2010. http://www.washingtonpost.com/wp-dyn/content/article/2010/07/16/AR2010071606252.html?sid=ST2010072106244.

Mora, Edwin. "U.S. Alleges Mexican Drug Cartel Rented Apartments in U.S. to Recruit Young Americans." CNSNews.com, January 11, 2011. Accessed January 19, 2011. http://www.cnsnews.com/news/article/federal-court-hear-case-mexican-drug-car.

Mower, Lawrence. "Search for Boy Taken from Home." *Las Vegas Review-Journal,* October 16, 2008. Accessed May 2, 2010. http://www.lvrj.com/news/31095764.html.

Myers, Amanda Lee. "Chandler Beheading Raises Fears of Drug Violence." *Arizona Star* (Associated Press), October 30, 2010. Accessed December 15, 2010. http://azstarnet.com/news/local/crime/article_c593bd79-e887-59e5-868a-a8179cfe830b.html.

National Clandestine Laboratory Register. US Drug Enforcement Administration. Accessed January 19, 2011. http://www.justice.gov/dea/seizures/index.html.

National Drug Threat Assessment 2010. National Drug Intelligence Center, US Department of Justice, February 2010. Accessed November 12, 2010. http://www.justice.gov/ndic/pubs38/38661/index.htm.

"National Forests Urge Awareness of Drug Operations." *Daily Reporter,* November 22, 2010. Accessed November 24, 2010. http://www.thedailyreporter.com/newsnow/x96441365/National-forests-urge-awareness-of-drug-operations.

"NorCal Cities Bring Pot Growing into the Light." FOX News (Associated Press), November 20, 2010. Accessed November 23, 2010. http://www.foxnews.com/us/2010/11/20/norcal-cities-bring-pot-growing-light/.

Nores, Lt. John Jr., and James A. Swan. *War in the Woods: Combating Drug Cartels on Our Public Lands.* Excerpted in *Crime Magazine,* November 14, 2010. Accessed November 20, 2010. http://www.crimemagazine.com/war-woods-combating-marijuana-cartels-our-public-lands.

North Carolina Drug Threat Assessment. National Drug Intelligence Center, April 2003. http://www.justice.gov/ndic/pubs3/3690/marijuan.htm.

NRA/ILA Firearms Laws for Arizona, NRA Institute for Legislative Action (AZ Rev. Statutes §§12-714, 13-2904, 13-3101, 13-3102, 13-3105, 13-31-07, 13-3109, 31-3112, 17-301, 17-301.1, 17-305, 17-312), February 2006.

NRA/ILA Firearms Laws for New Mexico, NRA Institute for Legislative Action (NM Stat. Ann. §§ 17-2-12; 17-2-33 through 35; 29-19-1 through 12; 30-3-8; 30-7-1 through 16; 32A-2-33), July 2006.

NRA/ILA Firearms Laws for Texas, NRA Institute for Legislative Action (TX Penal Code § 46.01 et seq. and TX Govt. Code § 411.171 et seq.), January 2008.

Olmos, José Gil. "The Mexican *Ninis.*" *Proceso* (Mexico), February 3, 2010. Accessed November 10, 2010. http://bit.ly/g9A0Ca/

"Operation Trident Results in Seizure of Thousands of Marijuana Plants Worth More Than $1.7 Billion." Press Release, US Drug Enforcement Administration, August 11, 2010. Accessed November 21, 2010. http://www.justice.gov/dea/pubs/states/newsrel/2010/sanfran081110.html.

Papenfuss, Mary. "Mexican Cartel Crew Indicted in San Diego Kidnap-Murders." Newser.com, August 14, 2009. Accessed April 28, 2010. http://www.newser.com/story/66901/mexican-cartel-crew-indicted-in-san-diego-kidnap-murders.html.

Peña, Alex. "No Mas: Mexico Students Unite to Stop Drug War." ABC News (online), December 23, 2010. Accessed December 29, 2010. http://abcnews.go.com/International/mas-mexico-students-unite-stop-drug-war/story?id=12462284.

Penhall, Karl. "Brave Few Break Mexico Drug War's Code of Silence." CNN Online, June 21, 2010. Accessed September 16, 2010. http://edition.cnn.com/2010/WORLD/americas/06/21/mexico.drug.war/index.html.

Peters, Katherine. "Losing Ground." *Government Executive,* December 1, 2010. Accessed November 20, 2010. http://www.govexec.com/story_page.cfm?filepath=/features/1203/1203s2.htm.

Phillips, Jen. "Mexico's New Super-Cartel Ups Violence in Power Play." *Mother Jones,* April 13, 2010. Accessed October 3, 2010. http://motherjones.com/mojo/2010/04/evolution-mexicos-cartel-war.

"Phoenix Bars Provide Recruiting Ground for Cartels, Authorities Say." FOX News (online), August 27, 2010. Accessed October 5, 2010. http://www.foxnews.com/us/2010/08/27/phoenix-bars-provide-recruiting-ground-cartels-authorities-say/.

"Police Lift Amber Alert for Abducted Las Vegas Boy." CNN Online, October 18, 2008. Accessed October 6, 2010. http://www.cnn.com/2008/CRIME/10/18/nevada.boy.kidnapped/index.html.

"Potent Mexican Crystal Meth on the Rise as States Curb Domestic Meth Production." Partnership for a Drug-Free America, January 25, 2006. http://www.drugfree.org/Portal/DrugIssue/News/Potent_Mexican_Crystal_Meth_on_the_Rise.

"PRI impulsa ley contra excesos militares [PRI Pushes Law Against Military Abuses]." *El Universal,* September 8, 2010. Accessed September 18, 2010. http://www.eluniversal.com.mx/notas/707353.html.

Preston, Julia. "Officers on Border Team Up to Quell Violence." *New York Times,* March 25, 2010. Accessed November 19, 2010. http://www.nytimes.com/2010/03/26/world/americas/26border.html?_r=1&src=tptw.

"Profile: Felipe Calderón." BBC News, September 5, 2006. Accessed November 16, 2010. http://news.bbc.co.uk/2/hi/americas/5318434.stm.

"Project Gunrunner." ATF Fact Sheet, Bureau of Alcohol, Tobacco, Firearms, and Explosives, Public Affairs Division, August 2008. http://www.atf.gov/publications/factsheets/factsheet-project-gunrunner.html.

Ramos, Jorge, Gerardo Mejía, and Ricardo Gómez. "Acuerdan una sola policía por entidad [Agreement on One Unified Police Force]." *El Universal,* June 4, 2010. Accessed September 22, 2010. http://www.eluniversal.com.mx/notas/685409.html.

Recio, Maria. "Obama May Send Guard to Help Stem Border Violence." *Houston Chronicle,* March 12, 2009. Accessed May 20, 2010. http://www.chron.com/disp/story.mpl/nation/6306226.html.

"Review of ATF's Project Gunrunner." US Department of Justice, Office of the Inspector General, Evaluations and Inspections Division, November 2010. Accessed March 4, 2011. http://www.justice.gov/oig/reports/ATF/e1101.pdf.

"Resignation in Mexican Missing Girl Paulette Case." BBC News, May 26, 2010. Accessed November 16, 2010. http://www.bbc.co.uk/news/10168243.

Riccardi, Nicholas. "Kidnapped Boy Is Safe." *Los Angeles Times,* October 20, 2008. Accessed May 6, 2010. http://articles.latimes.com/2008/oct/20/nation/na-kidnap20.

Rios, Viridiana. "Evaluating the Economic Impact of Drug Traffic in Mexico." Department of Government, Harvard University, 2007.

Ripley, Will. "Rancher's Last Stand." KRGV.com, November 25, 2010. Accessed November 25, 2010. http://www.krgv.com:80/news/local/story/Ranchers-Last-Stand/pBhPy5JwMUmR52HL7IB1Hg.cspx?rss=1652.

Roebuck, Jeremy. "McAllen Man Kidnapped, Held in Mexico Returned to U.S. Soil." *The Monitor,* November 30, 2009. http://www.themonitor.com/articles/mcallen-33018-soil-held.html.

Rosenberg, Mica. "Mexico Drug Cartels Use Gory Videos to Spread Fear." Reuters, August 4, 2010. Accessed September 6, 2010. http://www.reuters.com/article/idUSTRE6734E720100804.

———. "Mexico Marijuana Growers Learn New Tricks from U.S." Reuters, December 14, 2010. Accessed December 16, 2010. http://af.reuters.com/article/worldNews/idAFTRE6BD3LA20101214?sp=true.

Roséndiz, Francisco. "Nayarit: cancelan clases por miedo" [Nayarit: Classes Canceled due to Fear]. *El Universal,* June 16, 2010. Accessed September 6, 2010. http://www.eluniversal.com.mx/primera/35095.html.

Ross, Brian, Richard Esposito, and Joseph Rhee. "ATF: Phoenix Gun Dealer Supplied Mexican Cartels." ABC News, May 6, 2008. Accessed April 12, 2010. http://abcnews.go.com/Blotter/story?id=4796380&page=1.

Ruiz, Gustavo. "20 Kidnapped in Acapulco Had No Criminal Records." Associated Press, October 5, 2010. Accessed October 6, 2010. http://www.google.com/hostednews/ap/article/ALeqM5gMi5B2USfJStXxfqgWWr2xjRYpOgD9ILSLM01?docId=D9ILSLM01.

Sabalow, Ryan. "UPDATED: Marijuana on Public Lands: Herger Urges Feds to Devise a Strategy." Redding.com, July 29, 2010. Accessed November 24, 2010. http://www.redding.com/news/2010/jul/29/marijuana-on-public-lands-herger-urges-feds-to-a/.

Sanchez, Matt. "In Mexico, Journalists Are Becoming an Endangered Species." FOX News (online), August 18, 2010. Accessed September 6, 2010. http://www.foxnews.com/world/2010/08/18/mexico-journalists-increasingly-endangered-species/.

Sarré, Miguel. "Mexico's Judicial Reform and Long-Term Challenges." Presented at the Policy Forum: U.S.-Mexico Security Cooperation and the Merida Initiative, convened by the Mexico Institute of the Woodrow Wilson Center for International Scholars, Capitol Building, Washington, DC, May 9, 2008.

Schiller, Dane. "Mexican Cartels Infiltrate Houston." *Houston Chronicle,* March 7, 2009. Accessed July 12, 2010. http://www.chron.com/disp/story.mpl/metropolitan/6299436.html.

Schweigert, Cynthia. "Growing Marijuana on Public Land." WKBT.com, May 13, 2010. Accessed November 22, 2010. http://www.wkbt.com/global/story.asp?s=12473429.

"Secretary Napolitano Announces Major Southwest Border Security Initiative." Press Release, Office of the Press Secretary, US Department of Homeland Security, March 24, 2009. http://www.dhs .gov/ynews/releases/pr_1237909530921.shtm.

Seelke, Clare R. "Mexico-U.S. Relations: Issues for Congress." Congressional Research Service, March 17, 2010. Accessed March 11, 2011. http://www.dtic.mil/cgi-bin/GetTRDoc?Location=U2&doc =GetTRDoc.pdf&AD=ADA517310.

"Sheriff: Mexican Cartels Growing Pot in Georgia Parks." WSBTV.com, November 9, 2010. Accessed November 24, 2010. http://www.wsbtv.com/news/25675125/detail.html.

Smith, Michael. "Banks Financing Mexico Gangs Admitted in Wells Fargo Deal." Bloomberg.com, June 28, 2010. Accessed November 26, 2010. http://www.bloomberg.com/news/2010-06-29/ banks-financing-mexico-s-drug-cartels-admitted-in-wells-fargo-s-u-s-deal.html.

"Southwest Border HIDTA California Partnership." High-Intensity Drug Trafficking Areas, Office of National Drug Control Policy public website. Accessed May 18, 2010. http://www.ncjrs.gov/ ondcppubs/publications/enforce/hidta2001/ca-fs.html.

"Southwest Border Region—Drug Transportation and Homeland Security Issues." *National Drug Threat Assessment 2008.* National Drug Intelligence Center. Accessed October 5, 2010. http:// www.justice.gov/ndic/pubs25/25921/border.htm.

Southwest Border Violence: Issues in Identifying and Measuring Spillover Violence. CRS Report to Congress, Congressional Research Service, February 10, 2010. Accessed March 5, 2011, http://trac .syr.edu/immigration/library/P4351.pdf.

Stack, Patrick, and Clare Suddath. "A Brief History of Medical Marijuana." *Time,* October 21, 2009. Accessed November 22, 2010. http://www.time.com/time/health/article/0,8599,1931247,00 .html.

State of California Penal Code §§ 12001.5, 12020(a)(1).

State of California Penal Code § 12072(a).

State of California Penal Code § 12220.

State of California Penal Code § 12280.

State of California Penal Code §§ 12320, 12321.

Stern, Ray. "George Iknadosian, Accused of Supplying Mexican Cartels with Guns, Sues Arizona, City of Phoenix and Terry Goddard." *Phoenix New Times,* March 24, 2010. Accessed October 6, 2010. http://blogs.phoenixnewtimes.com/valleyfever/2010/03/george_iknadosian_accused_of_s.php.

Strange, Hannah. "Mexican Drug Gang Killers Cut Out Victims' Hearts." *Times* (UK), June 8, 2010. Accessed September 6, 2010. http://www.timesonline.co.uk/tol/news/world/us_and_americas/ article7145669.ece.

"Strategic Plan—Fiscal Years 2010–2016." Bureau of Alcohol, Tobacco, Firearms, and Explosives public website. Accessed May 13, 2010. http://www.atf.gov/publications/general/strategic-plan/.

Taylor, Phil. "Cartels Turn U.S. Forests into Marijuana Plantations, Creating Toxic Mess." E&E Publishing, July 30, 2009. Accessed November 21, 2010. http://www.eenews.net/public/Landletter/ 2009/07/30/1.

"This Is CBP." US Customs and Border Protection public website. Accessed May 12, 2010. http:// www.cbp.gov/xp/cgov/about/mission/cbp_is.xml.

Tobacco Control in Developing Countries. Published by the OUP for the World Bank and World Health Organization, 2000. Accessed April 14, 2010. http://www1.worldbank.org/tobacco/tcdc.asp.

"Trial: Kidnapping Victim 'Cooked' in Mexico." KGBT News, January 20, 2010. Accessed October 7, 2010. http://www.valleycentral.com/news/story.aspx?id=404432.

United States of America v. Uvaldo Salazar-Lopez. Criminal Complaint, US District Court of Nevada. Case 2:09-mj-00002-LRL-LRL, May 1, 2009. Accessed through PACER online.

"U.S. Foreign Economic and Military Aid Programs: 1980 to 2007." US Census Bureau website. Accessed September 14, 2010. http://www.census.gov/compendia/statab/2010/tables/10s1262.pdf.

"U.S. Guns Pour into Mexico." *Arizona Republic,* January 16, 2007.

"U.S., Mexican Authorities Investigating Cross-Border Tunnel near San Diego." US Immigration and Customs Enforcement public website, December 2, 2009. Accessed May 18, 2010. http://www .ice.gov/pi/nr/0912/091202sandiego.htm.

Vera, Rodrigo. "La Policía Federál pide auxilio [The Federal Police Asks for Help]." *Proceso* (online), August 2, 2010. Accessed September 18, 2010. http://www.proceso.com.mx/rv/modHome/detalle Exclusiva/81985.

Villagran, Lauren. "Probes by Authorities Sputter as Violence in Mexico Mounts." *Dallas Morning News,* October 7, 2010. Accessed October 7, 2010. http://www.dallasnews.com/sharedcontent/ dws/news/world/stories/DN-mexcrime_07int.ART.State.Edition1.488b5bf.html.

Villalba, Oscar. "Officials Say Gunmen Killed 17 at Party in Mexico." AOL News (Associated Press), July 19, 2010. Accessed September 6, 2010. http://www.aolnews.com/world/article/officials-say-gunmen-kill-17-at-party-in-mexico/19558786?icid=main%7Chtmlws-main-n%7Cdl1%7Clink 4%7Chttp%3A%2F%2Fwww.aolnews.com%2Fworld%2Farticle%2Fofficials-say-gunmen-kill-17-at-party-in-mexico%2F19558786.

"Violence Along the Southwest Border." Before the House Appropriations Committee, Subcommittee on Commerce, Justice, Science and Related Agencies, March 24, 2009. (Statement of Joseph M. Arabit, Special Agent in Charge, El Paso Division, Drug Enforcement Administration). http:// www.usdoj.gov/dea/speeches/s032409.pdf.

Wagner, Dennis. "Violence Is Not Up on Arizona Border Despite Mexican Drug War." *The Arizona Republic,* May 2, 2010. Accessed May 14, 2010. http://www.azcentral.com/news/articles/2010/05/ 02/20100502arizona-border-violence-mexico.html.

Wayland, Michelle. "DA: Brutal Kidnapping, Murder Crew Dismantled." NBC San Diego (online), August 14, 2009. Accessed May 6, 2010. http://www.nbcsandiego.com/news/local-beat/DA-Brutal-Kidnapping-Murder-Crew-Dismantled----53146782.html.

West Texas High Intensity Drug Trafficking Area Drug Market Analysis 2009. National Drug Intelligence Center, March 2009. Accessed November 5, 2010. http://www.justice.gov/ndic/pubs32/32792/ production.htm#Transportation.

"Who We Are and What We Do." US Border Patrol public website. Accessed May 12, 2010. http:// www.cbp.gov/xp/cgov/border_security/border_patrol/who_we_are.xml.

Wilkinson, Tracy. "Mexico Army Handling of Civilian Death Inquiries Questioned." *Los Angeles Times,* May 5, 2010. Accessed September 2, 2010. http://articles.latimes.com/2010/may/05/world/la-fg-mexico-dead-civilians-20100505.

———. "Mexico Cartel Kills Four in Car Bombing." *Los Angeles Times,* July 17, 2010. Accessed August 24, 2010. http://articles.latimes.com/2010/jul/17/world/la-fg-mexico-car-bomb-20100717.

———. "Mexico Moves Quietly to Decriminalize Minor Drug Use." *Los Angeles Times,* June 21, 2009. Accessed September 14, 2010. http://articles.latimes.com/2009/jun/21/world/fg-mexico-decriminalize21.

———. "Mexico Sees Inside Job in Prison Break." *Los Angeles Times,* May 18, 2009. Accessed November 16, 2010. http://articles.latimes.com/2009/may/18/world/fg-mexico-prison18.

"Window on State Government—Demographics." Texas Comptroller of Public Accounts public website. Accessed March 29, 2010. http://www.window.state.tx.us/specialrpt/tif/population.html.

Zeta Online. "CAF asesina a military." http://www.zetatijuana.com/html/Edicion1803/Principal.html.

INDEX